Quality Assurance

Also by Diana N. T. Sale and published by Macmillan:

Quality Assurance. Essentials of Nursing Management
  Series, 1990.

*Quality Assurance for Nurses and Other Members of the Health
  Care Team,* 2nd Edition. Essentials of Nursing
  Management Series, 1996.

Quality Assurance

A Pathway to Excellence

Diana N. T. Sale

palgrave
macmillan

First published 2000 by
MACMILLAN PRESS LTD
Houndmills, Basingstoke, Hampshire RG21 6XS
and London
Companies and representatives throughout the world

ISBN 10: 0-333-74992-8
ISBN 13: 978-0-333-74992-0

A catalogue record for this book is available
from the British Library.

This book is printed on paper suitable for recycling and
made from fully managed and sustained forest sources.
Logging, pulping and manufacturing processes are
expected to conform to the environmental regulations
of the country of origin.

Editing and origination by
Aardvark Editorial, Mendham, Suffolk

Transferred to digital printing 2003

Printed and bound in Great Britain by
CPI Antony Rowe, Chippenham and Eastbourne

This book is dedicated to my daughters,
Jo and Caroline

Contents

List of Figures

x

Preface

In the document *The New NHS, Modern, Dependable,* published in December 1997 (DoH, 1997), the government set out its plans for a new National Health Service (NHS). Within this document lie the foundations for an NHS with quality at its heart:

> The new NHS will have quality at its heart. Without it there is unfairness. Every patient who is treated in the NHS wants to know that they can rely on receiving high quality care when they need it. Every part of the NHS, and everyone who works in it, should take responsibility for working to improve quality. (DoH, 1997)

This vision is shared by people who work in the NHS and have been striving to achieve this for many years. The information contained within the pages of this book is intended to help health professionals to apply the various principles and approaches to quality assurance so that quality of care can be improved for patients and clients, and to follow the pathway to excellence.

In order to use the tools of quality assurance effectively, it is important to understand some of the history and early approaches to monitoring the quality of care. Those readers who have read my two previous books will recognise part of Chapters 1 and 2, in which I have traced the history of quality assurance from its early days in Roman times through to the nineteenth and twentieth centuries. This journey takes us up to 1999 and on to the new millennium. Systems such as Qualpacs, Phaneuf's Nursing Audit and Monitor provide good examples of quality assurance tools that take the first steps towards making the measurement of patient care more objective.

Chapter 2 offers a review of some of the best known and most widely used quality assurance theories, including those of Donabedian and Maxwell. There is still a need to have a clear and comprehensive understanding of setting and monitoring standards. Standards are an essential part of clinical audit, guidelines and pathways as they allow for objective measurement. Standards are the baseline against which to measure the effectiveness of care, so they must be well written, research based and measurable. The section on standard setting is a revised, updated and shortened version of an approach that I described in my two previous books, being based on the work of Professor Alison Kitson *et al.* and the Royal College of Nursing. It is a simple yet effective approach, which sets standards using structure, process and outcome criteria as defined by Avedis Donabedian.

Chapter 3 looks at Total Quality Management, or Continuous Quality Improvement (CQI) as it is known when applied in a health care setting. CQI is what quality assurance is all about because it is the continuous effort to improve the quality of care and to demonstrate that improvement. This approach to quality assurance has been used in health care for many years, with varying degrees of success, and lessons can be learned from its structured approach and its emphasis on the involvement of and ownership by the staff, and encompasses the desired outcome of satisfied patients/clients. I have described a Quality Improvement Project which is an example of a structured approach to problem solving that could equally be applied as part of the process of developing care pathways.

Some professionals are still struggling with clinical audit, the particular problems appearing to concern the lack of true participation of the multidisciplinary team in all stages of the audit. There is still a place for uniprofessional audit, but in order to demonstrate a real improvement in patient care, as a result of clinical audit, the whole multidisciplinary team needs to be actively involved (see Chapter 4). Clinical audit has an essential part to play in monitoring the effectiveness of care pathways, especially the documented variances from the pathway. These should be highlighted and used as topics for clinical audit in order to explore the reasons for common variances and to establish a way in which to reduce them and implement the necessary changes. The National Centre for Clinical Audit has been very successful in developing a large database of audits to support professionals in their quest for improving the quality of patient care through clinical audit.

Chapters 5, 6 and 7 expand on the more recent initiatives, which include clinical effectiveness, clinical guidelines, evidence-based practice, clinical governance and integrated care pathways. There is an enormous amount of information on these in the journals, so I have briefly explained the principles, benefits and problems associated with them and given some examples of how these approaches may be applied in practice. At the end of these chapters, readers will find some useful addresses and sources of information to help with the development of quality in their own organisations.

In Chapter 5, I have included some extremely well-written guidelines to support the care and treatment of patients suffering from depression. The guidelines were developed with representatives from Dorset Health Authority, Dorset Community Trust and Dorset Healthcare. Dr Nick Kosky, a psychiatrist, was the lead clinician, and the resulting guidelines are now used for the care and treatment of people suffering with depression across the whole county of Dorset. The guidelines are based on sound, current research, which enables evidence-based practice to be the basis of care for all patients with depression. Using evidence-based guidelines helps to ensure that all patients receive care that is delivered to the same standard, to preset outcomes and by all the professionals involved in the delivery of care. An ongoing review of the guidelines is essential to ensure that they are kept up to date and continue to reflect good practice as part of clinical governance.

In the government's White Paper *A First Class Service: Quality in the NHS* (DoH, 1998), clinical governance is defined as 'a framework through which NHS organisations are accountable for continuously improving the quality of their services and safeguarding high standards of care by creating an environment in which excellence in clinical care will flourish'. In Chapter 6, I have described a system of audit – Probe – which was designed and piloted by myself and Gayle Garland, from the University of Leeds. Probe has been designed to support Trusts and primary care groups (PCGs) through the first steps towards clinical governance.

Probe takes a clinical probe such as medicines and slices through the organisation to establish whether the safe and therapeutic prescribing and, administering of medicines is supported by corporate, clinical and self-governance. This includes a review of the procurement and safe storage of medicines, an assessment of the medical staff's knowledge and skills required for the therapeutic prescribing of medication, observation of the safe administration of medicines, the quality of information given to patients and the level of patients' understanding about the medicines they are taking and whether or not they are making informed choices and decisions. The same principles apply to the Trust's or PCG's choice of a clinical probe, such as the care programme approach, the care of leg ulcers, postoperative pain control and so on. Finally, the third probe is one which explores how effectively quality assurance has been implemented throughout the organisation. The methodology and approach to this audit are explained in detail in Chapter 6.

It is my belief that integrated care pathways are the most effective route to clinical governance as their development requires the multidisciplinary team to track the patient's care journey, through process mapping, from the GP to the acute services, the community hospital and back home to the care of the GP. The process of developing a care pathway includes a comparison of the present pathway to current, valid research, and then re-engineering the pathway in the light of this evidence. Care pathways improve the patient's care journey, may reduce the length of stay or enable a quicker rehabilitation of patients to their homes, and result in continuity of evidence-based care. When pathways are shared with patients and their families, the benefits include improved information, resulting in informed choices and a better understanding of their care.

Again, in order to demonstrate how the theory works in practice, I have included, in Chapter 7, three examples of pathways. The first was developed by Mr Nick Carty, a consultant surgeon at Salisbury NHS Trust, and his team, and Dr Graham Jagger (GP) and his primary care team. The pathway is a breast-care pathway, which led to changes in the staffing structure and clinical processes, which have resulted in a more efficient, effective and responsive service for the patients. The second pathway was developed by Dorset Community NHS Trust, led by the project leader Kate Sneider, and included both multidisciplinary and inter-agency teams. This pathway is for the care and treatment of patients with schizophrenia. The final pathway was also contributed by Dorset Community NHS Trust, being a pathway for the care of patients attending for day surgery at a community hospital; this was led by Carole Annetts. All these pathways track the patient's journey and re-engineer the process based on valid evidence. An ongoing review of integrated care pathways is essential to ensure that they are kept up to date and continue to reflect good practice as part of clinical governance.

I have left accreditation to the end of the book as in all aspects of quality assurance there is a need for an organisation to take a step back and take that longer, more detached look at the quality of care it is providing. This is really only achieved through the objective eyes of the external auditor. There are various systems of accreditation in the UK, which are described in Chapter 8. However, the reason this chapter is called 'Accreditation, with a Difference' is that it applies to a pilot study in Dorset involving two nursing homes that have been developed into Practice Development Units (PDUs), which will be accredited through the University of Leeds. If the pilot is successful, which at the time of writing it was certainly proving to be, the system will be extended to other nursing homes. The reason for developing nursing homes as PDUs was to support the staff in their desire to deliver evidence-based practice, to empower the residents and the staff, to improve the quality of care and generally to raise the profile of nursing homes among the profession of nursing and the general public.

Clinical effectiveness, clinical guidelines and integrated care pathways all depend on knowing where to find the evidence to support the most clinically and cost-effective treatments, drugs and other aspects of clinical practice. It is sometimes hard to know where to start, how to get the evidence. Research results are not easily accessible, and it is often difficult for busy professionals to find their way through the ever-increasing body of research and the ever-growing number of guidelines. The National Institute for Clinical Excellence will support professionals by providing advice on best clinical practice and the effectiveness of interventions. There are, however, many other sources of information, so at the end of Chapters 5, 6 and 7, I have included some useful addresses, web sites and telephone numbers of organisations through which to start the quality assurance journey to track down the evidence in order to support good practice.

References

Department of Health (1997) *The New NHS, Modern, Dependable.* London: HMSO.

Department of Health (1998) *A First Class Service: Quality in the New NHS.* London: HMSO.

Acknowledgements

I should like to thank the following people who kindly allowed me to use some of their work in this book, first, Professor Alison Kitson, Clare Morrell and Gill Harvey (Royal College of Nursing), for material on standard setting; I was privileged to be part of the group that worked on this methodology with Alison Kitson and Helen Kendall, in the early days of standard setting in the UK. Thanks are also due to the publishers Appleton-Century-Crofts for extracts from the Nursing Audit by Phaneuf and the Quality Patient Care Scale (Qualpacs). Permission was kindly granted by Newcastle-upon-Tyne Polytechnic Products Ltd to reproduce extracts from Monitor, and by the Juran Institute for extracts from their work on Quality Improvement Projects.

My thanks go to consultant surgeon, Dr Nick Carty and his team at Salisbury NHS Trust, and to Dr Graham Jagger (GP) and his team, for the breast-care pathway. Acknowledgement is also due to Dorset Health Authority, Dorset Community Trust and Dorset Healthcare, who worked together with the lead consultant psychiatrist, Dr Nick Kosky, to produce some excellent guidelines for treating patients with depression. In addition, Dorset Community Trust allowed the use of their pathway for the care and treatment of patients with schizophrenia, led by Kate Sneider, and also their pathway for patients attending community hospital for day surgery, led by Carole Annetts.

I would also like to thank Susan Hamer from the University of Leeds for the innovative work with Practice Development Units in Nursing Homes. Also Gayle Garland with whom I worked on the development of 'Probe', a clinical governance audit tool.

My sincere thanks go to Pam Homer, a much-respected colleague and friend, who patiently read through the book and offered both advice and encouragement.

DIANA SALE

1

An Introduction to Quality Assurance

Background

> The new NHS will have quality at its heart. Without it there is unfairness. Every patient who is treated in the NHS wants to know that they can rely on receiving high quality care when they need it. Every part of the NHS, and everyone who works in it, should take responsibility for working to improve quality. (DoH, 1997)

Quality assurance is firmly on the government's agenda, and this chapter explores some of the history that led to the emergence of clinical governance. As the chapter charts progress through the years, some of the quality assurance instruments and methods that have shaped the way in which we measure quality will be explored.

Early history

The earliest studies of quality assurance were probably undertaken by the Romans, who reported on the efficiency of their military hospitals. It is also possible that the monks gave an account of their work in caring for the sick. Probably the first documented evidence of the evaluation of nursing care dates back to the eighteenth century, when John Howard and Elizabeth Fry described the quality of patient care in the hospitals that they visited.

In the 1850s, Florence Nightingale (1858, 1874) evaluated the care delivered to the sick. She kept notes on her observations and used the information to establish the level of care being provided, and to improve care in areas that were sub-standard.

During the American Civil War, Louisa M. Alcott (1960) wrote about the quality of nursing care in *Hospital Sketches*, which was published in 1863. In this, she described the contrast between the chaos of the 'Hurly-Burly House' and that of the organised and compassionate care seen at the Armoury Hospital.

In the USA in 1917 a compilation of minimum standards was published and the Hospital Standardization Programme came into being in 1918 (McCleary, 1977). The programme was financed by the American College of Surgeons and had approved 3,400 hospitals by 1952 (Stephenson, 1978). Isabel Stewart (1919) looked at ways of measuring the quality of nursing care and the effective use of resources. She developed an 8-point list known as Stewart Standards, using professional opinion rather than a rating scale. The 8-point list included:

- safety
- therapeutic effect
- economy of time
- economy of energy and effort
- economy of material and costs
- finished workmanship
- simplicity and adaptability.

In 1936, Miss G. B. Carter and Dr H. Balme (1936) published a book on the importance of evaluating care. They recommended that a multidisciplinary team, consisting of the ward sister, the doctor and the administrator, should discuss the progress and evaluate the care of all patients by reviewing the medical and nursing record at the end of the month.

The 1950s

Between 1950 and 1954, Reiter and Kakosh (1953) developed a system based on the classification of patients into three categories. This classification looked at the way in which nurses planned to work with patients:

- type 1 – professional, the nurse working with the patient, as in rehabilitation;
- type 2 – curative, the nurse 'doing things' for the patient, such as dressings, treatments and specific tasks;
- type 3 – elementary, custodial or palliative care, that is, nursing care being given to a comatose or unresponsive patient.

Reiter and Kakosh developed a series of questions to assess the effectiveness of each type of care. Their work, after its publication, led to a study of communications as a focal point of quality in nursing.

In the USA in 1958, Abdellah (1958) developed the method of matching staffing levels to the measurement of quality of care for patients in a large hospital. She chose to measure the level of dissatisfaction expressed by patients, nurses and other individuals. Over a period of time, Abdellah established 50 of the most common causes of dissatisfaction and developed a weighting value for each one. The area of dissatisfaction was rated from 5 to zero; thus, for example, an unconscious patient who was left unattended, and therefore at risk, would have scored 5, whereas a minor dissatisfaction would have scored zero. The scores were then totalled. A high score indicated poor nursing, whereas a zero score meant that the ward was excellent.

Measuring what goes wrong is, however, rather a negative approach to evaluating a ward as it does not measure the positive qualities present. This method did not establish that staffing level equated with quality of care; in fact, it proved that there was little correlation between the number of staff and the quality of care. Neither did this system offer solutions for resolving dissatisfaction and improving the quality of care.

The 1960s

In 1961, Abdellah identified three types of criterion measures in nursing – physiological, sociological and psychological – all of which had to meet certain requirements in terms of validity, reliability, discrimination, relevancy and appropriateness.

In California in 1964, Drew (1964) undertook a survey of 21 hospitals to establish what quality assurance techniques were being used. It was established that 42 different techniques were being used, falling into the following categories:

- comments from patients and others;
- special rounds of patient units;
- checks and tests on procedures;
- patient and other records;
- other, for example inspection teams from outside agencies, nurse consultants, infection control nurses and so on.

The survey highlighted that each hospital was using at least one quality assurance tool, but there was a lack of co-ordination and information sharing between hospitals in the same area. Drew stressed the need for a sharing of techniques in order to establish a uniform and complete system of quality control.

Since then, nurses all over the world have, to a greater or lesser degree, evaluated the care given to their patients. In Europe, it has really only been since 1960 that the evaluation of nursing care has become structured and resulted in systematic studies.

In 1969, Donabedian (1969) divided the evaluation of quality of care into the evaluation of the structure in which care is delivered, the process and the outcome criteria.

In the 1960s, British nursing underwent an enormous change with the introduction of the recommendations of the Salmon Report (DoH, 1966). With the implementation of this Report came the introduction of industrial management techniques and the idea of improving efficiency and saving money in the NHS.

The 1970s

In the 1970s, accountability and cost-effectiveness in the delivery of health care became a major issue, leading to the development of systems to help nurses determine the quality of their practice. The nursing process from the USA was also introduced in the 1970s and has been adapted and implemented, to a greater or lesser extent, throughout the UK.

In the USA in the 1970s, three important instruments for measuring the quality of nursing care were developed:

- *The Slater Nursing Competencies Rating Scale* (1975) is an 84-item scale arranged into six subsections that identify nurse–patient interventions or interactions on behalf of the patient. The scale can be used concurrently or retrospectively and evaluates the competence of the nurse while delivering patient care by observing and measuring the nurse's performance against predetermined standards within the scale.
- *Qualpacs* (Figure 1.1), published in 1974, was developed by two professors, Wandelt and Ager (1974) and their faculty members at Wayne State University College of Nursing, USA. Many of the items were derived from the Slater Nursing Competencies Rating Scale. Qualpacs is used to evaluate the direct and indirect interaction of nursing staff with patients.

  Qualpacs uses a method of concurrent review that is designed to evaluate the process of care at the time it is being provided, including a review of the records, a patient interview asking the patient to comment on certain aspects of his or her care, and direct observation of the patient's behaviours related to predetermined criteria. Also involved are staff interviews asking the staff to comment on specific aspects of patient care, and staff observation – observing nursing behaviour related to predetermined criteria.

  The scale contains 68 items divided into six categories:

1. *psychological*: individual (15 items)
2. *psychosocial*: group (8 items)
3. *physical* (15 items)
4. *general* (15 items)
5. *communications* (8 items)
6. *professional implications* (7 items)

Date_____

Patient (name or no):   Rater (name or no):

INTERACTIONS RECORD: AM/PM

No:

Time:

	5	4	3	2	1	ρ	0	

PSYCHOSOCIAL: INDIVIDUAL

Actions directed toward meeting psychosocial needs of individual patients:

No.	5	4	3	2	1	ρ	0	Code
1. Patient receives nurse's full attention *D	X / 5		X / X / 6		X / 1			11–12 / 12 / 3
2. Patient is given an opportunity to explain his feelings *D								13–14
3. Patient is approached in a kind, gentle and friendly manner *D								15–16
4. Patient's inappropriate behaviour is responded to in a therapeutic manner *D								17–18
5. Appropriate action is taken in response to anticipated or manifest patient anxiety or distress *D/*I								19–20
6. Patient receives explanation and verbal reassurance when needed *D								21–22
7. Patient receives attention from nurse with neither becoming involved in a non-therapeutic way *D								23–24
8. Patient is given consideration as a member of a family and society *D/*I								25–26
9. Patient receives attention for his spiritual needs *D/*I								27–28
10. The rejecting or demanding patient continues to receive acceptance *D/*I								29–30
11. Patient receives care that communicates worth and dignity of man *D								31–32
12. The health aspects of the patient's personality are utilised *D/*I								33–34
13. An atmosphere of trust, acceptance and respect is created rather than one of power, prestige and authority *D								35–36
14. Appropriate topics for conversation are chosen *D								37–38
15. The unconscious or non-orientated patient is cared for with the same respectful manner as the conscious patient *D								39–40
AREA 1 MEAN								41–42–43

*D indicates that direct observation is appropriate and *I indicates that indirect observation is appropriate. *D/*I indicates that either method may be used.

Source: Wandelt and Ager (1974). *Quality Patient Care Scale* (New York: Appleton-Century-Crofts).

Figure 1.1   Qualpacs – Quality Patient Care Scale

Data must be held in STRICT confidence and MUST NOT BE FILED with patient's record
All entries to be completed by trained clerk

1. Name of patient: (LAST) (FIRST)	2. Sex	3. Age	4. Admission date	5. Discharge date

6. Name of institution	7. Floor	8. Medical supervision	Private ☐	Ward ☐	OPD/Clinic ☐

9. Complete diagnosis(es):

10. Admitted by referral form	Physician on staff ☐	MD not hospital affiliated ☐	Clinic/OPD ☐	11. Via emergency ☐

12. Patient discharged to:	Self-care ☐	Family care ☐	PHN agency ☐	Other ☐	Died ☐	Unknown ☐

13. If patient died:	MD present ☐	MD promptly notified ☐	Family present ☐	Family promptly notified ☐	14. If patient Catholic: last rites given YES ☐	NO ☐

15. All nursing entries signed by name and dates:	YES ☐	NO ☐	16. Nursing entries show whether made by professional, practical, student nurse, or other	YES ☐	NO ☐

17. Patient's clothing, valuables and other personal items were accounted for in accordance with policy:	YES ☐	NO ☐

		YES	NO
18.	Operative and other patient or family consent forms completed as required by policy	___	___
19.	A. Were there any accidents or other special incidents?	___	___
	B. If yes, chart indicates report was submitted to administration	___	___
	C. Or, report is part of chart	___	___
20.	A. Kardex in use	___	___
	B. If yes, Kardex becomes part of permanent chart	___	___
21.	Nursing care plan is recorded in the chart	___	___
22.	A. Nursing admission entry shows assessment of patient's condition:		
	physical	___	___
	emotional	___	___
	B. Nursing discharge entry shows assessment of patient's condition		
	physical	___	___
	emotional	___	___

Source: Phaneuf, (1976) *Nursing Audit Self-regulation in Nursing Practice*, 2nd edn (New York: Appleton-Century-Crofts).

Figure 1.2 Nursing Audit part 1 – hospital or nursing home audit

- *Phaneuf's nursing audit* (Figure 1.2) (1972) is a retro-spective appraisal of the nursing process as reflected in the patient's records. There are 50 items in the audit, which was devised around the seven functions of nursing described by Lesnik and Anderson (1955) in their book *Nursing Practice and the Law.*

Changes in the health service

In the UK in 1974, the government reorganised the NHS and set up Area Health Authorities by means of the National Health Service Reorganisation Act 1973. These authorities were abolished in 1982 with the creation of District Health Authorities, each with its own Community Health Council (DHSS, 1981).

All this change and development led to increased accountability for the quality of the service. In 1984, the government set up the Office of the Health Service Commissioner to investigate complaints of maladminis-tration (DHSS, 1983, 1985). This did not include 'clinical judgement', but the Ombudsman was able to comment on the way in which complaints were handled and the quality of patient care management.

During the 1960s and 70s, investigations were carried out concerning poor practice, particularly in large insti-tutions caring for the mentally ill and mentally handi-capped. This led to the formation of the Hospital Advisory Service for mental illness and elderly care groups, and of the National Development Team/Group for the mentally handicapped. Both these bodies are responsible for inspecting clinical areas and establishing the level of clin-ical practice. They report on good practice and criticise bad practice. Other forms of audit of quality come from the regular inspection of the academic or validating bodies for training: National Boards for nursing and the Royal Colleges for postgraduate doctors. Both promote good prac-tice and have the ability to withdraw training from author-ities if it is found to be unsatisfactory.

There have also been government reports that reflect quality, including that of the Royal Commission on the National Health Service (DHSS, 1979) and the Griffiths Report (DHSS, 1983).

Accreditation in the USA

In 1971 in the USA, it was established that audit review alone could not promote an improvement of patient care. Consequently, the Joint Commission on Accreditation of Hospitals established standards of nursing care in 1971 (Palmer, 1978), giving a more objective and systematic review of patient care and performance. There is also documented evidence of standard setting at a national level in Canada (Canadian Council on Hospital Accreditation (CCHA) 1952) (Wilson, 1983), in Australia (Australian Council of Hospital Standards, 1979) (McCue and Wilson, 1981) and in New Zealand (Joint Commission on Accreditation for Hospitals, 1987) (Darby and Cane, 1987). In 1979 in the Netherlands the National Organisation for Quality Assurance in Hospitals in the Netherlands (CBO) was formed (Roerink, 1987).

In the USA, accreditation is linked with funding. If standards fall below predetermined levels, the hospital organisation is in jeopardy of losing its federal or state funding. The hospital accreditation programmes demand evidence that a hospital has a system of quality assurance. Medical audits have developed into medical record audits, which examine in detail the records post-discharge, nowadays often by computer. Some of these hospitals employ a team of people to examine the records and report their findings to a quality assurance committee (see also Chapter 7).

Rush Medicus

In 1972, the Rush Medicus (Hegyvary and Hausman, 1975) instrument was developed by the Rush Presbyterian St Luke's Medical Center and the Medicus Systems Corporation of Chicago from 1972, being completed in 1975. This system evolved from research in two main areas:

- the development of a 'conceptual framework', stating what was being measured; as this constitutes a patient-centred approach, the nursing process and patient needs were the identified components;
- the identification of criteria for evaluating the quality of care within this framework.

Within the system, there are a series of objectives and sub-objectives, which represent the structure of the nursing process.

Criteria were simultaneously developed and tested to measure each of the sub-objectives within the six main objectives. These criteria have been written so that a 'yes' or 'no' response indicates the quality of care and, where appropriate, 'not applicable' can be applied. Each item is written in such a way as to minimise ambiguity and to ensure reliable interpretation and response on the part of the observers carrying out the study. A glance through the criteria will show that they are relevant to almost any situation of patient care.

The process itself is computerised, involving a simple dependency rating system, which enables the computer to select 30–50 criteria at random for individual patients according to their dependency rating. In order to test the criteria, information is gained by the following methods:

- questioning patients
- questioning nurses
- observing patients
- observing nurses
- observing the patient's environment
- observing the general environment
- examining records
- the observer making references.

Rush Medicus developed a method for evaluating the quality of nursing care for medical, surgical and paediatric patients, including the relevant intensive care units. Evaluation is achieved through the production of two indices, the first being an average score of the quality of patient care, and the second a score for the unit environment. Management scoring is on a scale of 0–100, a higher score indicating a better quality of care. The score obtained by the unit is an indication of the quality of care rather than being a measure of all aspects of the quality of care.

Monitor

In 1984 in the UK, Goldstone and Ball (1984) successfully adapted the Rush Medicus methodology to develop the tool Monitor. The original version of this was designed for use on acute surgical and medical wards; more recent versions have, however, been developed for use in care of the elderly wards and district nursing, followed by a version for mental health and paediatric wards in 1987. The midwifery and health visiting versions were published by Leeds Polytechnic in 1989.

Monitor has a patient-orientated approach and two main concepts: individualised patient care and patient needs. Linked with these concepts is the monitoring of the support services influencing the delivery of good standards of patient care.

Monitor is based on a master list of 455 questions concerning patient care. Only questions 8–150 are directed at the care of any one patient, these being grouped into four sections:

1. assessment and planning
2. physical care
3. non-physical care
4. evaluation.

Some typical questions representing the different sections of the Monitor patient questionnaire are shown below (Ball *et al.*, 1983).

Assessment and planning

- Is there a statement written within 24 hours of admission on the condition of the skin?
- Do the nursing orders or care plan include attention to the patient's needs for discharge teaching?

Physical care

- Has the patient received attention to his or her complaints of nausea and vomiting?
- Is adequate equipment for oral hygiene available?

Non-physical care

- Do the nursing staff call the patient by the name he or she prefers?
- Are special procedures or studies explained to the patient?

Evaluation

- Do records document the effect of the administration of 'as required' medication?
- Do records document the patient's response to teaching?

Monitor follows the structure of the nursing process, but the authors state that the clinical area being assessed does not have to be using this approach to patient care in order to use this tool.

Patients are classified into dependency groups (Figure 1.3).

DEPENDENCY GROUPS	FOUR LEVELS OF DEPENDENCY
Patients are classified into dependency groups according to the following factors: • personal care • feeding • mobility • nursing attention (frequency of nursing requirements) • other (including incontinence, preparation for surgery and severe behavioural problems)	• Minimal care • Average care • Above-average care • Maximum care

Source: Ball *et al.* (1983) *Monitor: An Index of the Quality of Nursing Care for Acute Medical and Surgical Wards* (Newcastle-upon-Tyne, Newcastle-upon-Tyne Polytechnic Products).

Figure 1.3   Dependency groups

The definitions of dependency are outlined in Figure 1.4.

CATEGORY I – MINIMAL CARE
Patient is physically capable of caring for himself but requires minimal nursing super-vision and may require treatments and/or monitoring (for example BP, TPR, clinical observations) by nursing staff.

CATEGORY II – AVERAGE CARE
Patient requires an average or moderate amount of nursing care, including some nursing supervision and encouragement. The patient may require some assistance with personal care needs as well as monitoring and treatments. Some examples would include:

- a patient past the acute stage of his disease or surgery
- a 3–4 day post-op cholecystectomy
- a diabetic patient for reassessment
- an independent patient requiring extensive investigative procedure

CATEGORY III – ABOVE AVERAGE CARE
Patient requires a greater than average amount of nursing care, including nursing supervision, encouragement and almost complete assistance to meet personal care needs. The patient usually requires medical support and sometimes the use of special equipment. Some examples would be:

- a patient after the acute phase of CVA (residual paralysis)
- a first day post-op radical mastectomy or cholecystectomy
- a debilitated, dependent elderly person
- a newly diagnosed diabetic requiring extensive health teaching and support from nursing staff

CATEGORY IV – MAXIMUM CARE
Patient requires very frequent to continuous nursing care along with close supervision by medical personnel and/or health team members, and/or support from technical equipment. Some examples would include:

- a quadriplegic in early rehabilitative stages
- a severely burned patient
- a comatose patient

Source: Ball *et al.* (1983) *Monitor: An Index of the Quality of Nursing Care for Acute Medical and Surgical Wards* (Newcastle-upon-Tyne, Newcastle-upon-Tyne Polytechnic Products). BP = blood pressure; TPR = temperature, pulse and respiration; CVA = cerebrovascular accident.

Figure 1.4   Monitor – definition of categories

There are four different questionnaires, each appropriate for a specific dependency category of patients. The criteria are presented as questions, and the information is gained from a variety of sources – by asking the nurse or patient, consulting the records, and observing both the environment and the patient. The questions are answered by a trained assessor with 'yes', 'no', 'not applicable' or 'not available'. The scoring system is 1 for 'yes' and 0 for 'no', the 'not applicable' or 'not available' answers being deleted. The total score is given as the percentage of 'yes' responses obtained. The closer the score is to 100 per cent, the better the standard of care being delivered.

In Pursuit of Excellence

In 1985, the Royal College of Nursing (RCN) Standards of Care Project was set up, with the intention of establishing the academic background to quality of care and encouraging the nursing profession to set and monitor standards. The RCN published two significant papers – *Standards of Nursing Care* (RCN, 1980) and *Towards Standards* (RCN, 1981) – that are essential reading for anyone interested in the history of quality assurance. Professor Alison Kitson's work with the RCN led to the active setting and monitoring of standards within the nursing profession; her published work includes 'Indicators of Quality in Nursing Care – an Alternative Approach' (1986), 'Taking Action' (1986), and with Helen Kendall, 'Rest Assured' (1986).

In 1987, the RCN produced a position statement on nursing, *In Pursuit of Excellence* (RCN, 1987). The steering group that produced this statement set down three main principles: equity, respect for persons and caring. The group then provided nine statements to enable nurses to move to the provision of a quality service based on core concepts.

Working for Patients

In 1983, when the Griffiths recommendations and general management of health care were introduced, quality assurance and the establishment of standards and review mechanisms became the responsibility of all general managers at regional, district and unit level.

In 1985, Alain Enthoven, an American university professor, studied the organisation of the NHS and suggested that it could be improved by the introduction of an 'internal market model'. He envisaged a system that would enable district managers to use services more efficiently. In summary, each district would receive, under a formula drawn up by the Resource Allocation Working Party, a per capita revenue and capital allowance. The district would then be responsible for the provision of comprehensive care for its own resident population but not for patients from other districts without current compensation at negotiated prices. The district would buy and sell services to and from other districts and the private sector.

In January 1989, the Government launched the White Paper *Working for Patients* (DoH, 1985). This covered a wide range of issues and initiatives, including the implementation of the internal market based on a system of contracting for services between purchasers and providers, the extension of the Resource Management Initiative and the formal introduction of medical audit.

Community Care Act 1990

This legislation facilitated the development of the process of contracting between the purchaser and the provider units. The provider units, in the form of NHS Trusts and Directly Managed Units, were responsible for meeting specifications for services as laid down in the contract with the purchaser (commissioner). The purchaser (commissioner) was looking for value for money and quality care from the providers.

Medical audit

As part of the NHS reforms, the government facilitated
the development of programmes intended to measure and
improve the quality of care within the NHS. One particular initiative was the development of medical audit. Over
the years, there have been studies that have audited the
quality of medical care, including a survey of general practice by Collings (1950). Collings established that there was
poor quality of care, his survey contributing to the formation in 1952 of the College of General Practitioners, now
known as the Royal College of General Practitioners
(RCGP). Collings' study observed current practice and
found it to be lacking, but his findings did not directly
change the delivery of care. However, another study, 'The
Confidential Enquiry into Maternal Deaths' (Godber,
1976), focused on the reasons for inadequate care, the
results of this leading to changes in practice and a reduction in the number of maternal deaths.

In 1967, in the Cogwheel report, audit was described as
a proper function for practising clinicians, but there was
still a distinct dearth of mechanisms for monitoring the
effectiveness of patient care. Thus, in the 1970s, the General
Medical Council was criticised for its inability to stop doctors
overprescribing heroin and other addictive drugs to
patients, and there were concerns that Britain had not
become involved in audit.

In the 1960s, a series of events, for example the UK
national quality control scheme for clinical chemistry
analyses in hospital laboratories and the establishment of
the Hospital Advisory Service in 1969, led to a more active
approach to audit. The Royal Commissions in 1976 (the
Alment report) and 1979 (the Merrison report) emphasised the importance of audit. In 1975, radiologists established a working party on the use of diagnostic radiology
(Roberts, 1988), and later, in 1977, the Royal College of
Physicians founded the Medical Service Group (Clarke and
Whitehead, 1981). In 1978, the Conference of Senior
Hospital Staff passed a resolution on medical audit.

During the 1980s, there was more activity from the RCGP as they took the initiative on quality of the service in general practice, and issued a further policy statement, *Quality in General Practice* in 1985 (RCGP, 1985). Then, in 1984, the government signed a declaration that effective mechanisms for quality of health care would be in place by 1990 (WHO, 1984). The Department of Health published the White Paper *Working for Patients* (DoH, 1985), and in 1987, the Royal College of Surgeons declared a requirement that regular audit was necessary for training posts to be recognised. In 1989, the Royal College of Physicians published a report on Medical Audit.

The introduction and early progress of medical audit was slow, but it has gathered speed during the past 10 years. Perhaps because of the NHS tradition of professional autonomy, audit has been seen as operating in separate areas: medical audit, clinical audit and nursing audit. During the 1990s, however, there has been an ever-increasing number of audits undertaken by professionals, either as a uniprofessional group or on a multidisciplinary basis.

King's Fund Organisational Audit

In November 1988, the quality assurance programme at the King's Fund Centre organised a conference to consider the development of national standards for the organisation of health care. Six District Health Authorities – Brighton, East Dorset, North Derbyshire, North West Hertfordshire, Nottingham (Queen's Medical Centre) and West Dorset – were selected to participate in the project. In addition, two independent hospitals, the Hospital of St John and St Elizabeth and AMI Chiltern, joined the project.

A project steering group looked critically at existing systems for setting and monitoring national standards, principally those models of accreditation used in the USA, Canada and Australia. The group considered the Australian system to be the most appropriate on which to build its own model, with reference to the Canadian system as appropriate. The King's Fund Organisational Audit was established in 1989, with the development of national standards for acute hospitals. By 1994, approximately 150 hospitals had been surveyed by the King's Fund Organisational Audit, this extending into health centres and GP practices in 1992 with the Primary Health Care Project. Organisational audit became accreditation in 1995.

Accreditation in the UK

Accreditation is a method that is used to address the issues of evaluating the quality of health services provided. It is the:

> professional and national recognition reserved for facilities that provide high quality health care. This means that the particular health care facility has voluntarily sought to be measured against high professional standards and is in substantial compliance with them. (Limongelli, 1983)

Accreditation is a system of organisational audit made up of three stages:

1. the *development* of organisational standards that are concerned with the systems and process for the delivery of health care; the standards are developed in consultation with the relevant professional organisations and are revised annually to ensure that they reflect current health care trends;
2. the *implementation* of standards, the various accreditation agencies providing support material and guidelines on the interpretation of standards;
3. the *evaluation* of compliance with standards by means of a survey, conducted by a team of trained surveyors chosen for their expertise in a specific health care service.

Accreditation differs from both registration and licensing in that it is not a statutory but a voluntary system (Higgins, 1985).

The Audit Commission .

The Audit Commission was created to enhance efficiency and financial probity in local government. As a result of the 1989 White Paper, its remit was extended to the NHS. Since October 1990, the Audit Commission has been responsible for the external audit of the NHS in England and Wales. The Audit Commission has responsibility for reviewing the financial accounts of all health service bodies and examining the health authorities' use of resources in terms of economy, efficiency and effectiveness. Each year, the Commission publishes around six detailed audits, some of its most recent studies covering the topics of:

- mental health (1995)
- accident and emergency (1996)
- fractured neck of femur (1996)
- maternity services (1997)
- anaesthetics (1998)
- children's and adolescents' mental health services (1998)
- district nursing (1999)
- locum doctors (1999).

The aim of the Audit Commission is to help people who work in, and manage, the NHS to deliver the best possible service within the financial resources determined by government. Every year, the Audit Commission publishes a number of reports on health topics that have been researched at a national level. It then ensures that local audits are carried out covering each topic. The national reports are not intended to be comprehensive surveys because most of the detailed information is collected by auditors during the audits that follow the reports' publication. Instead, the reports are intended to highlight the national issues established through the study. The national studies are carried out by teams consisting of professionals of relevance to the subject. They involve a detailed examination of a number of study sites, with the combination of published research and an analysis of national data. The study team is supported by an advisory group consisting of individuals with a close interest in the subject.

The local studies are undertaken by various firms of management consultants as well as the district audit staff. The auditors follow the Audit Commission guidelines, review local policies and procedures, interview staff, observe the particular service, and review activity and staffing data. They also review national guidelines, information, activity and staffing data. At the end of each study, a report is written that is discussed with the management team, and an action plan is agreed and drawn up with the main objective of improving the service for the patient.

The Patient's Charter

In 1991, *The Patient's Charter* (DoH, 1991) was launched, setting out a number of national rights and service standards that every patient could expect. Seven out of the 10 rights in the Charter were already in existence, for example the right to be treated on the basis of need regardless of ability to pay, and the right to be registered with a GP. Two new rights concerned not being on a waiting list for treatment for more than 2 years, and receiving detailed information about local health services, including waiting times and quality standards. Patients were also granted a right to a full and prompt investigation of any complaints. The rights in the Charter are not, however, legal rights.

Under the NHS Reform Act, a Clinical Standards Advisory Group, accountable to the Secretary of State, was established to evaluate the impact of the reforms upon standards of care in the NHS.

Clinical risk management

The publication in 1993 of the NHS Management Executive document *Risk Management in the NHS* (NHSME, 1993) resulted in Trusts implementing comprehensive systems for reporting adverse outcomes and serious incidents. These reports are used to develop a database of information to enable the Trust to identify common patterns and prevent incidents in the future. Risk may be defined as 'the reduction of harm to an organisation, by identifying and, as far as possible, eliminating risk' (NHSME, 1993). The aims of clinical risk management are (Clements, 1995):

- reducing and, as far as possible, eliminating harm to the patient;
- dealing with the injured patient:
  - continuity of care
  - swift compensation for the justified claimant;
- safeguarding the assets of the organisation:
  - financial
  - reputation
  - staff morale;
- improving the quality of care.

Complaints

In 1996, the process of complaints in the NHS underwent an alteration. The aim of this change was to reduce inconsistency in responding to and investigating complaints, and to introduce more openness with the participation of lay people.

The New NHS, Modern, Dependable

In December 1997, the Government launched the White Paper *The New NHS, Modern, Dependable* (DoH, 1997), in which it set out its plans to modernise the NHS by abolishing the internal market and enabling health professionals to focus on patients. It stressed that 'local doctors and nurses, who best understand patients' needs, will shape local services'. Patients will be guaranteed national standards of excellence so that they will have confidence in the quality of the services they receive.

In 1997 and 1998, locality commissioning pilot projects were set up with the aim of developing more locally sensitive services. This White Paper was an endorsement of the strengths and potential developments in primary care and the establishment of primary care groups (PCGs). It had the following objectives:

- To remove obstacles to integrated care.
- To develop services that are responsive to local needs.
- To reduce variations in health care.
- To work in partnership to provide integrated care.

The paper outlined four levels of PCG:

1. advising and supporting the health authorities in commissioning care;
2. managing the health care budget for its area as part of the health authority;
3. becoming established as a free-standing body accountable to health authorities for commissioning care;
4. becoming established as a free-standing body accountable to health authorities for commissioning care, as well as having added responsibility for the provision of community health services for the population.

In January 1998, a consultation paper outlining a National Performance Framework (DoH, 1998) was released, consisting of six areas.

1. *Health improvement*, which covered the overall health of populations, reflecting social and environmental factors, individual behaviour and NHS care.
2. *Fair access* to the provision of services in relation to need, including geographical, socio-economic, demographic and care groups.
3. *Effective delivery of appropriate health care*, including clinical effectiveness, evidence-based practice, and care that is appropriate to need, timely, in line with agreed standards, provided according to best practice and delivered by appropriately trained and educated staff.

4. *Efficiency*, for example the cost per unit of care or outcome, and the productivity of labour and capital.
5. *Patient/carer experience*, which includes being responsive to individual needs and preferences, assuring patients of skill, care and the continuity of the service, and involving patients in making informed choices and decisions. Patients are to be treated within an acceptable length of time, and easy access to care within an acceptable environment should be ensured.
6. *Health outcomes of NHS care*, which refers to reduced level of risk factors, disease, impairment and complications of treatment. There should also be improved quality of life for patients and carers, and a reduction in the number of premature deaths.

This performance framework was created with the aim of monitoring the performance of the NHS and improving quality.

In 1998, the government published its White Paper *A First Class Service: Quality in the New NHS* (DoH, 1998), its main elements being:

- clear national standards for services and treatments through National Service Frameworks and a National Institute for Clinical Excellence;
- the local delivery of high-quality health care, through clinical governance underpinned by modernised professional self-regulation and lifelong learning;
- monitoring progress through a commission of health improvement, a framework for assessing performance and a national survey of patient and service user experience.

By April 1999, a total of 481 PCGs had been set up. The proposed timetable, subject to legislation, is for the first primary care Trusts to become operational from April 2000 and for 1999–2000 to be used as a developmental period for PCGs and those community Trusts wishing to progress to primary care Trust status. The outcome of this venture will be awaited with great interest as the process of assuring quality takes another step forward.

References

Abdellah, F. 1958 *Effects of Nursing Staffing on Satisfaction with Nursing Care*. Illinois, American Hospital Association Monograph.

Alcott, L. M. 1960 *Hospital Sketches*, edited by B. Z. Jones. Cambridge: Belknap Press of Harvard University Press.

Alment Report 1976 *Competence to Practice*. Committee of Enquiry into Competence to Practice. London: HMSO.

Baker, A. 1976 The Hospital Advisory Service, in G. McLachlan (ed.) *A Question of Quality*. London: Oxford University Press, 203–16.

Ball, J. A., Goldstone, L. A. and Collier, M. M. 1983 *Monitor: An Index of the Quality of Nursing Care for Acute Medical and Surgical Wards*. Newcastle-upon-Tyne: Newcastle-upon-Tyne Polytechnic Products.

Carter, G. B. and Balme, H. 1936 *Importance of Evaluating Care*.

Clarke, C. and Whitehead A. G. W. 1981 The Collaboration of the Medical Services Group to the Royal College of Physicians to improvement in care, in G. McLachlan (ed.) *Reviewing Practice in Medical Care: Steps to Quality Assurance*. London: Nuffield Provincial Hospital Trust, 33–40.

Clements, R. V. 1995 Essentials of Clinical Risk Management, *Quality in Health Care*, **4**: 129–34.

Collings, J. S. 1950 General Practice in England Today: A Reconnaissance, *Lancet*, 555–85.

Darby, D. and Cane, L. 1987 The New Zealand Accreditation Programme: Not 'Reinventing the Wheel'. *Australian Clinical Review*, **7**(27): 168–70.

Drew, J. 1964 Determining Quality of Nursing Care, *American Journal of Nursing* **64**(10): 82–5.

Donabedian, A. 1969 Medical Care Appraisal – Quality and Utlization, in *Guide to Medical Care Administration*, vol. II. New York: American Public Health Association.

Department of Health 1966 Report of the Committee on Senior Nursing Staff Structure (Salmon Report). London: HMSO.

Department of Health 1991 *The Patient's Charter*. London: HMSO.

Department of Health 1985 *Working for Patients*. London: HMSO.

Department of Health 1997 *The New NHS, Modern, Dependable*. London: HMSO.

Department of Health 1998 *National Performance Frameworks*. London: HMSO.

Department of Health 1998 *A First Class Service: Quality in the New NHS*. London: HMSO.

Department of Health and Social Security 1981 *The NHS (Constitution of District Health Authorities)*. London: HMSO.

Department of Health and Social Security 1983 *NHS Management Enquiry*. London: HMSO.

Department of Health and Social Security 1985 *Report of the Committee on Hospital Complaints Procedure.* London: HMSO.

Department of Health and Social Security 1979 *Report of the Royal Commission on the National Health Service* (The Merrison Commission). Cmnd 7615. London: HMSO.

Department of Health and Social Security 1983 NHS Management Inquiry (The Griffiths Management Report). London: DHSS.

Dollery, C. T. 1971 The Quality of Health Care, in G. McLachlan (ed.) *Challenge for Change.* London: Oxford University Press.

Godber, G. 1976 The Confidential Enquiry into Maternal Deaths, in G. McLachlan (ed.) *A Question of Quality.* London: Oxford University Press, 24–33.

Goldstone, L. and Ball, J. 1984 The Quality of Nursing Services, *Nursing Times,* **29**(8): 56–9.

Hegyvary, S. T. and Hausman, R. K. D. 1975 Monitoring Nursing Care Quality, *Journal of Nursing Administration,* **15**(55): 17–26.

Higgins, J. 1985 A Consultation on the Accreditation of Residential Care Homes, Nursing Homes and Mental Nursing Homes: A Report of, and Commentary Upon, a Conference Held at the King's Fund Centre on 25 January 1985, Project Paper no. 56.

Kitson, A. 1986 Indicators of Quality in Nursing Care – An Alternative Approach, *Journal of Advanced Nursing,* **11**(2): 133–44.

Kitson, A. 1986 Taking Action, *Nursing Times,* **3**: 52–4.

Kitson, A. and Kendall, H. 1986 Rest Assured, *Nursing Times,* **27**: 28–31.

Lesnik, M. J. and Anderson, B. E. 1955 *Nursing Practice and the Law,* 2nd edn. Philadelphia: Lippincott.

Limongelli, F. 1983 Accreditation: New Standards Published. *Dimensions in Health Services,* **60**: 18–19.

McCleary, D. 1977 Joint Commission on Accreditation of Hospitals – Twenty Five Years of Promoting Improved Health Care Services. *American Journal of Hospital Pharmacy,* **34**: 951–4.

McCue, H. and Wilson, L. 1981 Hospital Accreditation in Australia: Evaluating Health Care. *Medical Journal of Australia,* **2**: 221–3, 226.

Merrison Report 1979 Report of the Royal Commission on the NHS (The Merrison Commission) London: HMSO.

NHS Management Executive 1993 Risk Management in the NHS. Leeds: DoH.

Nightingale, F. 1858 *Notes on Nursing.* London. Harrison and Sons.

Nightingale, F. 1874 Address from Florence Nightingale to the probationer nurses in the Nightingale Fund School at St Thomas's Hospital who were formerly trained there. Printed for private use 23 July 1874. Nutting Collection, Teachers College, Columbia University.

Palmer, R. E. 1978 The March of History: Growing Regulations and Growing Costs. *Hospital Progress,* **59**(9): 58–61.

Phaneuf, M. C. 1972 *The Nursing Audit.* Detroit: Appleton-Century-Crofts.

Reerink, E. 1987 Quality Assurance in the Health Care System in the Netherlands. *Australian Clinical Review,* **7**(24): 11–15.

Reiter, F. and Kakosh, M. 1953 *Quality of Nursing Care: A Report of a Field Study to Establish Criteria 1950–1953.* New York: Graduate School of Nursing, New York Medical College.

Roberts, C. J. 1988 Annotation: Towards the More Effective Use of Diagnostic Radiology: A Review of the Work of the Royal College of Radiologists' Working Party on the More Effective Use of Diagnostic Radiology, 1976–1988, *Clinical Radiology,* **39**: 3–6.

Royal College of General Practitioners 1985 *Quality in General Practice.* London.

Royal College of Nursing 1980 *Standards of Nursing Care.* London: RCN.

Royal College of Nursing 1981 *Towards Standards.* London: RCN.

Royal College of Nursing 1987 *In Pursuit of Excellence.* Position Statement on Nursing. London: RCN.

Stephenson, G. W. 1978 At Hand: Bureaucratic Surveillance. *Hospital Progress,* **59**(9): 50–7.

Stewart, I. 1919 Possibilities of Standardisation of Nursing Techniques, *Modern Hospital,* **12**(6): 451–4.

Wandelt, M. A. and Stewart, S. D. 1975 *Slater Nursing Competencies Rating Scale.* Detroit: Appleton-Century-Crofts.

Wandelt, M. A. and Ager, J. W. 1974 *Quality Patient Care Scale.* New York: Appleton-Century-Crofts.

Wilson, J. 1983 The Canadian Hospital Accreditation Program. *Canadian Nurse,* **79**: 48–9.

Williamson, J. D. 1973 Quality Control, Medical Audit and the General Practitioner, *Journal of the Royal College of General Practitioners,* **23**: 697–706.

Whitehead, T. 1976 Surveying the Performance of Pathological Laboratories, in G. McLachlan (ed.) *A Question of Quality.* London: Oxford University Press, 97–117.

World Health Organisation 1984 *Targets For Health For All.* Geneva: WHO Regional Office for Europe.

Further reading

Fawcett, R. 1985 Measurement of Care Quality, *Nursing Mirror,* **160**(2): 29–31.

Illsley, V. A. and Goldstone, L. A. 1986 *Guide to Monitor.* Newcastle-upon-Tyne: Newcastle-upon-Tyne Polytechnic Products.

Jelinek, R. C., Hausmann, R. K. D., Hegyvary, S. T. and Newmann, T. F. A. 1976 *A Methodology for Monitoring Quality of Nursing Care.* Publ. no. (HRA) 76–25. Bethesda, MD: US Department for Education, Health and Welfare.

Jelinek, R. C., Hausmann, R. K. D., Hegyvary, S. T. and Newmann, T. F. A. 1976 *Monitoring Quality of Nursing Care,* Part 2, *Assessment and Study of Correlates.* Publ. no. (HRA) 76–7. Bethesda, MD: US Department of Education, Health and Welfare.

Jelinek, R. C., Hausmann, R. K. D., Hegyvary, S. T. and Newmann, T. F. A. 1977 *Monitoring Quality of Nursing Care,* Part 3, *Professional Review for Nursing: An Empirical Investigation.* Publ. no. (HRA) 76–7. Bethesda, MD: US Department of Education, Health and Welfare.

Kemshall, H. and Pritchard, J. 1997 *Good Practice in Risk Assessment and Risk Management,* 1 and 2. London: Jessica Kingsley.

McCall, J. 1988 Monitor Evaluated, *Senior Nurse,* **8**(5): 8–9.

Sale, D. 1990 *Quality Assurance.* Essentials of Nursing Management Series. Basingstoke: Macmillan.

Sale, D. 1996 *Quality Assurance for Nurses and Other Members of the Health Care Team.* Essentials of Nursing Management Series, 2nd edn. Basingstoke: Macmillan.

Sale, D. 1998 *Garantia Da Qualidade Nos Cuidados De Saude, para os profissionais da equipa de saude.* Lisbon: Principia.

Whelan, J. 1987 Using Monitor – Observer Bias, *Senior Nurse,* **7**(6): 8–10.

Useful address

Institute of Risk Management
6 Lloyds Avenue, London EC3N 3AX
The Institute produces several textbooks on the subject.

2

Approaches to Quality Assurance

There are numerous concepts and theories associated with the ever-increasing base of knowledge on the subject of quality assurance, so much so that it was difficult to choose which to develop in this chapter. In order to arrive at a 'shortlist', those which were essentially useful in practice were chosen. There is a danger that quality assurance could become an academic exercise when the whole point is actively to improve patient care in a practical way. The following approaches to quality assurance are included in this chapter:

- the quality assurance cycle;
- Donabedian's approach to defining standards and criteria as developed by the Royal College of Nursing (RCN) into the dynamic standard-setting system;
- Maxwell's six dimensions;
- Donabedian's seven attributes of health care.

The chapter starts by offering a definition of quality assurance and goes on to look at the various levels of evaluation.

Defining quality assurance

There are many definitions of the term 'quality assurance' written by people who have researched the subject thoroughly. A definition that seems both appropriate and easily understood is that given by Williamson (1979):

> Quality assurance is the measurement of the actual level of the service provided plus the efforts to modify when necessary the provision of these services in the light of the results of the measurement.

Another description, according to Schmadl (1979), is as follows:

> The purpose of quality assurance is to assure the consumer of nursing of a specified degree of excellence through continuous measurement and evaluation.

The word 'quality' is defined by the *Concise Oxford Dictionary* as 'degree of excellence', and the word 'assurance' as 'formal guarantee; positive declaration'. Thus, from these definitions, 'quality assurance' may be interpreted as a formal guarantee of a degree of excellence.

Levels of evaluation of quality of care

There are various levels at which the evaluation of the quality of care may take place (Figure 2.1).

At the top of the pyramid, there is what might be described as a 'national level'. This level, since the publication of the government's White Paper *A First Class Service: Quality in the NHS* (DoH, 1998), comprises the National Service Frameworks, which will set out common standards across the UK for the treatment of particular conditions, and the National Institute for Clinical Excellence (NICE). NICE will act as a nationwide appraisal body for new and existing treatments, and disseminate consistent advice on 'what works and what doesn't'. The Commission for Health Improvement (CHI) is also at this level. CHI is a new national body set up as part of the White Paper, to support and oversee the quality of clinical governance and clinical services. Examples of other programmes offering an evaluation of the quality of care at this level are the Audit Commission and King's Fund Accreditation, and The Bristol University Hospital Accreditation schemes. At this level, the organisation is measured against preset standards or criteria set by an organisation outside the Trust or health care facility.

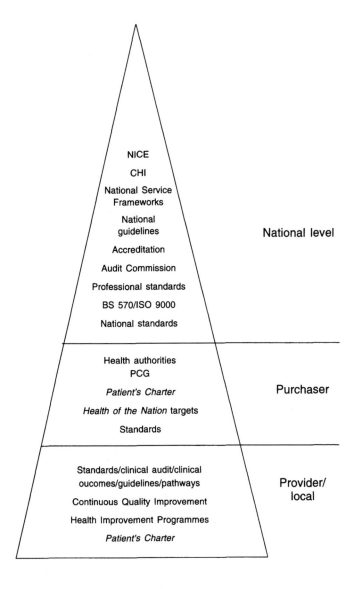

NICE

CHI

National Service
Frameworks

National
guidelines

Accreditation

Audit Commission

Professional standards

BS 570/ISO 9000

National standards

National level

Health authorities
PCG

Patient's Charter

Health of the Nation targets

Standards

Purchaser

Standards/clinical audit/clinical
oucomes/guidelines/pathways

Continuous Quality Improvement

Health Improvement Programmes

Patient's Charter

Provider/
local

NICE = National Institute for Clinical Excellence.
CHI = Commission for Health Improvement.
PCG = Primary Care Group.

Figure 2.1   Levels of evaluation of the quality of care

Also at this level, there is a place for standards set by the Royal Colleges and professional organisations such as the Chartered Society of Physiotherapists. Other standards at this level include *The Patient's Charter* and any British Standard BS 5750 and ISO 9000.

The next level is that of the purchaser and specific areas of quality assurance, which may make up part of the contract as indicators of quality or specified standards. The quality issues addressed in the contract may focus on *The Health of the Nation* targets, *The Patient's Charter*, or areas of concern identified by the consumer or through the Community Health Council. The purchaser will also focus on national issues that have arisen from other studies or reports. This level includes any Trust or organisational standards that may have been set by the purchaser and any national standards.

The next level, at the base of the pyramid, is the most important level – the clinical area, wards, departments, unit, clinics, GP practices and so on. Here, the quality assurance activities may be varied and numerous.

Until recently, quality assurance was monitored by groups of professionals, often in isolation from the rest of their professional colleagues. However, this does not reflect everyday practice, as in the majority of health care settings, the patient is cared for by a team of professionals. For example, the patient admitted for surgery is not cared for exclusively by a surgeon: the nursing staff have a part to play, the anaesthetist is involved, and the patient may need the services of the radiologist, the pathologist, the pharmacists, the therapist, the phlebotomist, the ECG technician, the porters, the clerks and many others. By measuring the quality of care delivered by just one group of staff within the team, we are only measuring a small part of the care given. As a result, what we do not measure is how the care delivered by one professional impacts upon the care given by another. There is also an opportunity to be more efficient and effective by discussing who does what, when, how and why, and by identifying the outcome for the patient.

Evaluation of quality of care

There are a variety of conceptual models of evaluation that have been published and may be used by any person, from any background, as a model of evaluation. Lang's model (1976) was adapted by the American Nurses' Association and modified by Vail in 1986, when an eighth step was added. Lang's model was also adapted by the Royal Australian Nursing Federation to include 11 steps, as shown in Figure 2.2. The model can also be adapted as shown in Figure 2.3, for use by a quality assurance committee, or by the ward sister, charge nurse, head of department or other professional in his or her particular clinical area.

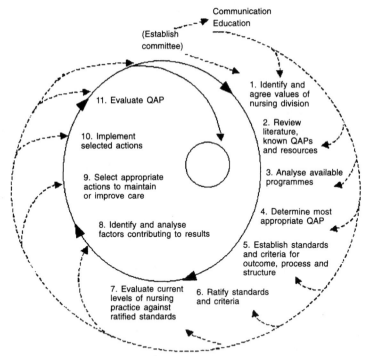

Source: N. Lang (1976) – Issues in Quality Assurance in Nursing, *ANA Issues in Evaluative Research*.

Figure 2.2   Steps in implementing a quality assurance programme (QAP)

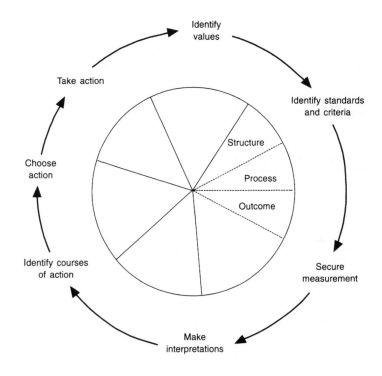

Figure 2.3   An adapted quality assurance model

The quality assurance cycle

Identify values

The first step of the quality cycle is to get together with colleagues in the particular clinical area and write a philosophy of care. To do this, one needs to discuss one's personal beliefs concerning patient care, the profession's code of conduct, beliefs about the uniqueness of individuals and their human rights, the philosophy of care of the Trust or organisation and society's values. This does not have to be a long, detailed account but simply a summary of everyone's beliefs as members of a caring team of professionals.

Set objectives

The next step is to set some objectives – what it is hoped to achieve by measuring the quality of care. This should include the measurable effect of care given to patients and the performance of the staff involved in the delivery of patient care.

Describe patient care in measurable terms

Before quality of care can be measured, the team members must be able to describe what they do. To this end, it is necessary to identify standards and criteria. On reviewing the literature, it can be seen that a number of tools have been developed and are in use all over the country. Many approaches are based on criteria and standards, and can be categorised into a structure, process and outcome framework. Some of these tools' authors favour the measurement of process, others outcome.

Secure measurement

To measure the quality of care, the appropriate tool must be selected. The tools are essentially data collection systems using retrospective and concurrent audit, that is, systems for collecting information that, when collated, will give an indication of the quality of patient care for a particular ward or department.

Evaluation of the results

The evaluation of the results involves comparing 'what is' with 'what should be' and then identifying what needs to be done to achieve quality care.

Taking action – completing the cycle

'Taking action' is achieved by developing a plan to ensure that care is given according to the agreed standard. If this last vital step is not taken, there has been little point in the exercise, and there will be no improvement in patient care. Where standards are found to be low, or where there is a poor quality of care, action must be planned and taken to change practice, returning one to the start of the cycle.

Standards of care

There has been a great deal of standard-writing activity all over the UK. Some standards are excellent, and there is evidence that the use of standards in general has improved patient care, but there are also areas where activity is not as dynamic. On my visits around the country in various guises, I ask to see the ward or department's standards of care. In some cases, what can only be described as a tome of standards is lifted from the shelf and, after the dust has been blown off its cover, it is then handed to me. Within this large folder, there may be dozens of standards, probably written by a manager or the lead person responsible for quality assurance some time in the early 1990s. The staff cannot say what the standards are about, when they were last monitored or how they are used to monitor patient care. In order for standards to have an impact on patient care, they need to be written by the people who deliver care every day, and to reflect current research-based practice.

There should only be about five or six current standards. Once a standard can easily be achieved, it should be replaced by another standard that will improve patient care. However, the old standard may occasionally be reviewed and monitored to check that its outcomes are still being achieved. If the standard is not being achieved, action must be taken to ensure its achievement – and thus the standard is brought back into the system.

Every member of staff should be involved in both the setting and the monitoring of standards. Standards should reflect the expertise of the caring teams and the specific care required for the patient in that particular clinical area. Standards must be evidence based and dynamic – always moving, always changing to ensure or improve the quality of patient care – rather than just a paper exercise.

In order to improve the use of standards as an instrument to monitor the quality of care for patients on a day-to-day basis, an approach to monitoring standards that will help to achieve this will be briefly described. The monitoring of outcomes is simplified, more succinct and part of everyday care rather than being formal monitoring on a planned basis, for example every 4 or 6 months.

The following framework is the one used by the RCN (Kitson, 1986) which is based on the work of Donabedian (1969). Although this framework has been used to set standards in nursing, it has also been successfully used by staff from the professions allied to medicine, and by multidisciplinary teams. It is very simple and straightforward, and could be adapted to set standards anywhere. The questions listed below are those most commonly asked by people embarking on setting standards:

- How do I choose a subject on which to write a standard?
- How many standards do I have to write?
- What good will it do?
- What is the difference between a standard, a policy and a procedure?
- Where do standards fit in with clinical audit, clinical effectiveness and evidence-based practice?
- How can we write standards or even think about standards when we are short staffed, hard pressed and under pressure?
- How do we monitor standards?

All of these questions are addressed in the following description of how to set and monitor standards.

In 1969, in the USA, Donabedian divided the evaluation of quality of care into the evaluation of the structure in which care is delivered, the process of care and the outcome of care (Donabedian, 1969). His findings are still highly valued, forming the basis of much of the work on quality assurance that is taking place worldwide.

Quality of care is the responsibility of everyone involved in health care and it has never been more important than it is today. There are a variety of reasons for the ever-increasing focus on quality assurance. For example, the general public's expectations of the quality of care that they should receive has been raised through the publication of *The Patient's Charter*. Patients and relatives are encouraged to complain if the service is not satisfactory, and their views on the quality of care are actively sought by staff providing a service. There is also the presence of the press ready to pick up on care and services that 'go wrong', with resulting bad publicity for the organisation concerned. Finally, by raising the patients' expectations of the quality of care through the use of care pathways which are shared with the patient and clearly describe the quality of care that the patient should receive.

Standards can be used as a means of monitoring the effectiveness of care in both guidelines and care pathways. For example, a care pathway may have explicit outcome standards that are measured at critical points of the pathway. These outcomes may be monitored concurrently as care progresses, or retrospectively after the patients go home as part of clinical audit.

Both the government's White Papers *The New NHS, Modern, Dependable* (DoH, 1997) and *A First Class Service: Quality in the New NHS* (DoH, 1998), outline the way forward. With *The New NHS* came the introduction of a statutory duty for quality improvement at local level in the form of clinical governance. Standards play an essential part in a clinical governance framework, clinical audit, clinical effectiveness initiatives, the development of guidelines and integrated care pathways, as well as a vehicle for implementing evidence-based practice. Apart from this, there is, and always has been, professionals' desire to deliver good-quality care for their patients.

Setting and monitoring standards of care and quality assurance are separate issues, although they are sometimes discussed as though they are the same. For example, it may be stated that standards are poor, implying that quality is poor, and this leads to the misconception that standards and quality assurance are one and the same – but this is not the case. A standard is an instrument with which to measure the quality of care as part of quality assurance (Figure 2.4).

What are standards of care?

Standards are valid, acceptable definitions of the quality of care. Standards cannot be valid unless they contain criteria to enable care to be measured and evaluated in terms of effectiveness and quality. Standards written without criteria can be likened to a ruler without any measurements marked upon it that is used to attempt a scale drawing: the 'measurements' would be only an estimate and therefore inaccurate and variable.

Why do we need standards of care?

Well-written standards enable professionals to describe, in measurable terms, the care they provide for patients, what is required to carry out that care and what the expected outcome will be. Perhaps we have in the past not been explicit about what we do, and this has led to people from other backgrounds having a less than clear idea about our roles and responsibilities. In the late 1970s and early 1980s, the health service, in particular the nursing service, was faced with cutbacks and enormous change. The RCN was concerned about a reduced number of nurses and falling standards, so a working group was set up to develop ways of measuring the quality of nursing care.

This group produced two documents: *Standards of Nursing Care* (RCN, 1980) and *Towards Standards* (RCN, 1981). Although these two documents apply specifically to nursing, they are equally applicable to the professions allied to medicine and other members of the health care team, as may be seen in the four main themes detailed below.

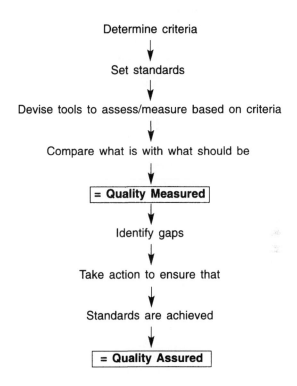

Figure 2.4   Quality measured, quality assured

In *Standards of Nursing Care*, four main themes were put forward:

1. Nurses should develop their own standards of care, and the profession should agree on acceptable levels of excellence.
2. Good nursing is planned, systematic and focused on mutually agreed goals.
3. Agreed standards provide a baseline for measurement.
4. Standards of care influence nursing practice, education, management and research.

In *Towards Standards*, the working party identified eight prerequisites for successful, professional setting and control of standards of nursing care, which may again be applied to other professions and members of the health care team. These are:

1. a philosophy of nursing
2. the relevant knowledge and skills
3. the nurse's authority to act
4. accountability
5. the control of resources
6. the organisational structure and management style
7. the doctor–nurse relationship
8. the management of change.

In summary, the document identified the need for a statement of the underlying values and philosophy to guide nursing practice before quality nursing care could be assured. The philosophy had to be agreed and made explicit. The following factors were linked with the philosophy:

- There must be a clear identification of the skills and knowledge required by the nurse in order to carry out care effectively. The nurse must be given the authority to act and be accountable for that action.
- Of the eight factors listed above, accountability is key to the formation of professional standards. Nurses must be clear about the extent of their authority, responsibility and accountability, which must be matched with the necessary authority to carry out their job effectively.
- The last four factors relate to the control of the nursing system. Managers and senior nurses must be prepared to provide nurses with the appropriate manpower and equipment to do the job effectively. There must be a recognition of the nurses' need to control appropriate resources, to manage the service and to enjoy a relationship of mutual respect with other professionals. Finally, nurses must be in a position to initiate and manage change, a principle implicit in general management.

How standards can be used

Standards can be used to obtain information to:

- monitor care
- assess the level of service
- identify deficiencies
- communicate expectations
- introduce new knowledge
- make explicit what professionals do.

The quality assurance cycle and standards

It is important to understand where standards fit into the quality assurance cycle (Figure 2.5). It has always been very difficult to describe care in measurable terms, but standards help us to do just that.

Describing

The first part of the cycle is the 'describing' part, and it is helpful to start by writing a philosophy of care. This is really a statement about what we believe we are doing to help and care for our patients or clients: Why are we here? What do we believe we are doing? This does not have to be a highly academic statement but should be a few words describing that belief. From this come the objectives – what one hopes to achieve. Once the team have written their philosophy and objectives, it will become apparent what standards must be written in order to measure the effectiveness of the philosophy and objectives. Thus, the first step is to describe what is done in measurable terms. Standards and criteria are identified in order to establish and measure the quality of the service.

Measuring

The next part of the cycle is measuring the standards. It is not possible to measure the quality of care unless it has

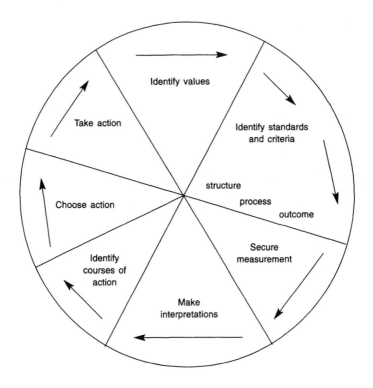

Figure 2.5 The quality assurance cycle

been accurately described in measurable terms. Once the standard has been measured, the results should be reviewed; criteria not achieved should be identified and interpretations made about compliance with the standard.

Taking action

The last and most important step is taking action – comparing what should be with what is, and taking action to ensure that the quality of care is assured. The cycle is then re-entered to ensure that improvements have been made.

Who writes standards?

Earlier in this chapter, we outlined the levels of evaluation; the level that this particular part of the chapter relates to is the 'local' level. The National Service Frameworks, which will set out common standards across the UK for the treatment of particular conditions, and NICE will act as a nationwide appraisal body for new and existing treatments, and disseminate consistent advice on 'what works and what doesn't'. There are already a large number of guidelines and pathways that are evidence based, but in order to monitor their effectiveness, or to develop existing standards to meet local requirements or situations, professionals need to be able to evaluate and write standards.

Local standards are written by staff working in clinical areas. They are written on topics that they select and are relevant to the needs of both staff and patients/clients. Standards are often written to solve a problem, but they may also be written for an area of concern or one of particular interest or good practice. Standards may be set and monitored as part of clinical audit, the development of guidelines and integrated care pathways.

Being involved in setting and monitoring standards of care means being committed to looking at what one does and being prepared to take appropriate action to change things to improve the quality of patient care. All standards should be research based, which means establishing sound, proven reasons for practice. Setting standards is about taking an extra look at what one does – not giving care that is ritualistic, unnecessary or of no proven value.

Standards are developed by professionals or any member of the health care team working in a particular area or with a specific concern group. These standards are statements that are specific and concern activities in wards and units. They are presented in statements of performance to be achieved within an agreed time and are *acceptable, achievable, observable* and *measurable.*

Terminology used in standard setting

There is an enormous amount of jargon used in the setting and monitoring of standards, but in order to write standards, it is important to understand the relevant terminology.

A standard statement

A standard statement is a professionally agreed level of performance, appropriate to the population addressed, which reflects what is acceptable, achievable, observable, and measurable. The first part of this description – 'A standard statement is professionally agreed' – means that a group of professionals or members of the health care team get together and, in discussion, agree a standard, taking into account research findings and changes in practice.

The first and vital step in standard setting is beginning the provision of continuity of care for the patient. The discussions about 'what we do' and 'who does it' prior to setting the standard are highly valuable as they may identify duplication of effort by professionals, differences in the way in which care is given and a debate on what should be done by whom, how and when.

The standard statement should include the indicators of quality. For example, 'Every patient receives a safe medicine regime' could be strengthened by an indicator of quality and the word 'effective'. Thus, the standard statement would read 'Every patient receives a safe and effective medicine regime.'

The second part of the statement – 'which relates to a level of performance' – means establishing what the nurse is trying to achieve for the patients/clients within the resources available, and reaching the desired outcome. 'Appropriate to the population addressed' means to the care group for which the standard is written, taking into account the patient or client's and relatives' needs, negotiating care with patients or clients and developing shared plans of care. The standard may be written for children, for patients admitted for surgery and so on.

Criteria

Criteria may be defined as descriptive statements of performance, behaviours, circumstances or clinical status that represent a satisfactory, positive or excellent state of affairs. A criterion is a variable, or item, that is selected as a relevant indicator of the quality of care. Criteria make the standard work because they are detailed indicators of the standard and must be specified to the area or type of patient.

Criteria must be:

- *measurable,* illustrating the standard and providing local measures;
- *specific,* giving a clear description of behaviours, action, situation or resources desired or required;
- *relevant,* being identifiable items that are required in order to achieve a set level of performance. It is possible to think of numerous criteria but it is essential to learn to be selective and pick out only those criteria which are the relevant indicators of quality of care and which must be met in order to achieve a set level of performance;
- *clearly understandable,* so they should each contain only one major theme or thought;
- *clearly and simply stated,* in order to avoid being misunderstood;
- *achievable,* it being important to avoid unrealistic expectations in either performance or results;
- *clinically sound,* thus being selected by practitioners who are clinically up to date and base their knowledge on sound research or evidence;
- *reviewed periodically,* to ensure that they are reflective of good practice based on current research;
- *reflective of all aspects of the patient or client status,* that is, physiological, psychological and social.

In summary, a criterion must be:

- a detailed indicator of the standard;
- specific to the area and type of patient or client;
- measurable.

The standard should be thought of as a tape measure or ruler, and the criteria as the measurement marks. The criteria allow measurement of the standard statement.

There are three types of criteria:

- structure
- process
- outcome

When thinking about and writing a standard, it is easier to start with the outcome and work backwards, working on the theory that if you know what you want to achieve, it is easier to establish what you need to do to get there.

Outcome criteria

Outcome criteria describe the effect of the care – the results expected in order to achieve the standard in terms of behaviours, responses, level of knowledge and health status, in other words what is expected and desirable described in a specific and measurable form.

Consider the following headings:

The professional can state...
The patient can state...
There is documented evidence...
The professional observed...

One of the reasons for developing the outcome criteria into immediately measurable criteria is to ensure that standards are measured all the time as part of the evaluation of care. Many professionals see the measurement of standards as 'someone else's responsibility' rather than part of patient or client care. Outcomes that are not being achieved need to be corrected immediately and not left for quarterly or 6-monthly formal monitoring.

Monitoring outcomes

Outcome criteria can be very broad, for example 'The discharge was carried out in accordance with the individual's needs and wishes.' This outcome requires a separate monitoring tool in order to measure the patient's satisfaction. An alternative is to state the outcome criteria, as shown in Figure 2.6.

THE STANDARD:
Every patient's discharge is discussed and planned with the patient/carer to meet his/her individual needs.

OUTCOME	YES	NO
Ask the patient/carer: • Was the discharge plan discussed with him/her? • Does the plan meet his/her needs?		
Review the patient's record: • There is a documented assessment of the patient's needs prior to discharge • There is a documented discharge plan • The discharge plan has been completed		

Figure 2.6 Outcome criteria stated in a format that can be monitored as part of every patient's care

The standard is measured for all patients as part of the process of their discharge. Any outcome criteria that are not achieved are investigated and corrected at the time of the discharge as part of ensuring good-quality care.

Process criteria

Process criteria describe what action must take place in order to achieve the outcome that has already been set. These may be:

- the assessment techniques and procedures;
- methods of the delivery of care;
- methods of intervention;
- methods of patient, client and relative or carer education;
- methods of giving information;
- methods of documenting;
- how resources are used;
- the evaluation of the competence of staff carrying out the care.

The following headings indicate the areas to include in process criteria – what must be done to meet the standard statement and the outcome:

The professional assesses...
The professional includes in the plan...
The professional does...
The professional reviews...
The professional and the patient or client...

Structure criteria

Structure criteria may be seen as a 'shopping list' of requirements, of what must be provided in order to achieve the standard, considering the items of service that lie in the system, such as:

- the physical environment and buildings;
- ancillary and support services;
- equipment;
- staff: number, skill, mix, training and expertise;
- information: agreed policies and procedures, rules and regulations, protocols, guidelines, research and evidence;
- the organisational system.

In summary, criteria state:

- what we need to meet the standard;
- what must be done to meet the standard;
- the expected results or outcome.

It is important to remember that the criteria describe the activities to be performed, whereas the standard states the level at which they are to be performed. The criteria are like the strings on a puppet, making the standard come alive. By following this process, patient or client care can be measured by comparing actual practice against the stated criteria and then checking to see whether the activity has met the agreed standard.

The standard is written for a specific care group

This is the target group of patients, clients or staff for whom the standard is written, such as 'care of the elderly' patients, 'patients in the recovery room', patients with a specific problem, such as diabetes, or those recovering from a cerebral vascular accident, 'mother and baby' clients, 'children', 'clients in the community' and so on.

Achieve by date and review by date

It is important to decide when the standard will be achieved and to set and record a realistic date. The team must also discuss and decide when it would be reasonable to review the standard and decide whether it is still relevant, achievable, acceptable and in line with current practice and research. If it is not, it should be removed from the system and replaced by an appropriate standard. It is important to realise that standards set today are not set in tablets of stone forever but should be reviewed and rewritten; they are dynamic and change as the patient's or client's needs change, as new research changes practice, as patients or clients change or as staff alter.

The good news is that standards should only be a page long. If they go on for longer, one may well be rewriting

the procedure book. It is very easy to write down every-
thing that comes to mind in relation to a problem, but it
is more difficult to be succinct and only include the indicators of quality.

Checking standards

Once the standard has been written, it should be checked
that the criteria:

- describe the desired quality of performance;
- have been agreed;
- are clearly written (and not open to misinterpretation);
- contain only one major thought;
- are measurable;
- are concise;
- are specific;
- are achievable;
- are evidence-based;
- are clinically sound.

Methods of monitoring standards

There are two approaches to monitoring standards:

- retrospective evaluation
- concurrent evaluation.

Retrospective evaluation involves all the assessment
methods that occur after the patient or client has been
discharged. Concurrent evaluation involves assessment that
takes place while the patient or client is still receiving care.
Figure 2.7 lists the approaches used to assess the quality
of care. Concurrent evaluation is perhaps more valuable
as it gives staff the opportunity to correct any negative
outcomes while the patient is still in their care. This
approach is further developed in Figure 2.8.

AT THE END OF AN EPISODE OF CARE	AS CARE IS BEING GIVEN
Retrospective evaluation of the quality of nursing care may be affected by:	*Concurrent evaluation may be affected by:*
Post-care patient interview Post-care patient questionnaire Post-care staff conference Audit of the records	Assessment of the outcome Patient interview Conference between patient, staff and relatives Direct observation of care Measurement of the competency of the nurse Audit of the records

Figure 2.7   Retrospective and concurrent evaluation of care

YES	NO	N/A	MONITORING STANDARDS
			Retrospective/concurrent evaluation Questions to be answered Developed from the criteria in the standard Auditor checks the criteria in question form: ● Asks the patient about care given ● Asks the staff about care given ● Observes care given/structure of area and reviews documentation ● Responds by answering 'yes', 'no' or 'not applicable' Response should be 100 per cent 'yes'. Any 'no' answers should be investigated and an action plan developed; a date should be set to remonitor standards

Figure 2.8   Monitoring standards using
retrospective and concurrent evaluation

Approaches to monitoring standards

Type 1. As discussed earlier, the process of monitoring standards may be made simpler and more effective by writing the outcome criteria in a form that requires a 'yes' or 'no' answer. It should be remembered that each outcome criterion must contain only one question or theme. Consider, for example, 'The patient states that he has a discharge plan that was discussed with him'. This is difficult to measure as he may have a plan but it may not have been discussed with him. There are thus two criteria in one, and this needs to be split into:

- There is a discharge plan.
- The plan has been discussed with the patient.

Type 2. An alternative approach is to take criteria from structure, process and outcome and turn them into a list of questions. Each question is then used as an indicator which requires a 'yes' or 'no' answer. The total number of 'yes' answers may be added together to calculate a score and demonstrate whether or not the standard has been achieved.

There are various methods of monitoring standards, of which the most commonly used are described below.

Retrospective monitoring. Retrospective monitoring involves all assessment mechanisms carried out after the patient has been discharged. These include:

- *Closed-chart auditing,* which is the review of patient records and the identification of the strengths and deficits of care. This can be achieved by a structured audit of the patient's records.
- A *post-care patient interview,* which is carried out when the patient has left the hospital or care has ceased in the home, and involves inviting the patient and/or family members to meet to discuss their experiences. The interview may be unstructured, semi-structured or structured using a checklist or questionnaire.

- *Post-care questionnaires,* which should be completed by the patient on discharge. They are usually designed to measure patient satisfaction.

Concurrent monitoring. Concurrent monitoring involves all the assessments performed while the patient is in hospital and receiving care. These include:

- *Open-chart auditing,* which is the review of the patient's charts and records against preset criteria. As the patient is still receiving care, this process gives staff immediate feedback.
- *Patient interview or observation,* which involves talking to the patient about certain aspects of care, conducting a bedside audit or observing the patient's behaviour against preset criteria.
- *Staff interview or observation,* which involves talking to and observing nursing behaviour related to preset criteria.
- *Group conferences,* which involve the patient and/or family in a joint discussion with staff about the care being received. This leads to problems being discussed and improved plans agreed.

The various types of measurement need to be discussed by the group and the most appropriate method selected.

Questionnaires

The techniques for asking questions have been thoroughly researched, and there are many different approaches. Payne (1951), Maccoby *et al.,* (1968) Gordon (1969) and Oppenheim (1979) all provide excellent discussions on the art of asking questions. Ward *et al.* (1982) give many examples of different approaches to patient surveys. From these findings and recommendations, the following points arise.

- Questions should be phrased so that they do not patronise the respondent while at the same time being easily understood, thus meeting the intellectual abilities of a cross-section of society.

- Questions must be expressed simply and clearly, making sure that words and phrases with more than one meaning are not used.
- Ask questions one at a time. Do not include two topics in one question, for example 'Was your discharge planned and negotiated with you?': the care may have been planned with the patient but not necessarily negotiated. It is best to ask two separate questions as the answers could be very different.
- Questions should be short.
- Give the respondent an opportunity to write his or her comments down.
- Respondents tend to choose a middle answer if given the choice; a simple 'yes' or 'no' answer will overcome this problem.
- A respondent may sometimes show a bias by answering 'yes' to every question. To avoid this, first ask a question requiring a positive answer and then later in the questionnaire ask the same or a similar question for which a negative response is needed. Including different forms of the same question can also check for consistency and misunderstandings.

These are only a few suggestions, but they may help when preparing a questionnaire to monitor a standard.

The care plan

The patient's or client's care plan is a very effective method of monitoring a standard. Other documents, such as the discharge checklist, patient records and other routinely used documents, may also be a useful source of information.

The final stage

The final stage in standard setting is to compare current practice with the standard and to act on the monitoring result. If the standard has not been achieved, the team needs to check why:

- Is the standard achievable?
- Is the standard realistic?

If the answer to these questions is 'no', the standard should be reviewed and revised. If however, it is achievable, an action plan should be developed to ensure that practice meets the standard.

As demonstrated in Figure 2.4, the measurement of standards is not 'quality assured'. Quality assurance only occurs when the gaps have been identified following measurement, and action has been taken to ensure that standards are achieved and the gaps are closed, so that the cycle can again continue.

Summary

It is important to remember that standards set at local level are written by those who are delivering the care. The very process of setting standards leads to a discussion about practice: who does what and how.

In any team of professionals, there will be a variety of people, all of whom were trained at different times, have different professional backgrounds and have varying amounts of experience and competence. Talking about practice gives everyone a chance to share their experience and expertise, this alone improving the quality of care. In order to have an agreed standard, there must be a consensus of opinion, which inevitably leads to improved continuity of care.

Continuity of care, practising according to research findings and keeping up to date can be potential problems, particularly for professionals working in isolation, and the process of setting standards is a very useful method of promoting good-quality care that is evidence based.

One of the main problems for groups of professionals setting standards is the lack of time available, during their working day, to set standards, particularly together as a multidisciplinary team. One seemingly successful solution to the problem is the principle of 'little and often', for

example using some of the time spent in routine meetings to set a standard. Most wards or departments meet to
discuss patient care, either for a report on patient care or
for a case conference. At the end of these meetings, liter-
ally a few minutes can be spent setting standards. Here is
an example of how this might be done:

- At the first meeting, discuss what the topic of the standard
  might be. Write these thoughts on a large piece of paper
  and leave it for those who were not at the meeting to add
  theirs.
- At the next meeting, try to draft the standard statement;
  again, write it up and leave it for comments.
- At subsequent meetings, add the process and the
  structure criteria to the standard.

Using this approach means that all members of staff are
involved, everyone in the team contributing to the standard. During these short sessions, there are opportunities
to discuss the content of the standard. Everyone agrees
the standard and has a clear understanding of the monitoring approach. As a result, there will, at the end of the
process, be a commitment and ownership to the standard,
and possibly changes in practice that will have already
improved patient care.

It is advisable to set a few standards, perhaps four or
five, so that the task does not become enormous. The standards will of course need to be changed when they can be
easily achieved, in order to ensure a continuous improvement of patient care. For example, if a ward or department sets five key standards and one is easily achieved,
this should be put on the shelf and a new standard established on another topic, perhaps in response to an area
in which care could be improved. The standard on the
shelf should occasionally be monitored to ensure it is still
being achieved, and be brought back into the system if
this is not the case.

Monitoring standards

Monitoring standards is like taking a 'snapshot' of the quality of care in order to establish the standard of care. If the standard is poor or there are problems, there may be a need to develop and set up a clinical audit so that solutions can be investigated, identified and implemented. Thus, the monitoring of standards may be seen as a snapshot of activity, and the process of clinical audit as a detailed portrait.

The standards displayed in Figures 2.9–2.17 demonstrate how standards are written and some of the reasons for writing the standards in order to improve patient care. Some of the standards contain the evidence base while others do not.

Maxwell's six dimensions of quality

In 1984 Robert Maxwell, then Secretary at the King Edward's Hospital Fund for London, wrote a paper in the *British Medical Journal* entitled 'Quality Assessment in Health'. Maxwell commented (1984a):

> Concern about the quality of care must be as old as medicine itself. But an honest concern about quality, however genuine is not the same as a methodological assessment based on reliable, evidence.

Maxwell's six dimensions (outlined below) arise from his belief that quality of care cannot be measured in a single dimension. Each of the six dimensions needs to be recognised separately; each requires different measures and different skills.

Acceptability

- How humanely and considerately is this treatment or service delivered?
- What does the patient think of it?
- How would I feel if the patient were my nearest and dearest?

Topic: Psychiatric Nursing Care Plan
Care Group: Mental Health Nursing

Date: 01/02/99
Results of Monitoring

Standard Statement: The nurse as key worker develops a care plan in partnership with the patient(s), with specific goals and nursing interventions to meet the individual needs of each patient.

Structure	Process	Outcome (Ongoing Monitoring Tool)	Yes	No

Nurses need to have:
 	
1. Information gathered from the psychiatric nursing assessment.
2. A knowledge of nursing models of care.
3. A knowledge of resources available.
4. A clinical environment in which the nurse has opportunities to discuss with others the development of nursing care plans.
5. A recognised system to record information.
 	
The standard was developed to improve record keeping and to encourage greater patient involvement in the process of planning and evaluating care.
	1. The nurse informs the patient of the key worker role and its responsibilities.
	2. The nurse, in partnership with the patient, uses a recognised nursing model to:
	  a. Assess and identify priorities of care.
	  b. Set realistic goals with review dates.
	3. The nurse discusses with the patient, multidisciplinary team members and significant others the development of plan of care.
		1. Each patient has a care plan.
		2. The care plan is up to date.
		3. The care plan reflects concurrent problems/goals.
		4. The patient states that he or she was involved in the development of the care plan.
		5. The patient states that he or she was involved in the evaluation of care.		

Figure 2.9 Psychiatric nursing care plan

Standard Statement: Each patient's discharge is planned from admission to ensure continuity of care.

Structure	Process	Outcome	Yes	No

• A registered nurse with skills and knowledge of community and social services.
• Multidisciplinary teams.
• A policy and procedures.
• Referral criteria for patients to community/social services.
• A discharge checklist.
 	
Evidence Base:
Neill J. and Williams J. (1992) *Leaving Hospital* London: NISW Research Unit
Audit Commission (1992) *Lying in Wait* London: Audit Commission
 	
Government Circulars:
DoH 1988 *Caring For People.* Cmmd 849
DoH 1989 *Discharge of Patients from Hospital* – HC(89)5 and LAC(89)7
DoH 1993 *Monitoring and Development Special Study 31 December, Agreements Reviewing the Implementation.* London
DoH 1994 *Hospital Discharge Workbook.* London
	• An anticipated discharge date is recorded in the patient's record on admission.
	• An assessment of the patient's home and social circumstances is documented on admission.
	• An ongoing assessment of the patient's needs is recorded.
	• The patient's discharge is discussed and planned with:
	  – The multidisciplinary team.
	  – The patient.
	  – The patient's family/carers.
	• All support services are organised and documented in the record.
	• The discharge checklist is completed prior to discharge.
		• The patient/family state that the plan was discussed with them.
		• The patient/family state the plan was developed with them.
		• All support services were organised prior to discharge.
		• The patient's length of stay was not extended due to discharge planning delays.
		• The patient states that the arrangements met his or her needs.
		
		Monitor all patients on discharge.		

Figure 2.10 Discharge from hospital (elderly care)

Topic: Comfort and Security in Outpatient Departments   **Date:** 01/04/99
Care Group: Outpatients   **Results of Monitoring**

Standard Statement: Each patient's stay in the outpatient department is made as comfortable as possible.

Structure	Process	Outcome	Yes	No

• Seats of variable heights.
• Refreshments.
• Health education reading material.
• Space for wheelchairs.
• Space for Zimmer frames.
• Lockers for clothing.
• Up-to-date reading material.
 	
The standard was written to improve the environment in an outpatient department.
	• The patient is welcomed to the outpatient department.
	• The staff ensure that:
	  – Suitable seating is available.
	  – There is space for patients in wheelchairs.
	  – There is space for patients using Zimmer frames.
	  – There is up-to-date reading material available (health education and general reading material).
	  – Patients are made aware of all facilities.
	  – Patients' clothes are kept secure.
	  – There are toys available for children, suitable for all ages.
	  – The temperature is constant:
	    ♦ Cool in summer.
	    ♦ Warm in winter.
		• The patient states that the facilities met his or her needs.
		• The patient states that the waiting area was comfortable.
		
		This standard is supported with a questionnaire distributed to patients on a 3-monthly basis to review the facilities offered by the department.		

Figure 2.11 Comfort and security in outpatient departments

Topic: Application of Therapeutic Heat
Care Group: Physiotherapy Patients

Date: 01/05/99
Results of Monitoring

Standard Statement: Prior to the application of therapeutic heat, the patient's skin is assessed with regard to the ability to detect heat to ensure that there is no tissue damage as a result of therapy.

Structure	Process	Outcome	Yes	No
• Physiotherapy. • Assessment. • Skills and knowledge. • Documentation. The standard was written in response to risk management issues.	• The physiotherapist: – Assesses the patient's skin ability to detect heat. – Records the findings in the patient's records. – Discusses the therapy with the patient.	• There is a documented assessment of the patient's skin sensation with regard to the ability to detect heat. • There is no damage to the patient's skin as a result of therapeutic heat. Monitor all patients.		

Figure 2.12 Application of therapeutic heat

Standard Statement: **Patients are supported through the endoscopy procedure by skilled nurses in order to reduce stress and anxiety.**

Structure	Process	Outcome	Yes	No
• Nurses' skills and knowledge. • Pre-procedural information. Evidence Base: Murphy, D. (1993) Managing Patient Stress in Endoscopy. *Gastro-enterology Nursing*, **16**(2): 72–4. Boore, J. (1997) Preoperative Care of Patients. *Nursing Times*, **73**(12): 409–11. Teasdale, K. (1995) The Nurse's Role in Anxiety Management. *Professional Nurse*, **10**(8): 509–12. May, C. (1990) Research on Nurse Patient Relationships: Problems of Theory, Problems of Practice. *Journal of Advanced Nursing*, **15**(3): 307–15. Teasdale, K. (1995) Theoretical and Practical Considerations of the Use of Reassurances in the Nursing Management of Anxious Patients. *Journal of Advanced Nursing*, **22**(1): 79–86.	• The nurse meets with the patient and discusses the procedure prior to the admission date. • The nurse gives the patient time to express fears and anxieties. • The nurse gives the patient the printed information about the procedure. • On the day of the endoscopy, the nurse confirms the patient's decision to have local anaesthetic cord spray. • During the procedure, the nurse observes the patient for signs of stress/anxiety and responds by reinforcing the patient's own coping strategies and other coping mechanisms, including relaxation, controlled breathing, distraction and cognitive therapy.	• Monitoring through a retrospective questionnaire to randomly selected patients: – Did you have sufficient information prior to the procedure? – Were you supported by the nurse throughout the procedure? – Were you physically stressed during the procedure? – Were you psychologically stressed during the procedure? – Would you have the procedure again without sedation? The standard was written as part of an ongoing review of current clinical practice against the listed evidence, in order to ensure good practice		

Figure 2.13   Endoscopy – day patient

Standard Statement: **The environment within which the patient is cared for minimises the opportunity for the patient to commit suicide by hanging.**

Structure	Process	Outcome	Yes	No

• Risk assessment.
• Criteria.
	• The nurse in charge of the ward undertakes a risk assessment to identify any potential risk areas.
	• Risk areas are reported.
	• Action is taken to minimise the risk.
	• Patients at risk of deliberate self-harm are assessed and a documented risk assessment is completed.
	• Patients are identified as being at risk of deliberate self-harm and kept under observation.
		• Pipes are boxed in.
		• There are non-weight-bearing:
		  – Rails in cupboards.
		  – Curtain rails.
		  – Rails for bed screens.
		  – Showers.
		  – Hooks on doors.
		  – Hooks in cupboards.
		• Stairways and landings are boxed in.
		• Patients at risk have a completed, documented risk assessment.
		
		Monitoring – Random audit at least 3-monthly of the environment. Ongoing monitoring of all patients at risk.		

Standard development occurred as part of a risk assessment for an acute inpatient area for mental health.				

Figure 2.14 Risk of suicide by hanging

Topic: Discharge
Care Group: Patients Receiving Speech Therapy

Date: 03/06/99
Results of Monitoring

Standard Statement: Each speech therapist adheres to the documented discharge criteria in order to ensure access to the service for new patients.

Structure	Process	Outcome	Yes	No

• Documented discharge criteria.
• Discharge policy.
	• An ongoing assessment of all patients.
	• A discharge plan is developed by the speech therapist for patients:
	  – Whose communicative abilities have reached normal limits.
	  – Considered to have no ascertainable defect on assessment.
	  – Or carers who fail to fulfil the agreed, negotiated contract.
	  – Who are, in the opinion of the speech therapist, unlikely to benefit from further intervention.
	  – Who fail to attend initial appointments without notification.
		• There is documented evidence of ongoing patient assessment.
		• The patient is discharged using the criteria as a baseline.
		• The patient's discharge was planned.
		
		Monitoring of all patients discharged from the speech therapist's caseload for a period of 1 month.		

The standard was written to ensure that patients were not kept on the caseload unnecessarily and that waiting lists were reduced, making the best use of the professional resources.				

Figure 2.15   Discharge from speech therapy

Topic:	Pain – Patient-controlled Analgesia (PCA)	Date: 03/08/99
Care Group:	Postoperative Patients	Results of Monitoring
Standard Statement:	All patients receiving pain relief by means of a PCA pump receive the prescribed medication, self-administered in order to control their pain to an acceptable level.	

Structure	Process	Outcome	Yes	No
• Nursing staff with intravenous drip administration training. • PCA guidelines. • Medicine policy and procedures. • PCA pumps. • Acute pain specialist. • Anaesthetist. Evidence Base: Collins, F. (1994) Pain: Patients in Control. An Evaluation of PCA. *British Journal of Theatre Nursing*, **3**: 9–13. Dening, F. (1993) Patient Controlled Analgesia. *British Journal of Nursing*, **2**: 274–7. DoH (1994) *Safety Action Bulletin. Syringe Pumps: Uncontrolled Infusion due to Syphonage*. London: HMSO. Kwan, A. (1996) Morphine Overdose from Patient Controlled Analgesia Pumps. *Anaesthetics and Intensive Care*, **24**: 254–6. Warwick, P. (1992) The Principles of PCA. *Nursing Times*, **88**: 38–40. Wells, J. (1991) Introducing PCA – the Gloucester Experience. *British Journal of Theatre Nursing*, **91**: 6–9. The standard was written to monitor the effectiveness of PCA.	• The anaesthetist selects the patient. • The anaesthetist discusses the use of PCA with the patient. • The anaesthetist writes up the prescription in the patient's day chart. • The nurse ensures that naloxone and anti-emetic medication are also prescribed by the anaesthetist. • The nurse reinforces the use of the PCA with the patient. • The nurse ensures that other opioids are not given while the PCA is in use. • Once the pump programme has been set up, it can only be altered by the anaesthetist, the specialist pain nurse and named nurses. • The nurse observes for signs of respiratory problems and responds as per the guidelines. • The nurse monitors the patient's pain to ensure that pain is controlled.	• The patient states that he or she was able to use the PCA. • The prescription for the drugs was written on the drug chart. • The patient states satisfaction with the pain control. • The PCA was administered safely. • There were no complications. Monitoring for all patients using PCA as part of the evaluation of care.		

Figure 2.16 Pain – patient-controlled analgesia (PCA)

Standard Statement: All nurse-led postoperative outpatient clinics are run efficiently and result in effective patient care

Structure	Process	Outcome	Yes	No

• Policy for the assessment of patients attending an orthopaedic nurse practitioner clinic.
• Policy and protocol for requesting clinical investigations.
• Integrated care pathway for patients undergoing orthopaedic surgery.
• Agreed list of patients who may be seen post-operatively in clinics run by the nurse practitioner.
• Qualified nurse practitioner.
• UKCC code of practice.
 	
The standard was written to monitor the introduction of nurse-led orthopaedic, postoperative, outpatient clinics.
	• The nurse practitioner checks that the patient meets the criteria to attend the nurse practitioner clinic.
	• The nurse practitioner:
	  – Assesses the patient.
	  – Examines the patient.
	  – Records the findings.
	• If problems are identified, the nurse practitioner:
	  – Refers the patient to the consultant (as per pathway).
	  – Requests clinical investigations (as per pathway).
	  – Records all treatment, advice given and decisions made (as per pathway).
	  – Refers to district/practice nurse if the problem requires further dressings.
	• If there are no problems, the nurse practitioner completes all the necessary documentation and discharges the patient (as per pathway).
	• Discharge letter to GP.
		• The patient meets the criteria to attend the nurse practitioner clinic.
		• The nurse-led clinic is run at the same time as the orthopaedic clinic.
		• Problems such as infection, reduced neurological or vascular status, loss of function or deep vein thrombosis were referred directly during the clinic.
		• The patient states that he or she was given time to discuss any problems.
		• The patient states that he or she was satisfied with his or her appointment with the nurse practitioner.
		• The documentation was completed.
		• The discharge letter was sent to the GP.
		• Access times to the orthopaedic registrar have been reduced.
		• The monitoring of outcomes through a random selection of patients at the time of discharge from the clinic.
		Peer review.		

Figure 2.17   Nurse practitioner services – nurse-led postoperative clinics

- What is the setting like?
- Are privacy and confidentiality safeguarded?

Effectiveness (for individual patients)

- Is the treatment given the best available in a technical sense, according to those best equipped to judge?
- What is their evidence?
- What is the overall result of the treatment?

Efficiency and economy

- Is the output maximised for a given input or, conversely, is the input minimised for a given level of output?
- How does the unit cost compare with the unit cost elsewhere for the same treatment or service?

Access

- Can people get this treatment or service when they need it?
- Are there any identifiable barriers to the service, for example distance, inability to pay, waiting lists and waiting times, or straightforward breakdowns in supply?

Equity (fairness)

- Is this patient or group of patients being fairly treated relative to others?
- Are there any identifiable failings in equity? For example, are some people being dealt with less favourably or less appropriately in their own eyes than others?

Relevance to need (for the whole community)

- Is the overall pattern and balance of the services the best that could be achieved, taking account of the needs and wants of the population as a whole? (Maxwell, 1984b)

To expand on his framework, Maxwell used the accident and emergency department services as an example:

1. *Social acceptability.* This could include the environment within the department and include privacy and standards of communication with the patient and the GP.

2. *Effectiveness.* Technical effectiveness might include the adequacy of equipment and staffing in the department, the incidence of complications, and some form of follow-up assessment.

3. *Efficiency and economy.* This would look at workload and unit cost comparisons with other accident and emergency departments.

4. *Access.* It is possible to assess access to this service in terms of ambulance response times and waiting times in the department.

5. *Equity.* This would include a review of the system of triage to establish that patients are given the correct priority of care and treatment.

6. *Relevance to need.* This would require further work in the form of a review and analysis of the different roles within the department, such as the services for major trauma, minor injuries and primary care.

By using these six dimensions, it is possible to assess the quality of the department as a whole rather than in a fragmented manner. Maxwell also stressed the need to keep the approach and system simple, while providing a framework within which the quality of care could be studied, discussed, protected and improved. He believed that this would take (Maxwell, 1984a):

> encouragement, experiment, and sharing of ideas and require a mixture of assessment methods including standard data analysis, sampling and follow up, professional peer review, consumer opinion tailored to an understanding of the multidimensional nature of quality itself.

Donabedian's seven attributes of health care

In 1990 Avedis Donabedian, a retired Professor of Public Health in the USA, wrote an article titled 'The Seven Pillars of Quality' (1990). In this, he describes:

the seven attributes of health care that define its quality:

1. Efficacy: The ability of care at its best to improve health.
2. Effectiveness: the degree to which attainable health improvements are realised.
3. Efficiency: the ability to obtain the greatest health improvement at the lowest cost.
4. Optimality: the most advantageous balancing of costs and benefits.
5. Acceptability: conformity to patient preferences regarding accessibility, the patient–practitioner relation, the amenities, the effects of care, and the cost of care.
6. Legitimacy: concerning all of the above.
7. Equity: fairness in the distribution of care and its effects on health.

Consequently, health care professionals must take into account patient preferences in assessing and assuring quality. When the two sets of preferences disagree the physician faces the challenge of reconciling them.

Donabedian's concept that quality of care has several dimensions was developed under the seven headings outlined above. He stated that quality of care is judged by conforming to a set of standards, which arise from three sources:

- the science of health care, which determines efficacy;
- individual values and expectations, which determine acceptability;
- social values and expectations, which determine legitimacy.

This expands the argument that quality cannot be judged by health care professionals alone but must include the patient's views and preferences as well as those of society in general. Donabedian also develops the debate surrounding the pursuit of each of the several attributes of quality, which can be mutually reinforcing, although the pursuit of one attribute may be in conflict with that of another, so a balance has to be achieved. The most common

conflicts arise when the preferences of society are at variance with the preference of individuals. For example, we
may as a society see the care offered in our acute Trusts
as being more of a priority than that given to patients with
mental health problems.

With this in mind, we move onto considering Continuous Quality Improvement, an approach that tries to put
into practice the theories, principles and dimensions of
quality assurance that have been outlined in this chapter.

References

Department of Health 1997 *The New NHS, Modern, Dependable.*
London; HMSO.

Department of Health 1998 *A First Class Service: Quality in the New NHS.*
London: HMSO.

Lang, N. 1976 *Issues in Quality Assurance Nursing, ANA Issues in
Evaluative Research.* Kansas City: American Nursing Association.

Donabedian, A. 1969 Evaluating the Quality of Medical Care, *Hilbank
Memorial Fund Quarterly,* **44**(2): 166–206.

Donabedian, A. 1990 The Seven Pillars of Quality, *Archives of Pathology
and Laboratory Medicine,* **114**: 14–16.

Gordon, R. I. 1969 *Interviewing Strategy: Techniques and Tactics.*
Homewood, IL: Dorsey Press.

Kitson, A. 1986 Indicators of Quality in Nursing Care – an Alternative
Approach, *Journal of Advanced Nursing,* **11**: 133–44.

Maccoby, E. *et al.* 1968 The Interview: A Tool of Social Science, in G.
Lindzey (ed.) *Handbook of Social Psychology,* vol. 1, *Theory and Method.*
Reading, MA: Addison-Wesley.

Maxwell, R. 1984a Quality Assessment in Health, *British Medical
Journal,* **288**: 1470–2.

Maxwell, R. 1984b Dimensions of quality revisited: from thought to
action, *Quality in Healthcare,* **1**(3): 171–7.

Oppenheim, A. N. 1979 *Questionnaire Design and Attitude Measurement.*
London: Heinemann.

Payne, S. I. 1951 *The Art of Asking Questions.* Princeton, NJ: Princeton
University Press.

Royal College of Nursing 1980 *Standards of Nursing Care.* London:
RCN.

Royal College of Nursing 1981 *Towards Standards.* London: RCN.

Schmadl, J. C. 1979 Quality Assurance: Examination of the Concept,
Nursing Outlook, **27**(7): 462–5.

Ward, M. J. *et al.* 1982 *Instruments for Measuring Practice and Other Health Care Variables,* vols 1 and 2. Boulder, CO: Westerns Interstate Commission for Higher Education.

Williamson, J. W. 1979 Formulating Priorities for Quality Assurance Activity: Description of a Method and its Application, *Journal of the American Medical Association,* **239**: 631–7.

Further reading

Audit Commission 1992 *Minding the Quality: the Audit Commission's Role in Promoting Quality in the NHS.* London: Audit Commission.

Cuthbert, M. 1984 Evaluating Patient Care, *Australian Nurses Journal,* **13**(8).

Donabedian, A. 1980 *The Definition of Quality and Approaches to its Assessment, vol. 1.* Michigan: Health Administration Press.

Donabedian, A. 1980 *The Definition of Quality and Approaches to its Assessment.* Ann Arbor, MI: Health Administration Press.

Kitson, A. 1988 Raising the Standards, *Nursing Times,* **84**(25): 28–32.

Kendall, H. and Kitson, A. 1986 Rest Assured, *Nursing Times,* **82**(35): 28–31.

Lang, N. 1976 *Issues in Quality Assurance in Nursing, ANA Issues in Evaluation Research.* Kansas City: American Nursing Association.

Sale, D. N. T. 1988 Raising the Standards – Down Dorset Way, *Nursing Times,* **84**(28): 31–2.

Sale, D. N. T. 1989 Participating in Standard Setting: Planning a Programme of Change, *International Journal of Health Care Quality Assurance,* **2**(2): 31–3.

Sale, D. 1990 *Quality Assurance,* Essentials of Nursing Management Series. Basingstoke: Macmillan.

Sale, D. 1996 *Quality Assurance for Nurses and Other Members of the Health Care Team,* 2nd edn, Essentials of Nursing Management Series. Basingstoke: Macmillan.

Sale, D. 1998 *Garantia Da Qualidade Nos Cuidados De Saude, para os profissionais da equipa de saude.* Lisbon: Principia.

3

Total Quality Management or Continuous Quality Improvement

This chapter seeks to explore the history of the principles of Total Quality Management (TQM), also known as Continuous Quality Improvement (CQI) when used in a health care setting. For the sake of clarity, the term TQM will be used throughout this chapter.

The introduction of TQM into health care in the UK in 1990 brought with it an opportunity for the providers of health care to address the issues surrounding quality assurance using a systematic approach. There were some key issues that led to the implementation of TQM. Over the past decade, the policy changes have focused on clinicians and the need for them to monitor clinical outcomes, ensure patient satisfaction and measure performance. Patients are increasingly knowledgeable about health care and want information about outcomes before making decisions about treatments and interventions. Additionally the managers of the services want care to be cost-effective and competitive.

In a traditional model of quality assurance, the key people or customers are the regulators, the focus being on individual clinicians and processes. The methodology of this traditional model concerns inspection and feedback, with a limited use of statistical information. A model of continuous improvement or TQM systematically addresses the needs of the internal and external customers. TQM is about strategy, processes and the use of epidemiology, statistics, population levels and outcome measurement.

The history of TQM

Many professionals dislike analogies between industry and the National Health Service (NHS), but their aims are surely similar. The manufacturing industries want cost-effective production and satisfied customers who make repeat orders and recommend the company to others. In the NHS, the aims are very similar: a quality service for patients that is cost-effective.

The concept of TQM originated in the USA during World War 2 from work by Dr W. E. Deming (1982) and J. M. Juran (1980), employees of the armaments industry. They recognised that putting quality first could reduce costs and improve productivity, over 85 per cent of quality failures normally coming from systems under the direct control of management. Phillip Crosby (1985), an American industrialist, highlighted the importance of the human resource within the business organisation, as a prime contributor to effective quality standards, by its active involvement in the process of continuous care.

In the 1970s, the Japanese flooded the international markets with good-quality products at competitive prices, which made many Western companies review their methods of production. Much of the success in Japan was accredited to the concept of 'quality circles', which many Western companies then developed.

Quality circles

Quality circles are a useful method of solving problems that may result in an improvement in the quality of care.

A quality circle is a group of between five and eight volunteers working in the same area who meet regularly to identify, select and solve problems. The solution to the problem is then implemented and monitored to establish whether the problem has been solved.

Quality circles were launched in Japan in 1962 as part of an overall quality assurance system. Lockheed Missiles and Space Company of California sent a team to Japan in 1973 who concluded that quality circles were not culturally based and it was vital to retain as much of the Japanese model as possible. The programme introduced into Lockheed was successful and led to the same approach in other American Companies such as Westinghouse, Harley Davidson, General Motors and Babcock and Wilcox. In 1974, quality circles were introduced in America by Lockheed, and 4 years later, Rolls-Royce of Derby became the first British company to do so. It was not until 1982 that the National Society of Quality Circles was formed in the UK. In North Warwickshire Health Authority, quality circles were implemented following the 1982 restructuring of the NHS, in order to gain greater staff involvement and participation.

How a quality circle works

As can be seen from Figure 3.1, a quality circle starts by brainstorming a list of problems. The group will inevitably identify a large number of problems, which then have to be sorted into those which can be dealt with, those for which help is needed and those which are really difficult, if not impossible, to solve.

The next stage is the selection of the problem. Out of the list of problems, there will appear a general theme, and the group select problems that will give them quick results. In this way, they will maintain the purpose and enthusiasm of the group as well as demonstrating their effectiveness.

The group then analyse the problem that has been selected, decide what facts are needed to solve the problem, and collect, record and interpret data relating to the problem. Solutions to the problem are discussed in consultation with all concerned, a number of options based on facts are established, and a solution is produced. The group then prepare a presentation for management outlining the solution.

Next, the chosen solution to the problem is planned and implemented. The situation is monitored to ensure that the problem is solved and the desired effect maintained. The final stage is the presentation to management, demonstrating an improvement in service and the recorded facts.

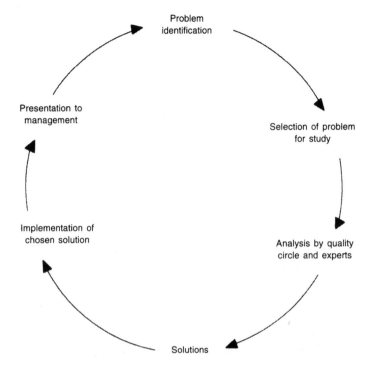

Source: M. Robson (1984) *Quality Circles – a Practical Guide* (Aldershot: Gower).

Figure 3.1   Quality circle

Members of the circle come from all disciplines and grades of staff who are working in the same clinical area. The only qualifications needed to be a member of a circle are the desire to solve problems that will lead to an improvement in the quality of patient care, commitment and plenty of enthusiasm.

Meetings are usually held weekly or fortnightly and last for a set period of time, usually 1 hour, even if all the business has not been finished. There is sometimes work for the members to do outside the meeting, for example researching solutions to the problem and gathering information. The minutes of the meeting are recorded and circulated to all members of the circle as well as to any other interested parties who may be able to help in solving the problem. These minutes serve two purposes: first, as a record of the meeting and, second, as a record of the group's progress towards a solution to the problem.

This may all sound very simple, but there is much more to a quality circle than a group of people who simply get together and solve a problem. There is a need for commitment on behalf of management to the work of a circle. There are also cost implications as training is required for the various roles that people take in order to develop an active and productive quality circle.

Key roles in a quality circle

Key people involved in a quality circle are:

- the co-ordinator
- the facilitator
- the leader
- the recorder.

Training for both the facilitators and the leaders is vital to the success of the quality circle programme; several training packages and books on the subject are available (see Further reading).

There has, however, been limited success using quality circles, not because of a failure of the concept, which is excellent, but because of problems including a lack of continuous senior, strategic management involvement and a lack of close working between departments. In addition, the concept is based on the notion that problems do occur, and, possibly most importantly, it is not based around the customer or user of the service. This has led to many organisations focusing on improving customer services. Ishikawa (1985) recognised that training is the firm foundation on which to base the total cultural change required by TQM. After the introductory sessions, training has to be related to individually identified training needs.

In Japan, businesses reviewed the way in which they operated and then went on to achieve the competitive edge based on producing better goods at better prices than those of their competitors in the West. This same philosophy may be used to improve the quality of service in the health service by looking critically at what is really needed to produce quality goods or, in this case, a good-quality service for patients. The factory needs to work well as a team, as does the hospital. If there are delays or defects in the service, customers will be dissatisfied with the service.

TQM in the UK

In 1990, the Department of Health (DoH) selected 23 demonstration sites to introduce a system of a managed approach to quality, or TQM. The sites ranged from departments within units, to hospitals and entire districts, these being in part funded by the DoH. Some common themes that help to define a total quality NHS emerged from the demonstration sites, including (NHSME, 1993):

- actively seeking patients' views and building organisations around their needs;
- encouraging staff to respond positively to patients' needs and suggestions;
- a commitment to quality by top management and professionals;
- creating a culture that encourages wide involvement and devolves responsibility to front-line staff;
- systematic training for staff to equip them with the skills that they need to participate in change;
- effective communications;
- continuous improvement based on systematic measurement.

Quality has always been an essential aspect of the delivery of professional care, but TQM has moved the focus from quality practised within the professions to that within the organisation as a whole. The key principles and strategies of TQM include:

- a customer focus
- teamwork and breaking down professional barriers
- a better management of resources.

TQM is a method of managing quality issues throughout every aspect of an organisation, ensuring that everyone gets it right, first time, every time. It is also about developing a culture in which all the staff strive to get it right, first time, every time and do not pass on errors and mistakes to someone else in the organisation.

TQM has been applied all over the world in manufacturing and service industries. It involves the whole organisation – everyone in every department – playing a part in addressing quality. Mistakes, errors and poor practice may be serious in a manufacturing organisation, but in the health care setting they can be devastating. The cost of poor-quality care can be greater than the cost of good-quality care.

Take as an example a patient admitted for a hip replacement operation. The patient is well prepared for surgery, the surgical intervention is excellent, and the patient returns safely to the ward. So far so good, but on the ward there is a problem: sickness has depleted the nursing staff, and there is no money in the budget to reinstate the total staffing complement with bank or agency staff. Thus, the nursing team is reduced to two members of staff for 28 patients, of whom 10 have returned from theatre that day. As a result, our patient is still lying on a rough theatre canvas, her skin already becoming reddened. The patient is not able to move herself around the bed and inevitably develops a pressure sore, which will take time to heal. This will slow down the rehabilitation process and increase the length of her stay, which will cost more – and this does not even take account of the unnecessary pain, discomfort and inconvenience she has been caused. There is also a 'knock-on' effect to the waiting list, leaving another patient in pain for longer than anticipated.

This is just one example of how a poor quality of care costs money, but there are many others – a delay in care being delivered, the unnecessary testing and treatment of patients, the necessity of repeating care to rectify errors, poor patient care and service, with non-compliance to explicit and implicit standards, errors and misjudgements leading to unnecessary and expensive litigation, and the recall of patients to repeat tests and treatments that perhaps were not done correctly the first time. Any working environment will surely supply several such situations.

Concept of TQM

The concept of TQM is fairly simple and straightforward. Any organisation requires 'processes' for ensuring that the service it provides is needed by the consumer and is of an acceptable standard. In a Department of Trade and Industry publication, Oakland (1989) outlined the TQM processes as follows:

The organisation should:
- focus on the needs and expectations of its market and its consumers;
- achieve top quality performance in all areas of its activity (product, service and internal processes);
- install and operate procedures, simple and complex, necessary for the achievement of top quality performance;
- critically and continuously examine processes to reduce and remove non-productive activities, inefficiencies and waste;
- develop and monitor measures of performance, set standards against which this performance is measured and set required improvements;
- understand and develop an effective communication strategy;
- develop a non-hierarchical team approach to problem solving and delegating responsibility for change;
- develop good procedures for communication and feedback to staff at any level of good work;
- continuously review the above processes to develop a culture for never-ending improvement.

In the business world, companies constantly have to address issues of quality to ensure that they are not overtaken by their competitors: the consumer demands a high-quality product or service. Since the NHS reforms, this has also become the case in the health service. Patients' awareness and expectations have been raised by *The Patient's Charter*. The introduction of the internal market in 1991 meant that GPs referred patients to the service that was responsive, effective and efficient rather than to the hospital or service with long waiting lists or a history of poor quality. The introduction of the concept of clinical governance by the Labour government in 1997 (DoH, 1997) secured the future of continuous quality improvement.

TQM can enable a Trust to meet patients' needs through an organised approach to monitoring and enhancing the quality of care or service delivered by all the staff. In order to do this, there must be a commitment by all the staff to improving the quality of service to patients and their families.

In the past, there has within the NHS tended to be a 'top-down' approach to quality assurance, people with the responsibility for quality, developing standards and distributing them to wards and departments for comments prior to the standards being implemented. TQM is about the development of a culture in which all staff are involved in ways of improving care and are supported by a management system with the same commitment to quality improvement.

TQM is about meeting and exceeding the consumers' requirements. These may be the requirements of GPs, patients and patients' families. To do this, there must be ways of establishing what the patients and GPs require of the service and developing ways of responding to this need, by understanding not only the external customer, but also internal staff requirements.

Another key aspect of this approach is the monitoring of the standard of the service by a constant review of the key elements. It is necessary to ensure that the standards set are valid standards that are explicit, measurable, a true reflection of quality and inclusive of the views of patients and relatives using the service. The whole organisation needs to be clear about the need for compliance with these standards and the implications of non-compliance.

The key issue of all those mentioned is perhaps the issue of ownership and commitment to quality of care and service by all staff at all levels of the organisation. Historically, staff within the health service have been committed to delivering quality care and have worked hard to improve the care they give and the service they deliver. The main difference is that instead of having pockets of enthusiasm within the organisation, the whole organisation is part of a structured system of quality that is managed systematically. TQM should encourage each member of staff to be an active 'cog' in the quality wheel, to be loyal to the hospital and department, and support staff to deliver higher quality and cost-effective care and services.

In 1989, District Health Authorities were instructed to ensure that their units developed a systematic and continuing review of quality, using a format and contents determined locally but consistent with national and regional policies. They were instructed to monitor all aspects of quality of patient care and service, including outcome. The specific areas included:

- medical and clinical audit;
- reducing waiting times (both outpatient and inpatient);
- the specification of quality elements for contracts;
- measurable criteria or standards of care and service;
- improved appointment systems;
- information to patients;
- reception and public area arrangements;
- customer feedback on strategies;
- improved environments (for example, in accident and emergency).

A framework for making the Chief Executive of Trusts accountable to Parliament for the quality of clinical care through clinical governance is currently being developed. The TQM approach is about putting the needs of patients at the centre of every activity at every level of the organisation, with the support and involvement of management.

Three TQM managerial processes

TQM consists of three managerial processes, which create a continuous improvement in the performance of an organisation. These processes are:

- *Quality leadership* – clear plans to support and develop quality, and the resources to meet the goals in terms of manpower, capital expenditure, an explicit strategy and policy commitment to 'getting it right first time'.
- *A hospital-wide approach* – all the quality initiatives, processes, actions must be implemented throughout the hospital.
- *Continuous measurement and training* – training and development specific to the area in which the staff are working, which is related to the job. There is a continuous measurement of quality.

The Juran Institute identified practice that made top companies and institutions highly successful. These management processes and systems are known as TQM. According to the Juran Institute, TQM succeeds because it leads to:

- Delighted patients, purchasers, and other customers
- Satisfied professionals and employees
- Optimal outcomes and health status of populations
- Increased revenue
- Reduced costs.

The essential components of TQM

The essential elements of TQM are as follows:

- The prevention of failure: it is cheaper to prevent rather than correct problems, and it is also more positive and cost-effective than accepting that the problem is an inevitable part of life.
- Senior managers are seen to lead from the front.
- Everyone has responsibility for quality.
- Everyone 'gets it right, first time, every time'.
- The cost of quality is addressed and accounted for.

- Quality is the priority in all departments and services.
- There is a drive for continuous improvement. All the results achieved are reviewed as part of a process of continuous improvement.

TQM is essentially about achieving quality through the involvement of people, who are seen as assets to be nurtured, developed and encouraged to take responsibility for their actions and are recognised as an important part in the culture that is TQM.

TQM is built around the key 'customers' – patients, their families, purchasers and users such as consultants, the medical staff the nursing staff and the support staff.

In his book *Quality Without Tears* Crosby (1984) identified 14 steps in the quality improvement process:

1. Management commitment – to make clear where management stands on quality
2. Quality improvement team – to run the quality improvement process
3. Measurement – to provide details of non-conformance in a way that permits objective evaluation and correction
4. Cost of quality – to get attention for quality, priorities, problems and measure improvement
5. Quality awareness – to provide a method of raising the personal concern felt by all employees towards providing a quality service
6. Corrective action to provide a systematic method of resolving problems forever
7. Zero defects planning – to examine the various activities in preparation for the continuing phases of the Quality Improvement Project (QIP)
8. Education to provide the type of training all employees need to carry out their roles actively
9. Zero defects day – an event which lets every individual realise, through personal experience that there has been a change
10. Goal setting to turn intentions into action, by encouraging individuals to establish improvement goals for themselves and their work groups
11. Error cause removal – to give individuals a means of communicating to management the situations that make it difficult to improve
12. Recognition – to appreciate those who participate
13. Quality councils – to bring together appropriate people to share quality management information on regular basis
14. Do it all over again – to make sure the quality process never ends.

A Quality Improvement Project

Quality Improvement Projects (QIPs) are organised efforts to address a performance deficiency or issue in the quality improvement process. The essentials of a successful project are:

- a group of people being involved;
- the project being recognised by the organisation;
- process analysis;
- that it is driven by data and facts.

Steps of the QIP

The steps of the QIP, as illustrated in Figure 3.2, include four phases of a problem-solving approach:

- project definition and organisation;
- a diagnostic journey;
- a remedial journey;
- holding the gains.

Problem-solving Approach	
Project Definition and Organisation • List and prioritise problems • Define project and team	Remedial Journey • Consider alternative solutions • Design solutions and controls • Address resistance to change • Implement solutions and controls
Diagnostic Journey • Analyse symptoms • Formulate theories of causes • Test theories • Identify root causes	Holding the Gains • Check performance • Monitor control systems

Source: Methods and Tools of Quality Improvement, developed by Paul E. Plsek & Associates and copyrighted by the National Demonstration Project, 1991 (National Demonstration Project).

Figure 3.2   Steps of the Quality Improvement Project

As can be seen in Figure 3.2, there is a clear approach involved in solving the problem.

Step 1: List the problems in order of priority

- Problems may come from the group's brainstorming session.
- Patient satisfaction surveys can be studied.
- Complaints may yield useful information.
- National reports are another source of data.
- Further ideas can be gleaned from the results of audits and so on.
- Priorities may arise from, for example, data analysis, policy decisions and research.

Step 2: Define the project and the team

- The project is a problem that is to be solved.
- The team is composed of representatives from all sections of the organisation on whom the problem impacts.
- The project definition must be objective.
- The scope of the project must match the scope of the team.

Step 3: Analyse the symptoms

- A 'symptom' is the indication that a problem exists; it is not the cause of the problem. The benefits of analysing the symptoms are that it helps to clarify the problem, focuses effort, establishes the habit of collecting data and leads to a common understanding of the problem.

Step 4: Formulate theories of causes

- Problems can be caused by staff, patients, equipment, supplies, procedures and protocols, inaccurate data or bias measurements.
- The views of the different members of the team on the cause of the problem need to be established.

Step 5: Test the theories

- A theory is an unproven assertion about a cause.
- The collection and analysis of data will confirm or rule out the theory.

Step 6: Identify the root causes

- All the possible causes should be listed and reduced to specific ones.

Step 7: Consider alternative solutions

- A wide range of solutions should be gathered from the different group members. Be creative and innovative in your quest for a solution.

Step 8: Design solutions and controls

- The solutions should be evaluated and ranked in order.
- The solution selected will depend on cost, the time to implement it, potential resistance, its impact on other processes and so on.
- Solutions and controls must be designed, together with feedback systems and training plans.

Step 9: Address resistance to change

- The causes of resistance must be identified.
- There are two aspects to process changes: technical and social. Technically sound solutions will fail if the social impact is not addressed through training and support.

Step 10: Implement solutions and controls

- The prime solution is then applied and its results evaluated through a pilot study.
- The solution is revised as necessary.

Step 11: Check performance

- The implementation of the solution does not guarantee improvement. There is a need to review performance through the collection and analysis of data.

Step 12: Monitor control systems

- Maintain controls and seek continuous improvement.
- The group must be rewarded and recognised.
- Ways in which to replicate the project in other similar problem areas should be considered.

Common difficulties with TQM

Problems often encountered are:

- missing out a step in the process;
- a lack of time, analysis skills or objectivity;
- implementing the changes before the solutions have been thoroughly evaluated and tested in a pilot study.

The TQM approach is about putting the needs of the patient at the centre of every activity of the organisation, with the support and involvement of management, as demonstrated in Figure 3.3. The quest for CQI continues and is now supported by the government's 1997 White Paper introducing the concept of clinical governance and methods by which to increase the accountability of clinical teams. The consultation paper *A First Class Service* (DoH, 1988) sets out the way forward to ensure 'quality in the new NHS'. The next chapter looks at one approach to assuring the quality of care through clinical audit.

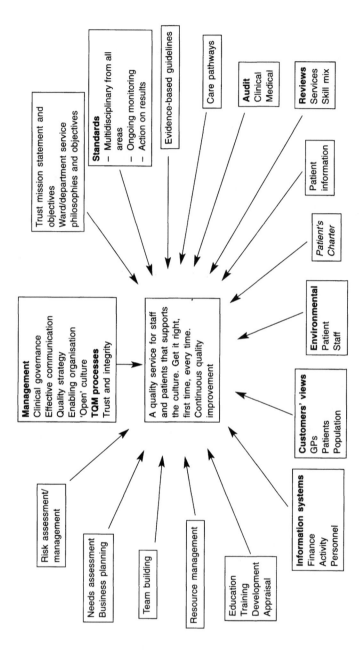

Figure 3.3 Total quality management (TQM) in health care

References

Crosby, P. B. 1984 *Quality Without Tears*. New York: McGraw-Hill.

Crosby, P. B. 1985 *The Quality Man*. London: BBC Enterprises.

Deming, W. E. 1982 *Quality, Productivity and Competitive Position*. Cambridge, MA: MIT.

Department of Health 1997 *The New NHS, Modern, Dependable*. London: HMSO.

Department of Health 1988 *A First Class Service, Quality in the New NHS*. London: HMSO.

Ishikawa, K. 1985 *Total Quality Control – the Japanese Way*. Englewood Cliffs, NJ; Prentice-Hall.

Juran, M. 1980 *Quality, Planning and Analysis*. New York: McGraw-Hill.

NHS Management Executive 1993 *The Quality Journey*. Heywood, Lancashire: Health Publications.

Oakland, J. 1989 *Total Quality Management*. Heinemann: Oxford.

Further reading

Berne, E. 1968 *Games People Play. The Psychology of Human Relationships*. London: Grove Press/Penguin Books.

Berwick, D. M. 1989 Continuous Improvement as an Ideal in Health Care, *New England Medical Journal*, **320**: 53.

Block, P. 1988 *The Empowerment Manager*. San Francisco: Jossey-Bass.

Carr-Hill, R. 1989 *The NHS and its Customers*. York: Centre for Health Economics, University of York.

Crosby, P. B. 1979 *Quality is Free. The Art of Making Quality Certain*. New York: MacGraw-Hill.

Deming, W. E. 1982 *Quality, Productivity and Competitive Positions*. Cambridge, MA: MIT.

Deming, W. E. 1982 *Out of Crisis*. Cambridge, MA: MIT Centre for Advanced Engineering Study.

Donabedian, A. 1985 *The Methods and Findings of Quality Assessment and Monitoring: An Illustrated Analysis*. Ann Arbor, MI: Health Administration Press.

Goldmann, D. 1997 Counterpoint: Sustaining CQI, *International Journal for Quality in Health Care*, **9**(1): 7–9.

Juran, J. M. 1979 *Quality Control Handbook*, 3rd edn. New York: McGraw-Hill.

Juran, J. 1988 *Juran on Planning for Quality*. New York: Free Press.

Juran, J. 1989 *Juran on Leadership for Quality: An Executive Handbook*. New York: Free Press.

Koch, H. C. H. 1991 *Training Manuals in TQM.* Brighton: Pavilion Publishing.

Koch, H. C. H. 1991 *Total Quality Management in Health Care.* Harlow: Longman.

Maguerez, G. 1997 Counterpoint: Integrating CQI in Health Organisations: Perspectives, *International Journal for Quality in Health Care,* **9**(1): 5–6.

Nerenz, D. 1997 Counterpoint: CQI in Health Care: Some Comments on 'Can it Really Work?', *International Journal for Quality in Health Care,* **9**(1): 3–4.

Oakland, J. 1989 *Total Quality Management.* Oxford: Heinemann.

Robson, M. 1984 *Quality Circles – a Practical Guide.* Aldershot: Gower.

4

Clinical Audit

Clinical audit is:

> The systematic critical analysis of the quality of medical care, including the procedures used for diagnosis and treatment, the use of resources and the resulting outcome and quality of life for the patient.

In the White Paper, *Working for Patients* (DoH, 1990), the government formally set out the need for medical audit by doctors in order to improve the quality of patient care. In 1991, this was extended to nursing, therapy professions and the professions allied to medicine, being developed into clinical audit. The government's White Paper *The New NHS, Modern, Dependable* (DoH, 1997) outlines the future shape and direction of the service, while *A First Class Service; Quality in the New NHS* (DoH, 1998) sets out the government's proposals for a radical and far-reaching set of quality reforms to the NHS. These include:

1. The introduction of a National Institute for Clinical Excellence (NICE). This is a new special health authority which has been established with responsibility for assessing the clinical and cost effectiveness of treatment and care, both new and existing, and providing guidance to the NHS on whether or not these approaches should be used. NICE is also responsible for directing national clinical audits in collaboration with the Royal Colleges and other professional bodies.
2. National Service Frameworks (NSFs) – these are templates for care in major service areas. They are developed nationally and then used locally by the NHS Executive and other health care organisations as a model on which to review and reshape services locally, with particular reference to the Calman-Hine reforms for

cancer services. The first two NSFs will be on coronary heart disease and mental health.

3. National framework for assessing performance – there will be a set of performance indicators that will be developed across six main areas of performance. This will allow the performance of health authorities and NHS Trusts to be compared and some of the data will be published in league tables.

4. Clinical governance – all NHS Trusts will be required to put in place new arrangements for clinical governance, defined as 'a framework through which NHS organisations are accountable for continuously improving the quality of their service and safeguarding high standards of care by creating an environment in which excellence in clinical care will flourish. (See Chapter 6.)

5. Commisssion for Health Improvement (CHI) – this is a new statutory body, reporting directly to the Secretary of State for Health. Its remit is to ensure that NHS Trusts have adequate systems of clinical governance in place and are implementing the guidance and national policies issued by NICE and the NHS Executive. CHI will visit each NHS Trust and have powers to access information, interview staff, and make recommendations for change where problems are identified.

The next chapter looks at clinical effectiveness, guidelines and evidence-based practice, but first we will outline a structured approach to clinical audit. It is clear that clinical audit is not the only instrument available for improving clinical effectiveness: there are protocols, guidelines, integrated care pathways, training, development and the implementation of research to support evidence-based practice. However, a well-executed clinical audit will help in the quest to establish whether clinical care is effective.

Reasons for clinical audit

Clinical audit gives professionals the opportunity to review clinical practice, to take a step back, to look at how care is delivered and the effects that care has on patients, and to consider whether or not this can be improved. As professionals, we have always undertaken activities such as this, but perhaps not using a structured approach and certainly not as a multidisciplinary team. Having used the clinical audit process to monitor the effect of care given to patients, there is an opportunity to take note of the results and to change the delivery of care. This is a chance to look at how things might be improved and how high-quality care might be delivered in a different, more effective way that would benefit the patient.

Benefits of clinical audit

- From the patient's point of view, this approach will lead to greater continuity of care from the multidisciplinary team.
- By looking at better ways of delivering care, we have an opportunity to raise the overall quality of care to a consistently higher level and constantly to improve the delivery of patient care.
- Clinical audit gives us an opportunity to reduce the number of clinical errors by looking at practice and identifying ways of delivering care that prevent mistakes and errors.
- Through clinical audit, it is possible to review the skills that staff have and how they are used, as these are often misplaced or misused.
- Clinical audit allows us to review the delivery of ineffective treatment where previously there has not been the opportunity to determine what is and is not effective.
- As a result of clinical audit, changes in practice may save time. This time may then be used more appropriately in areas that require specialised professional skills.
- The resulting changes to practice and the delivery of care may well improve cost-efficiency. The cost of poor-quality care is often significantly higher than that of delivering high-quality care 'right first time'.
- Clinical audit gives professionals the opportunity to develop their own standards. This is important because it

gives the staff a sense of 'owning' their own standards of care that reflect efficient, effective, good-quality care being delivered to patients.

- Clinical audit also encourages self-improvement, taking that longer look at what we do and how we do it, and asking whether it could be done better.
- If clinical audit is undertaken by a multidisciplinary team, this can lead to a greater understanding of how professionals perform in their own specialties and where the overlaps lie in the delivery of care between the different members of the team. It gives staff an opportunity to identify who is best suited to deliver certain aspects of care and to work as an effective team rather than as separate individuals.

As stated above, clinical audit provides an opportunity to question practice. Do staff continue to do things in the same old way? The answer to that is possibly 'yes' because there is not time to review procedures and instigate changes, but with clinical audit there is an opportunity to develop practice in order to move forward.

The approach to clinical audit described in this chapter links with the requirements for the completion of the form for the National Clinical Audit Centre database, and the work that supported the development of the criteria for the database.

The National Centre for Clinical Audit

In 1995, a partnership of 14 health care organisations was commissioned by the Clinical Outcomes Group (COG) of the Department of Health (DoH) to establish a national clinical audit information and dissemination centre. The COG identified the need for a centre that provided a national focus for clinical audit in order to ensure that existing and future audits were fully informed of similar or related projects. A prerequisite for the Centre was to encourage participation across all disciplines and professions in order to improve the quality of multidisciplinary clinical audit through sharing the principles of effective audit and examples of good practice. In this way, the Centre would contribute to the DoH's policy aims for clinical audit (National Centre for Clinical Audit, 1996).

The criteria for clinical audit were established through a series of road shows and questionnaires, leading to the final consensus on the criteria. This formed the audit database form, which was then piloted for 6 months, reviewed and revised. The resulting database of completed clinical audits is a valuable resource for information to support evidence-based practice and clinical effectiveness.

Clinical audit is a simple system that allows professionals to measure their performance, recognise good practice and, if necessary, make improvements. A clinical audit is not undertaken in isolation by one person but is developed with the help of colleagues and the support of management. Clinical audit is an essential part of the desire of every professional involved in patient care to deliver a high quality of care.

The audit cycle

The audit process is a cycle not dissimilar from the quality assurance cycle, as shown in Figure 4.1.

Observe current practice

The first part of the process is to observe current practice and make an assessment of its quality.

Set standards of care

The setting of standards is often seen as a difficult part of the cycle, and is discussed in detail in Chapter 2.

Compare expectations with reality

The next part of the cycle is to compare expectations with observed reality. Having established what the standards are,

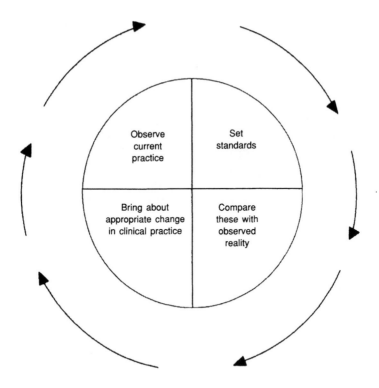

Figure 4.1   The audit process

these must be compared with clinical practice. What is the reality? Where are the gaps? Is there a difference between the standards that were set and the standards that actually apply when patient care is delivered? Having monitored the standards and identified the gaps, comparisons are then made. This will form the body of the clinical audit, which will be described in more detail later in this chapter.

Bring about appropriate change

This part of the cycle is perhaps the most important because it is about making appropriate change, if this is what is required. If areas for change have been identified, these must be agreed with colleagues. Changes in practice need to be carefully reviewed in order to ensure that they will result in an improvement to patient care. Having set up and implemented the alterations, these should then be monitored. The professional should observe the effects and improvements, as well as whether there are any problems associated with making the changes.

Four main principles of clinical audit

There are essentially four main principles that apply to the development of clinical audit, these being applicable to any clinical area and any professional group.

Define the objectives

It is important to remember that any effective care requires individuals to work as a team and depends on the members of the team holding the same values and expectations, so that confusion created by people working to different objectives can be avoided. Thus, the first step under this particular principle is to identify the mission statement of the organisation, and write the philosophy of care for the particular area in which the team is working.

Having identified the philosophy of care for a particular area, the next step is to identify the key objectives of the service. Many areas will already have been through this process while undertaking a recent 'Setting of Standards' exercise, so this will just be a continuation of work that has already been undertaken.

Develop standards and ways to measure them

Many professionals have already written their standards, and audit may be seen as a link between standard setting and a more in-depth monitoring of quality and audit. As discussed in Chapter 2, it is important to understand the 'jargon' and the words used so that areas of quality are not muddled. If professionals talk about 'auditing standards' instead of 'monitoring standards', this gives the impression that every standard needs to be audited in depth, which is of course not true.

The monitoring of standards should be seen as a 'snapshot' of activity looking at whether or not standards are being complied with and good-quality care is being achieved. If there is an area within those standards that the staff are having difficulty achieving, this may be the area that is highlighted and developed for clinical audit. In other words, audit should be seen to be a detailed portrait of the area of activity being monitored, and the monitoring of standards should be seen as a simple snapshot. If, on the other hand, the organisation does not have standards at this point and one is embarking on clinical audit, this is the moment to write the standards for the area that has been chosen for audit.

It is important to have written objectives because the standards should reflect the objectives and philosophy previously recorded. Standards make explicit the level of quality and become the benchmarks against which performance is judged.

Agree, implement and monitor change

Professionals should monitor the standards, identify current performance and compare what should be with what is. Gaps should be identified and action taken to ensure these are closed and that the audit cycle is completed. The clinical audit process will identify areas of excellence as well as areas in need of improvement. At this point in clinical audit, the ways of improving patient care must be discussed and agreed by the group.

Clinical audit is not something that is taken on by one person: it is achieved via a group of people. This means that the tasks and workload should be shared between members of the group, and individual people should be made responsible for specific areas of work that have been identified.

Communication

Within the organisation in which the clinical audit studies are taking place, there needs to be a communication strategy to publicise the purpose and outcome of audit so that the results may be shared for the benefit of patients throughout the organisation. This also has the advantage of preventing duplication of studies. Communication should not be limited purely to those professionals involved in audit but should be extended to patients and their relatives, particularly with regard to issues such as the audit of pain control.

Audits will be multidisciplinary, and the outcomes will affect people in a variety of departments who perhaps were not involved in the original audit. Communication should thus also be aimed at management, at policy makers and at those who are accountable for the resources, because without their support, the changes identified – with resource implications – may never take place.

Potential problems with clinical audit

One of the problems that has been identified within the principle of communication is the lack of involvement of management with the clinical audit process. Management involvement at the very beginning of the audit is vital and should include presenting management with:

- the objectives for the study;
- the area to be audited;
- the reason for the audit;
- a list of the people who are likely to be involved;
- the resources that are likely to be required;
- the potential outcome, with the potential changes to practice and resource implications all clearly identified.

It is important to gain management support from the beginning, because without it one may undertake an extremely worthwhile audit only to find that, when the results are discussed, the organisation cannot afford to implement the changes. This is very disheartening for everybody involved as much time and effort has been put into establishing an effective audit whose results cannot be followed through.

One of the main areas of concern during an audit is confidentiality, as patient records, information and data are often used to establish the findings within the audit. It is essential that there is a policy on confidentiality, that everyone is clear about what this means and that all data are anonymous. There may also be a variety of people involved in the audit, such as data collection clerks, secretaries, and other people who are not bound by a professional code of conduct, so this issue of confidentiality needs to be addressed and assured.

While undertaking clinical audit, poor practice involving a particular individual is sometimes identified. Prior to the study, it is important to establish what the policy and procedure are in the event of such a finding. This is one of the areas that causes anxiety to staff, who worry that they will be found to be doing something that is either inappropriate or negligent, and are concerned that they will be identified and taken to task. The organisation as a whole needs to have a very clear policy on what the procedure is in the event of poor practice being identified.

One of the reasons for setting clearly stated objectives at the start of the study, as well as standards defining the boundaries of the study, is to ensure that the study does not become too large. It is easy to become overenthusiastic and for the members of the group to say 'Wouldn't it be interesting if we looked at...', thus taking the group way beyond their original objectives and the boundaries of the study into the realms of a different investigation. Consequently it is essential to keep a very close eye on the size of the study.

Another problem with audit is the collection and collation of large amounts of data. Again, the group can become overenthusiastic about the collection of data and forget that someone has to analyse them. It is important to be selective about the data that are required and to ensure that the data collected are essential.

There are two major problems that will lead to a failed audit, there being little more depressing than an audit that is definitely beginning to fail. The first of these problems is the lack of understanding on the part of the group about what they are meant to be doing. It is important that members are given very clear guidelines on:

- what the audit is
- what the objectives are
- what the expected outcomes might be
- what their role is
- how they are expected to perform.

The second problem is the lack of commitment within the group that sets up the audit. Within a group, there may be staff who will say 'Why bother; what good will it do anyway?' This lack of commitment needs to be addressed before the audit starts, because people with this attitude will destroy the audit from within by devaluing it, so that the audit will be likely to fail. As stated above, this lack of commitment often arises from a lack of understanding and a fear that members will be identified as not performing. These fears and anxieties need to be overcome by careful training and support throughout the study.

The 11 steps to a successful audit

Having outlined the four principles of audit, the next step is to put these principles into practice. The cycle of audit activity that results in a systematic improvement in clinical practice can be described in 11 stages (Figure 4.2).

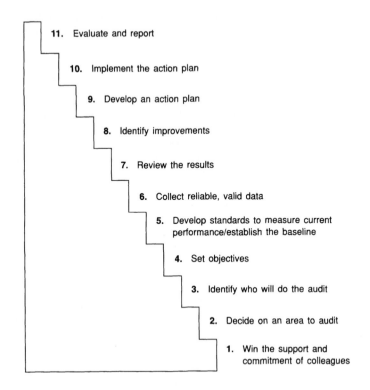

Figure 4.2   Eleven steps to clinical audit

Step 1: Win the support and commitment of colleagues

The first part of this step is to obtain support from management, as discussed above. Without their support, audit is likely to flounder because of the lack of resources. It is important to reiterate at this point that the involvement of management, through the presentation of clear objectives and the probable implications of the audit, will move the group closer to good communication with the managers. During this first step, it is a good idea to establish whether there are any specific resources available for audit. These may be in the form of data collection clerks, information technology systems or even other particular personnel with expertise or access to previous studies that are closely linked to the proposed audit.

The research undertaken at the beginning of this study, which looks at the mission statement and the objectives of the organisation followed by the team's own philosophy and objectives, will be key in demonstrating how the audit will fit into the clinical governance strategy. If this is the case, the audit is more likely to get support from management.

Step 2: Decide on an area to audit

If there are already standards, integrated care pathways and guidelines that are being monitored, and an area in which it is felt that performance could be improved has been identified, the selection of the area to audit is quite logical because it follows from the areas measured through the standards, pathways or guidelines. If, on the other hand, there has been no such activity, standards, pathways or guidelines have not been monitored and there are no particular areas that need to be audited, the following questions might help with making the decision:

- Review areas of clinical care and ask, 'Why do staff do it that way?' Then identify ways that it might be done and ask why staff do not use that method?
- Are there delays in the provision of care? If so, why do these delays occur, and what can be done to improve the timing of the provision of care?
- Discuss with colleagues whether or not patients suffer unnecessary complications. If they do, what can be done about it? In what specific areas do these complications occur?
- Discuss whether equipment is always used correctly, and if it is not, what can be done about it.
- Are the most suitably qualified people delivering the care? Who is doing what, and who should be doing what?
- A key area to address is whether or not clinical practice is safe. If not, why not, and how can it be improved?

- Would a change in resources improve the quality of care? What resources are available at present, what resources are required, and where do the gaps lie?

Clinical audit may be used to audit an integrated care pathway or some guideline for which outcomes are not being achieved, as well as areas of clinical care that are high volume, high risk or high cost. Audit may stem from a complaint or a critical incident, or from outside pressures such as a purchaser requirement, a *Health of the Nation* target, *The Patient's Charter*, or an area of care or concern raised by the Community Health Council or any other outside body.

Step 3: Identify who will do the audit

The group to conduct the audit will probably arise quite naturally from the chosen area in which the audit is being undertaken, be it a ward, department, a whole hospital, the patient's home or the community. As mentioned above, there may be key people available who will affect the choice or make up the group, and there will be several groups of people working at various levels of the organisation. It may be important to involve some of the managers with the audit to ensure that both sides of the clinical audit are taken into account, that is, clinical care and the management of that care.

In the UK, some clinical audits are currently still undertaken by uniprofessional groups, but the clinical audit of patient care should involve a multidisciplinary team approach in which everybody who has a part to play in patient care takes part. It is very difficult to isolate one group of professionals delivering patient care without taking into account how other professionals impact upon the care that has been given.

The initial activities within this third step produce a good opportunity to set up workshops and seminars to provide an impetus as well as to make sure that everyone is well informed and has a clear understanding, so that all may participate totally without feeling unsure of themselves.

Having identified the *scope* of the audit, a decision must be made on how much *time* should be spent on the audit. Staff who are involved in clinical audit already have a heavy professional workload delivering patient care, and this activity adds an extra burden. Thus, one needs to be realistic about how much time is required and how much time can be allotted to delivering a successful audit. At this point, it is also important to consider what the audit will require apart from time, for example:

- information technology
- the development of data collection forms
- secretarial support.

Evidence base

Clinical audit must be evidence based, in other words based on recognised research evidence that is proven to be effective, or on expert clinical judgement. This will involve a, probably computerised, literature search to establish current research findings. However, many audit topics deal with local issues, for which the literature may provide evidence that is of only superficial relevance. In this case, it is even more important to develop local standards and criteria through a discussion with the relevant stakeholders.

An evidence base may also be provided through existing protocols, national initiatives, professional consensus, peer group consensus, national guidelines, professional journals, national and regional organisations and so on (see also Chapters 5–7).

Step 4: Set objectives

The objectives should be set and agreed by the audit group. Objectives must be measurable, achievable and in line with the strategy and objectives for the audit programme and the organisation as a whole, as set out in the business plan and the clinical governance strategy.

Step 5: Develop standards to measure current performance

If there are no standards, or if existing standards have not been monitored, this is the moment to agree, write and set the standards specifically for the audit proposed.

Each standard should be broken down into measurable elements that will indicate whether or not it is being met. These are known as audit indicators or audit criteria, and are the criteria that have been established within the structure, process and outcome criteria of the standard. (For more information on standard setting, see Chapter 2.) The audit indicators are the foundations on which to collect data.

Establishing the baseline or identifying the level of current practice may also be achieved through a comparison with other centres, through clinical judgement or the assessment of current practice through direct observation.

Step 6: Collect reliable, valid data

There are already numerous potential sources from which to gather relevant data without gathering new data of one's own. The patient or client record is a key area. Care plans developed by nurses and other professionals also contain information that may be relevant to the particular audit. If there are guidelines being used to support care or as part of a pathway, there will be relevant data to collect. If the audit is part of the monitoring of a pathway, the information from the recorded 'variances' may be the data to collect. The audit may require a review of the complaints reports, so the auditor must establish who is responsible for the complaints received from patients and relatives, talk to them and establish whether there have been any complaints relating to the area of the selected audit. A further area that may be relevant is accident reports, indicating the number of patient falls or staff incidents, for example.

There are an enormous number of data to be gathered from Körner-based data. In 1980 a steering group was set up, chaired by Edith Körner, to look at Health Services information. The six main Körner reports were published between 1982–84, each report covering a major area of NHS activity on which management nationally, regionally and locally needed to collect data. These were hospital facilities and diagnostic services, patient transport, manpower, paramedical services, community services and finance. A key concept in the reports was the identification of minimum data sets, for example:

- NHS number (from 1993)
- patient's name
- patient's usual address
- post code of usual address
- DHA of residence
- sex
- marital status
- date of birth
- code of registered GP
- ethnic origin (from 1992/93).

These will provide information on length of stay, cases per consultant and bed occupancy. If this information is relevant to the audit, arrangements can be made to gather it from the finance department, information technology department or wherever it is held. If the location is in doubt, library staff will probably be able to say where the information can be obtained.

The audit may require new sources of information to be developed. It is important to try to keep this information to what is essential. It is also important to use forms that are already in existence to prevent the staff having to learn how new forms are to be filled in. This also saves money that might be spent on the reproduction of numerous new forms. If existing forms are not exactly what is needed, it may be possible to modify them. If not, a new form will need to be developed. The audit form must be clear and easy to understand and quick to complete. Again, it should be remembered that people are undertaking this task in addition to their usual workload; if there are several audits in progress at one time, staff will be spending a disproportionate amount of time completing audit data collection forms.

It may be necessary to conduct interviews with patients, clients or other service users. If the use of interviewing is to be one of the areas for collecting data, the key questions to be asked should be written down in an unambiguous fashion so that all the interviewers ask the same questions. This will facilitate collection of the data. It may be necessary to create a special audit questionnaire. In the majority of clinical audit studies, the staff are involved in observing and recording patient information and data. If this is the case, the forms on which they record data must be clearly designed, easy to understand and quick to complete. As it is in these areas that there may be problems with confidentiality, whatever is developed must be in line with the hospital's policy on confidentiality.

For the chosen topic to be audited, the data essential to the audit can be identified by answering the following questions:

- What are the purposes of the data?
- What data items are required?
- What are the sources of the data?

Sample size

Some thought must be given to sample size. The sample used must be large enough to meet the objectives of the audit but not so large that unnecessary time is spent collecting and collating data that are not required or have no purpose. The skills of a statistician may be helpful in making an accurate decision, but experience and clinical judgement will suggest what is reasonable.

Pilot the data collection systems

All aspects of data collection should be piloted to ensure that the data collected are accurate, reliable, ethical and valid. The data collection forms should result in the collection of data that meet the purpose as intended, are non-ambiguous and are straightforward to use.

Step 7: Review the results

Once the required data have been collected, the next step is the analysis. As this can take a great deal of time, it is essential to be sure that the data collected were really required and essential, and no more. Taking each indicator in turn, the auditor should quantify the degree to which the standards have been met and identify areas in which the service delivered has not conformed to the standards set. This needs to be clearly documented as the group collate and analyse the data.

During this process, the group may discover that one indicator has a significantly lower rate of achievement than others, or a pattern of failure may be emerging that indicates a need for a specific remedy. It is important to note down the indicators and the way in which the study is actually progressing, discussing these aspects at regular meetings of the whole group so that everyone is clear about progress.

Step 8: Identify improvements

Through an analysis of the data and peer group discussion, improvements to be made, if these are necessary, can be identified.

Step 9: Develop an action plan

The action plan should identify how the group intends to rectify any problems that the audit has identified. This action plan should specify the following:

- the improvement to be achieved;
- the actions that need to be taken;
- the resources (if any) that are needed;
- how their achievement can be measured;
- the timescale in which improvements should be achieved;
- who is responsible.

One method of exploring possible solutions is for the group to focus on one particular problem through brain-storming or using a mock solution in a systematic way. It is essential that ideas are explored on paper or within the group prior to using them in direct patient care. If the outcome of the audit indicates a change in the delivery of patient care, it is essential that those changes are piloted and the results monitored prior to implementation on a larger scale.

Step 10: Implement the action plan

Once the action plan has been drawn up and named people have been identified to co-ordinate certain aspects of the initiative, it is essential that the new strategy is put into effect. Any changes should reflect the results of the monitoring process, and these may have to be modified again after a further period of evaluation. This should not necessarily be seen as the end result, as there may need to be further changes to ensure that the delivery of care has been improved to the extent that was initially predicted.

Step 11: Evaluate and report

Once the group is confident that the standards are now firmly in place, that changes have been identified and that those changes when measured assure the group that the quality of care has been improved and can be sustained, the audit report can be prepared for all those involved in the service and for management. Re-auditing must be planned in order to check that patient care has improved.

Guidelines for success

Below are summarised the elements which can be said to lead to a successful audit:

- Commitment
  - Commitment to the study
  - A group of staff who are keen to be involved
- The scale of the study
  - Start with a small study
  - Be clear about the scope of the study
- Learn the key elements
  - Handling the data
  - Acquiring the evidence base on current good practice
  - Drawing up checklists
  - Devising ways of communicating
  - Developing resources
  - Acquiring additional relevant skills such as a critical appraisal of research, computer skills and so on
- Decisions to be made
  - How is the audit to be carried out?
  - What should be looked at?
  - How should it be studied?
  - What should be done with the results?
- Rules for success
  - Look at topics that are relevant to the group's work
  - Ensure that professional groups maintain responsibility for their own practice
  - Be clear about polices, procedures and confidentiality

– Ensure that the study is not too time-consuming
– Ensure that the group is representative of the team delivering the particular area of care
– Get the support of management
– Make sure that the audit cycle is closed and that advances or changes for the improvement of patient care demonstrated.

Examples of areas for clinical audit might include:
- patient information on diagnosis, treatment/care, and follow-up care;
- postoperative wound infections;
- the prevalence of pressure sores;
- immunisation uptake and health promotion;
- areas of high risk or high volume;
- staffing number and skill mix, including doctors, nurses, therapists, clerical staff and support staff;
- the security of records;
- the discharge of patients and follow-up care;
- the lifting and moving of patients;
- confidentiality;
- communication with staff;
- waiting times and waiting lists;
- guidelines for specific areas of care;
- integrated care pathways either to ensure that they result in good-quality care or to audit common 'variances'.

Issues surrounding clinical audit

Disadvantages

- There has to date been no national review of the effectiveness of clinical audit in changing or improving clinical practice.
- Clinical audit is not always multidisciplinary.
- Clinical audit programmes are not always prioritised and based on risk.
- Findings are not always implemented.

- There has been a lack of re-audits to establish whether patient outcome or care has improved as a result of an audit.
- A lack of ongoing training is apparent.

Benefits

- Standards are developed as part of the audit to ensure that the quality cycle is completed.
- A better understanding ensues of the care provided by other professionals in the health care team.
- The approach allows an objective audit of a specific area of care.
- There are opportunities to use and understand research.

General points in relation to clinical audit

Throughout the process of clinical audit, it is essential that key people within each area are made responsible for keeping the whole group informed of what is happening and how the audit is progressing, and for ensuring that the group meets to discuss findings, problems and the way forward. Key people from within each audit will benefit from spending some time networking with other people on other audits; this will help to prevent duplication, overlap, repetition and the replication of studies.

After an audit, it is interesting to note that staff are often highly encouraged about the process as it gives them a feeling of autonomy over their professional practice. There is a sense of achievement that they have the ability and the where-withal to make changes to improve patient care. They are usually inspired to go on the next audit, to take the next area and to try to improve the situation for their patients.

Setting up the first audit is the most difficult and also the most crucial. If an audit has been set up well and thought through, with a clear idea of what the outcome might be, the audit is often successful. Poor preparation for audit, with unclear objectives, poorly set standards that are neither monitorable nor measurable, and a vague idea of what the outcome might be, will often lead to an audit that falls apart half way through. This does not inspire people to go on to audit further areas. In fact, it has the opposite effect, making them feel 'Why bother?'

Sometimes the audit is not successful, and after the data collection and the implementation of change, the standard is still not achieved. This means that there needs to be a further change in practice in specific areas. The group should go back and look at the data collected and the documentation that was reviewed, and in general study the notes made on the audit as it progressed, trying to identify where the gaps were, what should have been reviewed and what was not reviewed.

The other area that needs to be considered when an audit is unsuccessful is how well the staff understood their role in the audit. Was there room for further educational sessions for the staff? Were the staff committed to the principle of audit, or did their lack of commitment contribute to the failure of the audit? Whatever the outcome, there will definitely be a greater understanding of the area of work that the group has undertaken, and a greater appreciation of other people's roles and responsibilities, as well as of how staff work as a team. There is nearly always a renewed commitment to professional competence, the competence in most cases breeding confidence.

Finally, the result of all this work is the development of explicit quality indicators and an improvement in patient care, which is, after all, what it is all about.

References

Department of Health 1988 *A First Class Service: Quality in the New NHS.* London: HMSO.

Department of Health 1990 *Working for Patients.* London: HMSO.

Department of Health 1997 *The New NHS, Modern, Dependable.* London: HMSO.

National Centre for Clinical Audit 1996 *Action Pack.* London: National Centre for Clinical Audit.

Further reading

Crombie, I. K., Davies, H. T. O., Abraham S. C. S. and Florey, C. Du V. 1993 *The Audit Handbook – Improving Health Care Through Clinical Audit.* Chichester: John Wiley & Sons.

Department of Health 1993 *Meeting and Improving Standards in Healthcare: A Policy Document on the Development of Clinical Audit.* EL(93)59. Heywood: DoH.

Department of Social Security 1972 *Management's Arrangement for the Reorganised NHS.* London: HMSO.

Fitspatrick, R. 1991 Surveys of Patient Satisfaction: 11. Designing a Questionnaire and Conducting a Survey, *British Medical Journal,* **302**: 1129–32.

Hopkins, A. 1990 *Measuring the Quality of Medical Care.* London: Royal College of Physicians.

Koch, H. 1981 *Total Quality Management in Health Care.* Harlow: Longman.

Kogan, M. and Redfern, S. 1995 *Making Use of Clinical Audit.* Buckingham: Open University Press.

Lewis, N. 1990 Nursing Audit, *International Journal of Health Care and Quality Assurance,* February: 30–3.

Mason, A. 1990 *Enabling Clinical Work in the South West.* Bristol: SWHRA.

National Audit Office 1995 *Clinical Audit in England.* HC 27 Session 1995–96. London: HMSO

National Centre for Clinical Audit 1997 *Information for Better Healthcare.* London: National Centre for Clinical Audit.

NHS Management Executive 1990 *Nursing Care Audit.* London: HMSO.

NHS Training Directorate 1994 *Getting Ahead with Clinical Audit: A Facilitator's Guide.* London: NHS Training Directorate.

RCP 1989 *Medical Audit: A First Report.* London.

Sale, D. 1996 *Quality Assurance for Nurses and Other Members of the Health Care Team,* 2nd edn. Essential of Nursing Management Series. Basingstoke: Macmillan.

Sale, D. 1998 *Garantia Da Qualidade Nos Cuidados De Saude, para os profissionais da equipa de saude.* Lisbon: Principia.

Shaw, C. 1989 *Medical Audit Hospital Handbook.* London: King's Fund Centre.

South Western Regional Health Authority 1989 *Regional Approach to Medical Audit.* Bristol: SWRHA.

Walshe, K. and Bennett J. 1991 *Guidelines on Medical Audit and Confidentiality.* Brighton: Brighton Health Authority/South East Thames Regional Health Authority.

Useful addresses

Eli-Lilly National Clinical Audit Centre
Department of General Practice, School of Medicine, Leicester General Hospital, Gwendolen Road, Leicester, LE5 4PW
Tel: 0116-258 4873
Conducts research and provides an information service with a focus on audit in general practice and across the primary/secondary care interface.

Intensive Care National Audit and Research
ICNARC, BMA House, Tavistock Square, London, WC1H 9HR
Tel: 0171-383 6451
Incorporates the work of the Cochrane Centre. Co-ordination in intensive and critical care medicine that promotes the need to access unbiased systematic reviews of available evidence.

National Co-ordinating Unit for Clinical Audit in Family Planning
University of Hull, Cottingham Road, Hull, HU6 7RX
Tel: (01482) 466051

Nursing and Midwifery Audit Information Service
Room 521, Royal College of Nursing Headquarters, 20 Cavendish Square, London, W1M 0AB
(or c/o Royal College of Midwives, 15 Mansfield Street, London, W1M 0BE)
Tel: 0171-629 7464
http://www.man.ac.uk/rcn/ukwide/nmais.htm

UK Clinical Audit Association
Room 9, Cleethorpes Centre, Jackson Place, Wilton Road, Humberston, South Humberside, DN36 4AS
Tel: (01472) 211492
Has a database of published clinical guidelines for clinical care.

5

Clinical Effectiveness, Clinical Guidelines and Evidence-based Practice

Since the early 1990s, there has been a growing interest in using the results of research to improve patient care. Over the past decade, this work has been advanced under a variety of titles, including clinical audit, clinical effectiveness, the implementation of research and evidence-based practice. The next three chapters in this book cover topics that play a fundamental role in clinical governance. This present chapter explores clinical guidelines, clinical effectiveness and evidence-based practice. A brief résumé, rather than a detailed account of each topic, is provided as these subjects are covered in depth in the professional journals. Sources of information to help with the development of each of these topics is included in Chapter 6.

Clinical effectiveness

The Department of Health (DoH, 1993) defined clinical effectiveness as:

> the extent to which specific interventions, when deployed in the field for a particular patient or population, do what they are intended to do, for example, maintain and improve health and secure the greatest possible health gain from available sources.

Professor Alison Kitson, at a conference in London in 1995 on 'Clinical Effectiveness – from Guidelines to Cost Effective Practice', described clinical effectiveness more poignantly as 'doing the right thing' and 'doing the thing right'. She went on to say:

The former requirement relates to the effective utilisation of research through mechanisms such as clinical guidelines, which are rigorously developed. The latter requirement relates to how such information is implemented.

The Royal College of Nursing (RCN, 1995) produced an excellent strategy document on clinical effectiveness, outlining the main elements of the process:

- the production of evidence through research and scientific review;
- the production and dissemination of evidence-based clinical guidelines;
- the implementation of evidence-based, cost-effective practice through education and change management;
- the evaluation of compliance to agreed practice guidance and the evaluation of patient outcomes, including clinical audit.

Achieving clinical effectiveness

To achieve clinical effectiveness, the government has introduced a framework of clinical governance within the National Health Service (NHS) Trusts and primary care (DoH, 1997):

> to ensure that clinical standards are met, and that processes are in place to ensure continuous improvement, backed by a new statutory duty for quality in NHS Trusts.

Clinical effectiveness as well as cost-effectiveness is to be evaluated and measured against national indicators of success.

The government 'proposes a new model which marries clinical judgement with clear national standards. It involves a partnership between the Government and the clinical professions.' This is described as the government's third way, which involves the setting of clear national standards but with responsibility for delivery being taken locally and being backed by consistent monitoring arrangements. National yardsticks, drawn up through joint working between the DoH and the professions, will guide local decisions by managers and clinicians, rather than tying their hands. The devolution of responsibility will be matched with accountability for performance, as it has to be in a national public service as important as the NHS.

- National standards will be set through National Service Frameworks as well as through a National Institute for Clinical Excellence (NICE). The standards will be set for major areas of care and disease groups. NICE was set up as a Special Health Authority in early 1999.

- There will be a Commission for Health Improvement (CHI), which will monitor the quality of clinical services at local level and tackle shortcomings. It will be able to intervene if necessary when there are problems. The CHI will also ensure that health care organisations fulfil their CHI responsibilities for clinical governance. It will monitor clinical practice and the implementation of NICE guidelines. It has been suggested that the CHI will visit all hospitals every 3–4 years. It is also anticipated that it will be given power to highlight cases in which Chief Executives and Chairs fail to ensure that quality care is provided to the local population, which might lead to their dismissal by the Secretary of State.

There is a wealth of information in the various professional journals about clinical effectiveness. Publications such as *Effective Health Care* bulletins offer a summary of research, but it is important to remember that these publications will become out of date, so other sources of new research and reviews should be found.

Critical appraisal

The current author has talked to professionals about using research findings; many of them feel that they lack the skills to critically appraise research or reviews. It may be helpful to look at the work of Crombie (1997), Sackett *et al.* (1997) and Swage (1998) as it is possible to break down the process of critical appraisal into some simple points that summarise what it is about:

- considering the relevance of a research question;
- evaluating the evidence to answer the question;
- assessing the relevance of the conclusion and the recommendations for practice;
- reviewing the research through the stages that make up the process of research, which include the title, abstract, introduction, literature review, methods, results, discussions and recommendations.

The following questions should then be considered (Crombie, 1997):

- Is the research of interest?
- Why was it done?
- How was it performed?
- What did it show?
- What are the possible implications for practice?
- Is the research for information only, or can it be used to support practice?

It may well be possible to attend, through the Trust's continuing education department, a course on critical appraisal, or read some of the books that specialise in research. Some of the books, papers, databases and sources of information that might be useful are listed at the end of this chapter.

Clinical guidelines

The work on guidelines has been developed since the publication of the DoH document *Clinical Guidelines: using Clinical Guidelines to Improve Patient care within the NHS* (DoH, 1996). The definition used, which is now widely accepted in the UK, is that recommended by the Agency of Health Care Policy and Research in the USA. This definition states that:

> Clinical guidelines are systematically developed statements to assist practitioner and patient decisions about appropriate health care for specific clinical circumstances.

The key words here are 'assist decision making', as guidelines do not replace the decision-making processes involving individual clinicians and patients.

The definition of local clinical guidelines or protocols is that they are locally adapted versions of the broad statement of good practice contained in national guidelines, including more operational detail (RCN, 1995).

From early 1999, for major areas of care and disease groups, NICE has produced and disseminated:

- clinical guidelines based on relevant evidence of clinical and cost-effectiveness;
- associated clinical audit methodologies and information on good practice in clinical audit.

In doing so, it will bring together work currently undertaken by the many professional organisations in receipt of DoH funding for this purpose (DoH, 1997).

At the time of writing, a number of organisations have drawn up clinical guidelines, for example:

- the medical Royal Colleges;
- the NHS Management Executive;
- academic institutions;
- the RCN;
- the Royal College of Midwives;
- the National Institute for Nursing in Oxford;
- the professional organisations representing professions allied to medicine;
- patient representatives organisations.

To develop one's own clinical guidelines is very time consuming, requiring much research to ensure that they are accurate and evidence based. It is highly likely that there are national guidelines that could be adapted to meet local requirements. If there are no national guidelines for the particular area of care that has been chosen, the following 10 steps to implementation, which were developed by the RCN (1995), are a well-structured approach to follow (see also Figure 5.1).

The main stages are guideline development, spreading the information, implementation, evaluation and review. The 10 steps to implementing guidelines are outlined below:

Step 1:

- Decide on the subject to address.
- Set up a group to develop a strategy.
- Involve other members of the multiprofessional team as well as management and patient/client representatives.
- Ensure the backing of the key players.
- Instil a sense of ownership of the guidelines among those who will be using them. Otherwise, no matter how good your guidelines are, they will not be successfully implemented.

Step 2:

- Spread the word among all those who will be affected.
- Explain how the change will benefit patient care.
- Use meetings, conferences, publications and any other way you can think of to raise awareness.

Step 3:

- When developing guidelines or adapting national guidelines to suit local conditions it's important to take account of any other quality improvement initiatives – don't work in isolation.

Step 4:

- Decide in what form you want to present the guidelines for example a booklet, a computer programme, a poster or a quick reference pocket-card. Be clear who your target audience is and how best to reach them.

Step 5:

- Check your guidelines using a reliable evaluation tool and make any necessary adjustments.

Step 6:

- Brief staff on the final version of the guidelines and set a date when the changes come into effect.

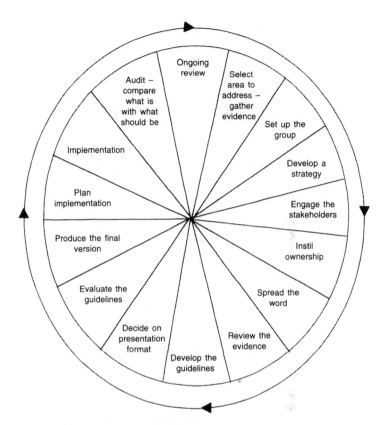

Figure 5.1   Clinical guidelines: implementation

Step 7:

- Devise a plan for implementing the changes assigning responsibility for various actions. Support staff carrying out the changes in every way you can – offer incentives, use 'opinion leaders' among your staff to get the message across and get feedback on how things are going.

Step 8:

- Reinforce the message. Remind people what it is all about.

Step 9:

- Carry out an audit comparing the outcome with what was happening before.

Step 10:

- Take action to ensure improvements are maintained by periodic review of the guidelines. The Royal College of Nursing 1995. *Clinical Guidelines – What You Need to Know* (Clinical Effectiveness Series).

Some potential areas for developing local guidelines are:

- those in which guidelines have been developed nationally and are available for adaptation, for example asthma, diabetes, head injury, the management of leg ulcers, cancer and hospital infection;
- areas of high volume, high risk and high cost;
- areas in which there are variations in practice with the potential for improvement.

The benefits of clinical guidelines are that they will:

- support the provision of high standards of health care;
- reduce unacceptable or undesirable variations in clinical practice;
- provide a basis for clinical audit;
- offer a way of implementing research findings;
- provide a means of ensuring research-based practice;
- facilitate an agreement between professionals concerning treatment;
- offer an interface between purchasers and providers that will establish cost-effective practice;
- help the purchasers of care to make informed choices;
- give managers useful data for establishing treatment costs.

Some issues surrounding guidelines

Accessing guidelines that are up to date

The 'New NHS' wants Trusts to ensure that the evaluation of good and innovative practice is systematically disseminated both within the Trust and, more widely, across the health service. Evidence-based guidelines have been developed by the Royal Colleges and a number of Trusts.

One of the problems for professionals is accessing the guidelines when they are needed and being totally sure that the guidelines are up to date from both a best practice and a legal point of view. To help to resolve this problem, software has been developed to allow the guidelines to be accessed via the Internet. One example is that of Chelsea and Westminster Healthcare, who have developed software for a set of evidence-based guidelines for obstetrics. The user is able to find the required guideline through a logical structure of headings and subheadings, or by searching through key words. The guidelines are kept up to date, changes being made when necessary in the light of current research. Such systems allow the user to copy a complete set of external guidelines, which will save an enormous amount of time and money, and support local practice.

Medico-legal problems

Guidelines may well be disclosed in legal proceedings in which there is alleged medical negligence. The plaintiff may attempt to demonstrate that guidelines were available but were not followed by the clinician, in which case the hospital will be in the position of justifying its decision not to follow the guidelines in the best interest of this particular patient. Thus, the completion of comprehensive documentation of a variance from the guidelines is vital not only for medico-legal purposes, but also for clinical audit.

Poor implementation of guidelines

The plans for implementation need to start at a very early stage in order to ensure that the key players are on board, that clinicians are clear about the benefits for the patient and that they are involved in the process, resulting in owner-ship of the guidelines. If they are not involved, the guide-lines will not be used, which will jeopardise continuity and quality of care.

Lack of multidisciplinary collaboration

The collaborative and multidisciplinary content of the group that develops and or adapts local guidelines is vital to the success of the development and implementation of the guidelines. Poor multidisciplinary teamworking will need to be addressed, although the process of developing/adapting guidelines, can if well facilitated, strengthen multi-disciplinary teamworking through discussions of the care that is given by the professionals involved and the expected outcomes for the patient.

Culture change

If clinical guidelines are to work, it will in some instances be essential to change the culture to one of 'lifelong learners' with a willingness to learn. To support this, Trusts must invest in equipping professionals with the skills to access and crit-ically appraise information and evidence, providing an envi-ronment that encourages and responds to learning.

In conclusion

Grimshaw and Russell (1993), in their discussion of guide-line development, argue that clinical guidelines must be scientifically valid, based on the best available scientific evidence, to be worthwhile.

Clinical guidelines provide an important route to promoting evidence-based practice and the basis for systematic audit. They are multidisciplinary, evidence based, focused on service priorities and reflective of patient interests. In summary, and drawing on the work of the Institute of Medicine of the USA, clinical guidelines must be:

- valid
- reliable
- reproducible
- clinically applicable
- clinically flexible
- clear
- multidisciplinary
- regularly reviewed
- well documented.

Guidelines should ultimately be shared with patients and their families so that they are able to make informed choices about care options. In Chapter 7, outlining the development of integrated care pathways demonstrates how guidelines support the delivery of evidence-based practice as part of a pathway for a specific area of care.

With the permission of Dorset Health Authority, Dorset Community NHS Trust and Dorset HealthCare NHS Trust, there is included here an example of a well-researched guideline that has been developed to support evidence-based care for patients with depression.

Guideline for the treatment of depression in secondary care

Background to the guideline

Clinicians and managers working in Dorset believed that there might be considerable variation in the treatment offered to patients referred with depression to secondary care services. There was also concern that the best available evidence was often not presented to clinicians in an easy and accessible form. It was therefore decided that a guideline should be developed to address these issues.

A working group was formed in January 1997, calling itself the Dorset Depression Group. The group contained mental health professionals from Dorset HealthCare NHS Trust, Dorset Community NHS Trust, Dorset Health Authority and the local social services department.

Literature was obtained through a number of search methods, including Psychlit, the Medline and Cochrane databases, and the Internet, using various search engines. Qualitative and recent review articles were also consulted. Pertinent papers were reviewed by members of the group who had a specific interest in or knowledge of the field. Papers that showed a scientific rigorous method were fed back to the group for further consideration; if the evidence was felt to be valid, it was included within the guideline.

The draft guideline was widely distributed and presented to secondary care multidisciplinary clinicians throughout Dorset for comments and suggestions. Focus Groups were also established to obtain users' views on the care and treatment of depression.

Following the consultation period and feedback from the Focus Groups, the guideline was amended to take into consideration various suggestions and recommendations; this included reviewing a number of research papers brought to the group's attention. Annual reviews of the guideline are planned to ensure that the guideline keeps up to date with new evidence.

It is hoped that this guideline will be used as a benchmark of best available evidence helping to improve practice.

Dorset Depression Group Members

- Dr Sue Bennett, Consultant in Public Health, Dorset Health Authority
- Dr Denise Cope, Consultant Psychiatrist for the Elderly, Dorset HealthCare NHS Trust
- Kevin Dudman, Community Mental Health Nurse, Dorset HealthCare NHS Trust
- Neil Failes, Senior Practitioner, Social Worker, Dorset Social Services

- Tim Hollingbery, Consultant Clinical Psychologist, Head of the Department of Psychological Therapies (Chairman of Committee), Dorset HealthCare NHS Trust
- Phil Kelly, Community Mental Health Nurse, Dorset Community NHS Trust
- Dr Nick Kosky, Consultant Psychiatrist, Dorset Community NHS Trust
- Christine Main, Head of Pharmacy, Dorset HealthCare NHS Trust
- Joyce Monteith, Acute Mental Health Ward Sister, Dorset HealthCare NHS Trust
- Dr Mynors-Wallis, Consultant Psychiatrist, Dorset HealthCare NHS Trust
- Dr Frances Small, Consultant in Public Health and Strategic Development, Dorset HealthCare NHS Trust
- Peter Thorne, Consultant Clinical Psychologist, Dorset Community NHS Trust
- Sheila Waters, Senior Occupational Therapist, Dorset HealthCare NHS Trust
- Sandra Hayward, Group Secretary, Clinical Development Facilitator, Dorset HealthCare NHS Trust.

Introduction to the guideline

Helping people who are clinically depressed is a complex, multifaceted task. Several factors must be considered, including a patient's preference, social/environmental variables, a patient's physical health and an understanding of the different forms of treatment for depression. There are also complexities associated with diagnosis and co-morbidity.

This guideline has been developed for the treatment of adults in secondary care. The guideline outlines some of the decision steps and considerations that may be addressed in treating depression. The basis of the guideline is the best available evidence. With developments in knowledge and further research, these guidelines will obviously change. They are part of a process of trying continually to improve the quality of clinical care and to provide efficient and cost-effective services based on sound clinical and research evidence.

This guideline is to be implemented whenever a diagnosis of depressive disorder is made. We recommend the use of the ICD10 classification system (WHO, 1992), in which the depressive disorder is rated as mild, moderate or severe. In addition, the risks of suicide, self-neglect and harm to others should be rated as low, medium or high. The severity of the depressive disorder, together with the assessment of risk, will guide treatment, as shown below.

The guideline is set out in four main sections. The first section sets out the appropriate assessment of a patient suffering from depressive illness, while the subsequent three sections outline the principles of pharmacological, psychological and psychosocial treatment.

The guidelines do not replace clinical decision making or responsibility. There will always be occasions when guidelines are not followed, but their presence can often remind clinicians to detail the reasons for taking various courses of action.

What is depressive illness?

Depressive illness is a common, disabling, sometimes chronic and potentially fatal illness, affecting about one in 20 adults in Britain (Le Pine *et al.*, 1997). It is more common in women than men, and is usually first diagnosed in the twenties or thirties, with another peak in later life. It does occur in children and adolescents, although it would appear to be less common than in adults.

The core symptoms of depression are pervasive low mood, a loss of interest or pleasure and a loss of energy. Additional symptoms are poor concentration, morbid thoughts (including those of suicide), feelings of either being unable to relax or of being slowed down, poor sleep, changes in appetite and weight, loss of libido and feelings of worthlessness or excessive guilt. There is commonly a marked decrease in effectiveness at work and social functioning (WHO, 1992).

Depressive illness is usually a remitting or relapsing condition. The majority of episodes will resolve spontaneously given enough time: about half will have resolved by 9 months, and the majority by 2 years. Unfortunately, about a fifth of people who develop a depressive episode will go on to be chronically depressed (Moyse, 1992). There is an increased rate of both attempted and completed suicide in patients with depression. The lifetime risk for completed suicide is about 10 per cent. Sufferers with chronic depressive illness are more likely than the general population to develop physical illnesses.

Treatment for depressive illness most commonly includes antidepressant medication. There will often be efforts made to help sufferers to deal with the factors that made them depressed or have prevented their recovery. Treatment is usually effective. Because of a variety of factors, only one in four sufferers of depressive illness currently receives adequate help.

Patients have the right to be treated in a sympathetic and humane way. It is to be expected that different treatment options will be discussed with the patient and that a clear explanation of their treatment will be given to them. Patients should have the opportunity to discuss their treatment and, if necessary, have aspects of it clarified.

Assessment/initial action

All patients in whom a diagnosis of depressive illness is eventually made will have had a clinical assessment. This assessment will have elicited symptoms and problems that will enable a diagnosis to be made. This diagnosis, together with an assessment of risk, will be recorded in the patient's clinical notes. For patients with a depressive illness, an assessment of the risk of suicide or self-harm is particularly crucial and should be clearly recorded in the clinical notes. Once a diagnosis and risk assessment has been made, a management plan will be implemented, as shown in Figure 5.2.

Classification	LOW RISK	MEDIUM RISK	HIGH RISK

MILD – see ICD10 classification for more details
 	
A. The general criteria used for depressive episode must be met.
B. At least two of the following three symptoms must be present:
  1. Depressed mood to a degree that is definitely abnormal for the individual, present for most of the day and almost every day, largely uninfluenced by circumstances, and sustained for at least 2 weeks.
  2. Loss of interest or pleasure in activities that are normally pleasurable.
  3. Decreased energy or increased fatigability.
C. An additional symptom or symptoms from the following list should be present, to give a total of at least four:
  1. Reduced concentration and attention.
  2. Reduced self-esteem and self-confidence.
  3. Ideas of guilt and unworthiness (even in a mild type of episode).
  4. Bleak and pessimistic views of the future.
  5. Ideas or acts of self-harm or suicide.
  6. Sleep disturbance.
  7. Diminished appetite.
 	
None of the symptoms should be present to an intense degree. Minimum duration of the whole episode is about 2 weeks.
	Consider:
	Brief therapies
	Psychosocial needs
	Referral back to primary care
	Medication
		Consider:
		Brief therapies
		Psychosocial needs
		Referral back to primary care
		Medication
		
		Arrange:
		Appropriate monitoring
			Consider:
			Brief therapies
			CBT
			Psychiatric opinion
			Psychosocial needs
			Hospitalisation
			Medication
			
			Arrange:
			Appropriate monitoring

MODERATE – see ICD10 classification for more details A. The general criteria for depressive episode must be met. B. At least two of the three symptoms listed for mild depression, criterion B, must be present. C. At least three (preferably four) of symptoms from criterion C must be present. Several symptoms are likely to be present to a marked degree, but this is not essential if a particularly wide variety of symptoms is present overall. Minimum duration of the whole episode is about 2 weeks.	**Consider:** Brief therapies CBT Psychiatric opinion Psychosocial needs **Arrange:** Appropriate monitoring Medication	**Consider:** Brief therapies CBT Hospitalisation Psychosocial needs **Arrange:** Appropriate monitoring Medication Psychiatric opinion	**Consider:** Brief therapies CBT Hospitalisation Psychosocial needs **Arrange:** Appropriate monitoring Medication Psychiatric opinion
SEVERE – see ICD10 classification for more details A. The general criteria for depressive episode must be met. B. All three of the symptoms in criterion B must be present. C. At least four other symptoms, some of which should be of severe intensity. However, if important symptoms such as agitation or retardation are marked, the patient may be unwilling or unable to describe many symptoms in details. An overall grading of 'severe episode' may still be justified in such instances. The overall episode should usually last at least 2 weeks, but if the symptoms are particularly severe and of very rapid onset, making this diagnosis after less than 2 weeks may be justified.	**Consider:** ECT Hospitalisation Psychosocial needs **Arrange:** Appropriate monitoring Medication Psychiatric opinion	**Consider:** ECT Hospitalisation Psychosocial needs **Arrange:** Appropriate monitoring Medication Psychiatric opinion	**Consider:** ECT Psychosocial needs **Arrange:** Appropriate monitoring Hospitalisation Medication Psychiatric opinion

A S S E S S M E N T

Source: Dorset Health Authority, Dorset Community NHS Trust, Dorset HealthCare NHS Trust, (1998).
CBT = cognitive behaviour therapy.

Outcome and screening measures

It may be helpful to employ screening instruments when assessing patients for the presence or absence of depression. It is recognised that, for tools to be suitable for routine clinical practice, they need to be brief and easily administered, and their scores easily interpreted. Screening instruments should also have known psychometric properties, established through research, relating to reliability and validity.

Three widely known and well-validated self-report instruments are recommended as follows:

1. *Beck Depression Inventory (BDI)* (Beck *et al.*, 1961). The BDI is useful for assessing the severity of depression and for monitoring change. Its administration takes about 3–5 minutes.
2. *Hospital Anxiety and Depression Scale (HADS)* Zigmond and Snaith, (1983). The HADS is useful for identifying cases of depression in those who are medically ill. It takes about 2–3 minutes to administer. The HADS contains items linked to key symptoms of depression and anxiety.
3. *Geriatric Depression Scale.* This is a self-report for use in the elderly.

These self-report measures can be useful in measuring change.

It should be noted that a diagnosis of depression cannot be made from the results of screening instruments alone.

Medication

Medication is a convenient and effective treatment option. Patients are, however, often fearful of medication because of concerns about side-effects and the risk of dependence; they should thus be reassured that antidepressant drugs do not cause dependence. Patients need to be warned of the common side-effects of the medications chosen, and this should be documented in the clinical notes (Figure 5.3).

Tricyclic antidepressants (TCAs)	Amitriptyline Clomipramine Dothiepin Imipramine Lofepramine Trimpramine
Selective serotonin reuptake inhibitors (SSRIs)	Cital Opram Fluoxetine Fluvoxamine Paroxetine Sertraline
Monoamine oxidase inhibitors (MAOIs)	Isocarboxazid Phenelzine Tranylcypromine
Reversible inhibitors of monoamine oxidase type A (RIMAs)	Moclobemide
Others	Mirtazapine Nefazodone Reboxetine Trazodone Venlafaxine

Source: Dorset Health Authority, Dorset Community NHS Trust, Dorset Health Care NHS Trust (1998).

Figure 5.3 Classes of antidepressant

Selection of antidepressants

The choice of antidepressant will be influenced by the following factors:

1. Previous patient response to particular drug (and a family history of a positive response to a drug) (Depression Guideline Panel, 1993).

2. The toxicity of the antidepressant if taken in overdose:
   - older tricyclic antidepressants (TCAs) are most lethal in overdose;
   - monoamine oxidase inhibitors (MAOIs) are of intermediate toxicity;

- selective serotonin reuptake inhibitors (SSRIs) and newer drugs possess a low toxicity (Henry, 1997).

3. The side-effects of the antidepressant:

- consider the likelihood of compliance with a particular class of drugs in view of:
  - the patient's history;
  - the patient's lifestyle;

- consider co-existing medical conditions:
  - avoid TCAs if there is a history of cardiac disease or narrow angle glaucoma, a risk of orthostatic hypertension or prostatic problems;
  - epilepsy: consider moclobemide, citalopram or sertraline.

4. The symptom cluster:

- agitation and the need for sedation may suggest:
  - a sedative antidepressant such as amitriptyline or trazodone;
  - supplementing the antidepressant with a brief (1–2 week) course of benzodiazepine or a phenothiazine;

- atypical symptoms might preferentially respond to an MAOI (Quitkin *et al.*, 1988, 1991);

- for obsessive-compulsive symptoms, consider clomipramine or an SSRI.

5. Cost

If an antidepressant is changed, the reason for the change should be documented in the patient's notes.

Antidepressant treatment is then continued for 4–6 weeks (Figure 5.4).

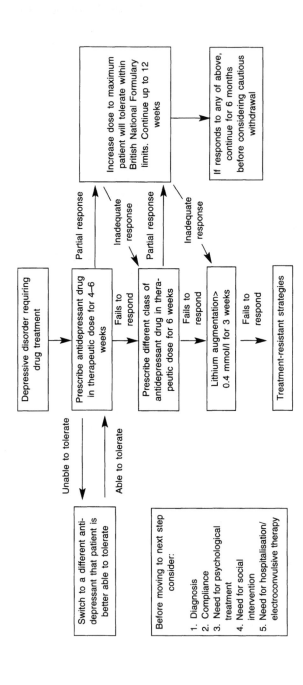

Figure 5.4 Guidelines for the treatment of depression in secondary care – pharmacological management of non-psychotic unipolar depressive disorder (see also Figure 5.5 for information on switching or changing antidepressants)

Source: Dorset Health Authority, Dorset Community NHS Trust, Dorset HealthCare Trust (1998).

Choice of second antidepressant if inadequate response to the initial drug

The following should be considered (see also Figure 5.5):

1. Switching to a drug with a different theoretical mode of action, for example from a noradrenaline reuptake blocker to a 5-hydroxytryptamine reuptake blocker, or a TCA to an MAOI.

2. Drug interactions, for example the untoward effects of combinations of drugs and the need for possible wash-out periods. An SSRI should not be used with an MAOI (because of the risk of serotonin syndrome), nor should a TCA be added to an MAOI. (The recommended procedure for this combination therapy is to allow a drug-free interval of at least 1 week and then start both drugs together at a low dosage, gradually increasing this to about half of the usual dose for each individual drug) (Katona and Barnes Thomas, 1985).

Lithium augmentation

Before starting lithium treatment, the patient should be warned of potential side-effects and this should be documented in the notes. Baseline tests of renal and thyroid function need to be carried out, as does the routine monitoring of lithium levels according to Trust guidelines.

Treatment resistance strategies

Several options are available, but there is little evidence for any one strategy being of particular benefit. A second opinion should be considered.

Positive response to medication

If the patient responds to a pharmacological intervention, the drug should be continued for at least 6 months (from recovery) before considering its cautious withdrawal.

TCAs and REBOXETINE	No significant problems reported	No significant problems reported	Care needed. Fluoxetine, paroxetine and fluvoxamine can double or triple TCA levels. Taper TCA dose to 50 mg/day. Start SSRI at usual dose and discontinue TCA over 1 week	No significant problems reported	Wash-out period of 5 times the half-life of the TCA recommended by manufacturer. No problems reported	Wash-out period: phenelzine 7–14 days; isocarboxazid 7–14 days; tranylcypromine 7 days and start at half dose for one week	No significant problems reported. British National Formulary recommends 1 week wash-out
SSRI	Care needed. See TCAs to SSRIs. Fluoxetine has a long half-life – care is needed up to 4 weeks after stopping. Stop fluoxetine and wait several days before starting TCA at low dose. Increase dose cautiously	Serotonin syndrome possible – careful observation with gradual changeover or wash-out period to minimise potential problems	Care – fluoxetine can increase levels of trazodone. Serotonin syndrome reported with trazodone and fluoxetine, and fluoxetine and paroxetine combinations. Gradual switch advised. See SSRIs to SSRIs	Care	Care	Wash-out period required: citalopram 7 days[1]; fluvoxamine 7–14 days[1]; fluoxetine 6 weeks[1]; paroxetine 2 weeks[1]; sertraline 1–2 weeks[1]	Wash-out period required of 4–5 times half-life[1]: citalopram 7 days; fluoxetine 6 weeks; fluvoxamine 5 days; paroxetine 5 days; sertraline 7–13 days
TRAZODONE/ NEFAZODONE	Occasional problems	Care needed. See SSRIs to trazodone/ nefazadone		Care	Care	Wash-out period 7 days[1]	Wash-out period required of 4–5 times half life[1]: trazodone 1–2 days; nefazadone 4 days
VENLAFAXINE	No significant problems reported	Care needed	Care needed	Care	No significant problems reported	Wash-out period 7 days[1]	No significant problems reported
MAOIs	Wash-out period 14 days[1]	Wash-out period 14 days[1]	Wash-out period 14 days[1]	Wash-out period 14 days[1]	Wash-out period 14 days[1]	Wash-out period 14 days[1]	Wash-out period 7 days
MOCLOBEMIDE	Occasional problems with clomipramine	No significant problems reported. Fluoxetine 14 days wash-out (Lilly).	No significant problems reported	No significant problems reported	No significant problems reported	No significant problems reported	
MIRTAZAPINE	No significant problems reported	No significant problems reported	No significant problems reported	No significant problems reported	No significant problems reported	Wash-out period 2 weeks	No significant problems reported

1 Manufacturers' summary of product characteristics.
Source: Dorset Health Authority, Dorset Community NHS Trust, Dorset HealthCare NHS Trust (1998).
TCA = tricyclic antidepressant, SSRI = selective serotonin reuptake inhibitor; MAOI = monoamine oxidase inhibitor.

Figure 5.5 Guidelines for the treatment of depression in secondary care – recommendations when switching or changing antidepressants

Notes on antidepressants

The number of deaths caused by drug overdose involving antidepressants, either alone or in combination with other drugs, exceeds 10 per cent of the number of annual national suicides (Henry, 1996).

The Fatal Toxicity Index (FTI) is used to express the number of fatal overdoses per million prescriptions for each drug, but takes no account of suicide by other methods. Comparing the FTI for different antidepressants shows a marked advantage for SSRIs and lofepramine. However, other factors, especially treatment failure, will also influence the overall suicide rate (Henry *et al.*, 1995).

Tricyclic antidepressants

Amitriptyline. This is an effective tricyclic with potent anticholinergic, sedative and weight-gaining properties. Because of its long half-life, sustained release preparations are expensive and unnecessary. It is toxic in overdose.

Dothiepin. Dothiepin is an effective TCA with sedative and anticholinergic effects. It is very toxic in overdose, linked with proconvulsive and cardiac arythmic effects (Crome, 1993; Buckley *et al.*, 1994).

Imipramine. This TCA is similar to amitriptyline and dothiepin but less sedative. Stimulant side-effects may be a problem, as may anticholinergic effects, especially in the elderly. Imipramine is toxic in overdose.

Lofepramine. Lofepramine shows minimal sedative effects and an impairment of memory and concentration compared with dothiepin. In some patients lofepramine may increase alertness. It is safe in overdose despite its metabolism to desipramine (Reif and Henry, 1996).

Selective Serotonin Reuptake Inhibitors (SSRIs)

Fluoxetine. Fluoxetine is licensed for depression with or without associated anxiety symptoms, although some patients may experience a degree of anxiety during the first week or two of treatment (Palazidou, 1997). It has an active metabolite with a long half-life of 7–9 days. A wash-out period of 5 weeks is necessary before starting treatment with an MAOI. Fluoxetine is safe in overdose and shows no cardiotoxicity (Henry, 1992; Henry *et al.*, 1995).

Citalopram. This drug is similar to fluoxetine but is a poor inhibitor of cytochrome P450–2D6 and may thus cause fewer adverse drug interactions (Baumann and Rochar, 1995).

Paroxetine. Paroxetine has early anxiolytic properties in addition to its antidepressant action and is useful for treating depression accompanied by anxiety (Palazidou, 1997). It has a shorter half-life (24 hours) than fluoxetine and no active metabolite. Extrapyramidal reactions and withdrawal syndrome have been reported to the Committee on Safety of Medicines (1993) more frequently than has occurred with other SSRIs. Withdrawal should be slow.

Sertraline. Sertraline is similar to fluoxetine but has a shorter half-life (25 hours), that of its active metabolite being 3.5–4.5 days. It is licensed for depression, including that associated with anxiety. Upward dose titration is needed more frequently than with fluoxetine, leading to increased cost (Nair *et al.*, 1995). The summary of product characteristics recommends that doses of 150 mg and above should not be used for more than 8 weeks.

Monoamine oxidase inhibitors

Isocarboxazid. Isocarboxazid is an irreversible inhibitor of the monoamine-oxidase enzyme. It interacts with tyramine in food and with other drugs, for example sympathomimetics, pethidine, clomipramine, SSRIs and venlafaxine.

Moclobemide. This drug is a reversible inhibitor of mono-amine oxidase. Compared with traditional non-reversible MAOIs, there are fewer side-effects (Nair *et al.*, 1995), including effects on sexual function (Phillip, 1993). Food interactions are also less likely, although they are possible with high doses (>600 mg) or if large quantities of tyra-mine are ingested. Moclobemide is effective across a broad range of depressive presentations, including agitated depression, rather than being limited to less typical subtypes (Paykel, 1995).

Phenelzine. Phenelzine is similar to isocarboxazid but possibly safer if combination, for example with a TCA, is considered.

Tranylcypromine. This is similar to isocarboxazid but has an amphetamine-like structure. It should never be used in combination with potentially interacting drugs. It may cause mild dependence, and it has stimulant properties; thus it should not be taken after 3.00 pm.

Others

Mirtazapine. With this noradrenergic and specific seroton-ergic antidepressant, anticholinergic and serotonergic side-effects seem less common, but somnolence and weight gain may be a problem.

Nefazadone. Nefazadone may cause nausea and restlessness in the early stages of treatment, and a stepwise increase of dose is advised. The incidence of sexual dysfunction may be less than with other antidepressants. Data from clinical trials show no significant difference between nefazadone and placebo in the incidence of psychosexual disturbance (Rickels *et al.*, 1994; Baldwin, 1996).

Trazodone. Trazodone has low cardiotoxicity and few anti-cholinergic side-effects, but is associated with a high incidence of nausea and drowsiness. Priapism is a rare side-effect.

Reboxetine. A selective noradrenaline reuptake inhibitor, reboxetine causes fewer anticholinergic side-effects and less cognitive and psychomotor impairment than do TCAs. Compared with fluoxetine, it causes a higher incidence of anticholinergic side-effects but less gastrointestinal ones.

Vanlafaxine. Vanlafaxine is a combined serotonin and noradrenaline reuptake inhibitor. There are only limited data to support the special properties of venlafaxine: fast onset, greater efficacy (Anderson, 1997); and efficacy in refractory illness (Nierenberg *et al.*, 1994). Further studies and clinical experience are needed to support these.

Electroconvulsive therapy

The use of lithium with electroconvulsive therapy (ECT) has been reported to cause severe memory loss, neurological abnormalities and a reduced antidepressant effect (Small *et al.*, 1980; Ferrier *et al.*, 1995). ECT may also facilitate lithium toxicity. One should consider withdrawing lithium treatment 48 hours prior to ECT and not restarting it until several days after the last treatment (Ferrier *et al.*, 1995).

Augmentation therapy

Lithium. Lithium has been shown to be an effective adjunct to TCAs (Austin *et al.*, 1991; Ferrier *et al.*, 1995) and MAOIs (Nierenberg and White, 1990). Published studies of lithium used with SSRIs are limited. Combining lithium with fluoxetine (Nelson and Byck, 1982) or sertraline (Fava *et al.*, 1994) has been shown to improve the response in patients resistant to treatment with an SSRI alone. The lithium augmentation of venlafaxine has not been studied; there have been three reports of adverse effects with this combination; but a definite casual link has not been established (see Figure 5.5).

Psychological treatments for non-psychotic unipolar depressive disorder (Figure 5.6)

For depressive disorders of mild or moderate severity, there is good evidence for the effectiveness of psychological treatment (Mynors-Wallis *et al.*, 1995). For those with severe depressive disorders, medication should be the first treatment option, although there is some evidence for the effectiveness of psychological treatment.

It is probable that, because of the limited availability of trained therapists, medication will be the first treatment option for most patients. However, there are relatively simple behavioural techniques that can be used by many disciplines. If such treatments are used, they should be documented in the clinical notes, together with an indication of their effectiveness.

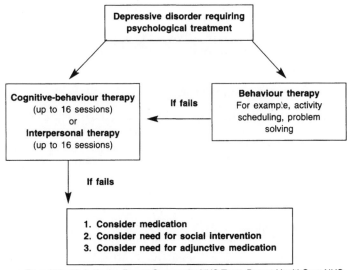

Source: Dorset Health Authority, Dorset Community NHS Trust, Dorset HealthCare NHS Trust (1998).

Figure 5.6 Guidelines for the treatment of depression in secondary care

Psychological treatment may be used as a first-line treatment for depressive disorders if:

- a suitably trained therapist is available, and
- the patient has a preference for this treatment; or
- medication is contraindicated because of physical illness or has not been effective in the past.

Psychological treatment may have a particular role if:

- the patient has not responded to medication;
- co-morbid conditions, for example personality disorders, are present.

Effective psychological treatments, although differing in their underlying rationale, show several common factors in that they:

- are structured;
- are goal orientated;
- focus on change in the here and now;
- remove blame from patient;
- instil the belief that there are actions that affect outcomes.

There are no established grounds for choosing between cognitive behavioural therapy and interpersonal therapy for the treatment of depressive disorders. There is less evidence, however, supporting brief psychodynamic treatments.

Cognitive therapy

Cognitive therapy is based on the theoretical rationale that low mood arises secondary to 'depressive cognitions'. Systematic errors of thinking have been identified, including selective attention to the negative features of a situation, magnification of the catastrophic implications of such situations, arbitrary inference, drawing a conclusion for which there is little or no evidence, overgeneralisation, drawing a general conclusion on the basis of a single incident, personalisation relating external events to oneself in an unwarranted way, and dichotomous thinking, that is, seeing every-thing as either black or white. These errors of thinking are underpinned by a set of faulty assumptions based on past experience, for example, 'Unless I do everything perfectly, I am a failure.'

Treatment typically comprises 15–20 structured sessions attempting to detect and counter these faulty assumptions and errors in thinking. Treatment is an active collabora-tive process that tests out assumptions and beliefs in real-life experiences rather than by persuasion or debate. Cognitive therapy has a behavioural component (active scheduling and the empirical testing of beliefs); hence treatment should be more precisely termed 'cognitive–behaviour therapy'.

Interpersonal psychotherapy

The rationale underpinning interpersonal psychotherapy is that depression occurs in the context of, if not actu-ally being caused by, relationship and social difficulties. If difficulties in these areas are satisfactorily dealt with, the symptoms of depression will resolve. Interpersonal psychotherapy emphasises the importance of the psychosocial environment and the understanding of psychiatric disorders. These ideas have been given empir-ical support by work implicating life events in the aeti-ology of depression. Stressful life events are often of a psychosocial nature, for example marital disharmony and bereavement. Furthermore, depressed patients have impaired social functioning, which improves with symp-tomatic recovering.

Interpersonal psychotherapy is a time-limited (12–16 week) psychological treatment that begins by describing the symptoms of depression and explaining that they are understandable and likely to resolve. Interpersonal therapy, like cognitive therapy, deals with events in the present rather than the past. The aims of treatment are the clarification and resolution of one or more of the following interper-sonal difficulties:

- prolonged grief reaction
- role disputes
- role transitions
- interpersonal deficits.

Behaviour therapy

Behaviour therapy for the treatment of depression encompasses several different therapeutic regimes. Behavioural formulations, however, share the hypothesis that depression results from inadequate or insufficient positive reinforcement. In general, there is a reduction in behaviours that have previously been positively reinforced. Without reinforcement, these positive behaviours occur at a lower rate, setting in motion a downward cycle that further reduces opportunities for reinforcement and eventually results in the symptoms of depression. Treatments include activity scheduling and social skills training.

Psychosocial interventions (Figure 5.7)

Many patients with depressive disorders have experienced a recent adverse life event or chronic life difficulties.

An assessment of psychosocial problems should be part of all assessments. If a specific problem area is identified, specific help could be offered alongside a drug or psychological treatment, or further, more detailed assessment and treatment might be offered by a member of the community mental health team, for example the community occupational therapist, community mental health nurse or social worker. If an intervention is provided it should be documented in the clinical notes, together with an indication of its effectiveness.

There has been little research in the field of social interventions for depression. Common sense and experience, however, suggest that help in sorting out psychosocial difficulties will help to lift mood. A list of psychosocial interventions is categorised within the flowchart in Figure 5.7.

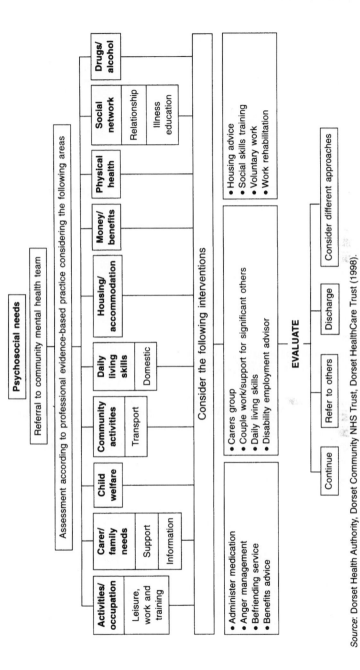

Figure 5.7 Guidelines for the treatment of depression in secondary care

Source: Dorset Health Authority, Dorset Community NHS Trust, Dorset HealthCare Trust (1998).

There is good evidence that behavioural therapies are helpful in the treatment of depression (see Psychological treatments), such treatments often focusing on psychosocial interventions. There is also evidence in primary care that problem solving is an effective treatment for depression (Mynors-Wallis *et al.*, 1995).

Evidence-based practice

Evidence-based practice, as defined by Long and Harrison (1996):

> is practice that reflects the aspiration that doctors and other clinical professionals should pursue their work of diagnosis, therapy and care on the basis of procedures, which are known, through research evidence, to be effective.

Over the past decade, there has been growing interest, across all the professions, in the use of the results of research to improve patient care. The terms applied to this activity include 'evidence-based practice', 'clinical effectiveness' and 'implementation of research findings'. In 1995, the NHS Executive published a booklet, primarily for the Chief Executives of Health Authorities and NHS Trusts, their teams and clinicians who have responsibility for developing local strategies, to improve clinical effectiveness (DoH, 1995). This booklet outlined the issues that the NHS Executive believed needed to be addressed in helping the service to develop more effective health care.

The booklet is divided into three sections: Inform, Change and Monitor. The section headed Inform describes the sources of information available and what is being planned for the future to make information more readily accessible. The section Change describes and suggests ways in which changes to services can be encouraged based on well-founded information on effectiveness. The section entitled Monitor describes ways in which changes to services can be assessed to demonstrate that change has resulted in improvement.

The booklet includes a section on milestones to be achieved, for example:

- Health authorities would report the delivery of success criteria for effectiveness by March 1996 and criteria for effectiveness by March 1997.
- NHS Trusts would:
  - have policies that involve patients;
  - develop local framework for clinical effectiveness;
  - have access to Centre for Reviews Dissemination database and Cochrane CD ROM/disk information;
  - foster clinical audit and the implementation of clinical guidelines and service guidelines;
  - support professional training, further education and skills training (for example, in critical appraisal techniques).

The Trust milestones were set as ongoing but should already be well established.

Implementing evidence-based practice

Sackett *et al.* (1997) advise that there are four stages to implementing evidence-based practice (Figure 5.8):

- identifying a problem;
- finding an answer through literature searches and critiques;
- implementing the changes;
- evaluating change.

In order for evidence-based practice to become part of the culture of the multidisciplinary team, it is important that the environment of the organisation is one that supports and nurtures evidence-based practice. As stated earlier in this chapter, it is about the provision of access to information and research, as well as the provision of training and development to acquire or increase skills such as critical appraisal, searching the literature and evaluating the research.

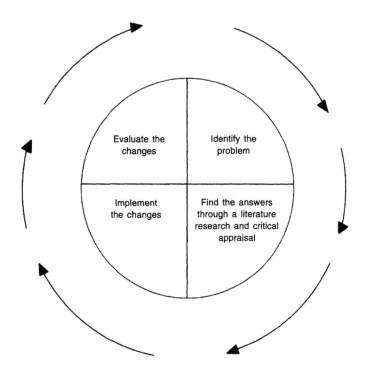

Figure 5.8   The four stages of implementing evidence-based practice

Finding the research through the library, journals or one of the organisations listed at the end of this chapter may be fairly straightforward. Once the research has been found, evaluating it can be the first major stumbling block. Evidence-based practice requires the practitioner to critically appraise and review the research in order to establish whether the findings are valid in the setting in which the study was conducted and, more importantly, whether the findings can be applied in the chosen clinical setting. If the answer to this fundamental question is 'no', the next piece of research should be tackled. If the answer is 'yes', the next step is to establish whether the approach used was comprehensive, whether there were sufficient data and so on. From the work developed by Milne and Chambers (1993), some key questions emerge:

- Are the literature search strategies explicitly designed and stated?
- Is the search strategy comprehensive?
- Is the issue of publication bias addressed?
- Are the methodologies of the individual studies appropriately reviewed?
- Are sufficient data given on the individual studies, (patients, diagnoses, therapies and outcomes)?
- If a quantitative overview is provided, is such an overview justifiable, given possible sources of heterogeneity?
- Are appropriate conclusions drawn for treatment recommendations (whether it is beneficial, equivocal or harmful) and future research?

Having successfully completed this process, research findings may be incorporated into practice through clinical guidelines and integrated care pathways, being evaluated through the clinical audit cycle to establish whether expected outcomes have been achieved.

Benefits of evidence-based practice

These include:

- a greater understanding of the area of care or practice;
- practice that is evidence based;
- practice that is cost-effective;
- improved quality of care;
- standardised care;
- the ongoing monitoring of the quality of care;
- fewer unacceptable or undesirable variations in clinical practice;

- better agreement between professionals concerning treatment;
- an interface between purchasers and providers that will establish cost-effective practice;
- help for the purchasers of care to make informed choices;
- a desire to learn more about research and a commitment to evidence-based practice.

Problems of implementing evidence-based practice

The implementation of the Culyer recommendations challenges Trust managers to nurture a climate that supports research and development initiatives. There has to be organisational commitment and leadership if research and development are to become part of the normal day-to-day business of Trusts. Unfortunately, there are a large number of managers without research training, which hinders this process and makes it difficult for practitioners to base their practice on research findings in a culture based on the principles of trial and error, and an historical approach of 'We have always done it this way'. This is a particular problem for the nursing profession.

There is also a lack of evidence. The amount of evidence available to some professions, including nursing, is often small and not always reliable or valid. Work undertaken by Appleby *et al.* in 1995 established that more than 70 per cent of the information available related to acute care treatments, these being dominated by pharmaceutical interventions. The authors also established that 79 per cent of the activities related to the medical profession, only 15 per cent concerning nursing. The amount of evidence available for nurses working in the community is, therefore, very limited.

Other difficulties are also encountered:

- a lack of dissemination of the findings of research;
- a lack of knowledge of the NHS Research and Development strategy;

- a dearth of training in research skills for both managers and clinicians;
- a lack of support in gaining these skills;
- time constraints;
- activity being additional to an already heavy workload;
- a lack of multidisciplinary teamworking;
- little knowledge and experience;
- problems in making changes in the light of research.

There are numerous sources of information to support evidence-based practice, a sample of which is listed below:

The Cochrane Database of Systematic Reviews, Oxford
UK Cochrane Centre NHS R&D Programme, Summertown
Pavilion, Middle Way, Oxford, OX2 7LG
Tel: (01865) 516300
Email: general@cochrane.co.uk
A very large collection of regularly updated, systematic reviews of the effects of health care. The database is developed from contributors to the Cochrane Collaboration, an international research initiative committed to 'preparing, maintaining and disseminating systematic reviews of the effects of healthcare'. The Cochrane Collaboration has two types of organisational unit: Cochrane Centres and Collaborative Review Groups.

Cochrane Library
The Cochrane Library began in April 1995 under the name of the Cochrane Database of Systematic Reviews and now includes other important related databases, including: the Cochrane Database of Systematic Reviews (CDSR): the York Databases of Abstracts of Reviews of Effectiveness (DARE), the Cochrane Controlled Trials Register (CCTR) and the Cochrane Review Methodology Database (CRMD). This is a regularly updated electronic library designed to provide the evidence required for making health care decisions.

NHS Centre for Reviews and Dissemination (NHS CRD)
University of York, Haslington, York, YO10 5DD
Tel: (01904) 433707
http://www.york.ac.uk/inst/crd
A facility commissioned by the NHS Research and Development Division. It identifies and reviews the results of good-quality health

research and then disseminates the findings within the NHS. The areas they cover are:

- *the effectiveness of care for particular conditions;*
- *the effectiveness of health technologies;*
- *evidence on efficient methods of organising and delivering particular types of health care.*

National Research Register (NRR)
NHS Executive HQ, Quarry House, Quarry Hill, Leeds, LS2 7UE
A register of research that may be found in health care libraries.

Promoting Action on Clinical Effectiveness (PACE)
King's Fund Development Centre, 111–113 Cavendish Square, London, W1M 0AN
Tel: 0171-307 2694
http://www.kingsfund.org.uk/pace/evidence.htm
Set up by the King's Fund in 1995, focusing on organisational development designed to ensure the implementation of evidence for specific clinical conditions. PACE circulate regular PACE Bulletins and discussion papers. Publications include Getting Started *(how to establish a local implementation project),* Creating Local Projects, Measuring Impact, Effective Communications *and so on.*

Critical Appraisal Skills Programme (CASP)
Old Road, Headington, Oxford, OX3 7LF
http://www.ihs.ox.ac.uk/casp/home.page.html
A training service to help health service decision makers to develop skills in the critical appraisal of evidence on effectiveness in order to promote the delivery of evidence-based health care. Produces a series of half-day workshops and an interactive CD-ROM for use in conjunction with the workshops or video conferencing, as a stand-alone package, or to reinforce learning. A distance learning pack is also available.

Health Care Evaluation Unit (HCEU)
St George's Hospital, Medical School, Tooting, London, SW17 0RE
A designated support unit for the National Research and Development Initiative located within the Department of Public Health

Sciences at St George's Hospital Medical School. The unit has a remit to assess the quality of nationally developed clinical guidelines.

Summary of sources of evidence:

Evidence can be obtained from:

- the Cochrane database;
- the Centre for Reviews Dissemination;
- local universities;
- centres for research and development;
- libraries;
- the clinical audit department;
- the National Centre for Clinical Audit;
- Practice Development Units;
- Nursing Development Units;
- professional bodies;
- information technology centres;
- voluntary and support organisations.

It is sometimes quite difficult to see how the new initiatives set out in this chapter will really affect everyday clinical care. The following chapters, on clinical governance and integrated care pathways, will help to demonstrate how theory can be put into practice. This is particularly true of the development of the care pathway, which the present author believes is the only way to deliver evidence-based care to patients and clients.

References

Allen, D., Curran, H. V. and Lader, M. 1993 Effects of Lofepramine and Dothiepin on Memory and Psychomotor Function in Health Volunteers, *Journal of Psychopharmacology*, **7**: 33–8.

Anderson, I. 1997 Lessons To Be Learnt from Meta-analyses of Newer Versus Older Antidepressants, *Advances in Psychiatric Treatment*, **3**: 58–63.

Appleby, J., Walshe, K. and Ham, C. 1995 *Acting on the Evidence. A Review of Clinical Effectiveness: Sources of Information, Dissemination and Implementation.* Birmingham: NAHA.

Austin, M. P. V., Souza, F. G. M and Goodwin, G. M. 1991 Lithium Augmentation in Antidepressant Resistant Patients: A Quantitative Analysis, *British Journal of Psychiatry,* **159**: 510–14.

Baldwin, D. S. 1996 Depression and Sexual Function, *Psychopharmacology,* **10**(suppl.): 30–4.

Baumann, P. and Rochar, B. 1995 Comparative Pharmacokinetics of Selective Serotonin Reuptake Inhibitors: A Look Behind the Mirror, *International Journal of Psychopharmacology,* **10**(suppl.): 15–21.

Beck, A. T., Ward, C., Mendelson, M., Mock, J. and Erlbaugh, J. 1961 An Inventory for Measuring Depression, *Archives of General Psychiatry,* **4**: 561–71.

Buckley, N. A., Dawson, A. H., Whyte, I. M and Henry, D. A. 1994 Greater Toxicity in Overdose of Dothiepin than of other Tricyclic Antidepressants, *Lancet,* **343**: 159–62.

Committee on Safety of Medicines/Medicines Control Agency 1993 Dystonia and Withdrawal Symptoms with Paroxetine (Seroxat), *Current Problems,* **19**: 1.

Crombie, I. 1997 *The Pocket Guide to Critical Appraisal.* London: BMJ Publishing.

Crome, P. 1993 The Toxicity of Drugs Used for Suicide, *Acta Psychiatrica Scandinavia,* **87**(suppl. 371): 33–7.

Department of Health 1993 *Improving Clinical Effectiveness.* London: HMSO.

Department of Health 1995 *Promoting Clinical Effectiveness – A Framework for Action in and Through the NHS.*

Department of Health 1996 *Promoting Clinical Effectiveness – A Framework for Action In and Through the NHS (The Culyer Report).* Londo: NHSE.

Department of Health 1996 *Clinical Guidelines: Using Clinical Guidelines To Improve Patient Care within the NHS.* London.

Department of Health 1997 *The New NHS, Modern, Dependable.* London: HMSO.

Depression Guideline Panel 1993 *Depression in Primary Care,* vol. 2, *Treatment of Major Depression Clinical Practice Guideline,* Number 5. Public Health Service, Agency for Health Care Policy and Research Pub. No. 93-0551. Rockville, MD: US Department of Health and Human Services.

Fava, M., Rosenbaum, J. F., McGrath, P. J. *et al.* 1994 Lithium Augmentation of Fluoxetine Treatment for Resistant Major Depression: A Double-blind, Controlled Study, *American Journal of Psychiatry,* **151**(9): 1372–4.

Ferrier, I. N., Tyrer, S. P. and Bell, A. J. 1995 Lithium Therapy, *Advanced in Psychiatric Treatment*, **1**: 102–10.

Grimshaw, J. and Russell, I. 1993 Achieving Health Gain Through Clinical Guidelines. 1: Developing Scientifically Valid Guidelines, *Quality in Health Care*, **2**: 243–8.

Henry, J. A. 1992 Toxicity of Antidepressants: Comparisons with Fluoxetine, *International Clinical Psychopharmacology*, **6**(suppl. 6): 22–7.

Henry, J. A., Alexander, C. A. and Sener, E. K. 1995 Relative Mortality from Overdose of Antidepressants, *British Medical Journal*, **310**: 221–4.

Henry, J. A. 1996 Suicide Risk and Antidepressant Treatment, *Journal of Psychopharmacology*, **10**(suppl. 1): 39–40.

Henry, J. A. 1997 Toxicity of Newer Versus Older Antidepressants, *Advances in Psychiatric Treatment*, **3**: 41–5.

Katona, C. and Barnes Thomas, R. E. 1985 *British Journal of Hospital Medicine*, September: 168–71.

Le Pine, P., Gastpar, J., Mendleson, M. and Tyler, J. 1997 On Behalf of the Depression Steering Committee. Depression in the Community in the first Pan-European Study of Depression. Depression Research in European Society, *International Clinical Psychopharmacology*, **12**: 19–29.

Long, A. and Harrison, S. 1996 Evidence-based decision making. *Health Service Journal*, **106**: 1–11.

Milne, R. and Chambers, L. 1993 Addressing the Scientific Quality of Review Articles, *Journal of Epidemiology and Community Health*, **47**(3): 169–70.

Moyse, J. 1992 How Recurrent and Predictable Is Depressive Disorder?, in Montgomery, S. and Rouillen, R. (eds) Long-term Treatment of Depression, *Perspectives in Psychiatry*, **3**: 1–13.

Mynors-Wallis, L. M., Gath, D. H., Lloyd-Thomas, A. R. and Tomlinson, D. 1995 Randomised Controlled Trial Comparing Problem Solving Treatment with Amitriptyzine and Placebo for Major Depression in Primary Care, *British Medical Journal*, **310**: 441–5.

Nair, *et al.* 1995 Moclobemide and Norrtiptyline in Elderly Depressed Patients. A Randomised Multicentre Trial Against Placebo, *Journal of Affective Disorders*, **33**: 1–9.

Nelson, J. C. and Byck, R. 1982 Rapid Response to Lithium in Phenelzine Non-responders, *British Journal of Psychiatry*, **141**: 85–6.

Nierenberg, A. A. and White, K. 1990 What Next? – A Review of Pharmacology Strategies for the Treatment of Resistant Depression, *Psychopharmacology Bulletin*, **26**: 429–60.

Nierenberg, *et al.* 1994 Venlafaxine for Treatment-resistant Unipolar Depression, *Journal of Clinical Psychopharmacology*, **14**(6): 419–23.

Palazidou, E. 1997 Development of New Antidepressants, *Advances in Psychiatric Treatment*, **3**: 46–51.

Paykel, E. S. 1995 Clinical Efficacy of Reversible and Selective Inhibitors of Monoamine Oxidase A in Major Depression, *Acta Psychiatrica Scandinavica*, **91**(suppl. 386): 22–7.

Phillip, M., Kohnen, R. and Benkert, O. 1993 A Comparison Study of Moclobemide and Doxiepine in Major Depression with Special Reference to Effects on Sexual Dysfunction, *International Clinical Psychopharmacology*, **7**: 149–53.

Quitkin, F. M., Stewart, J. W., McGrath, P. J. *et al.* 1988 Phenelzine Versus Imipramine in the Treatment of Probable Atypical Depression: Defining Syndrome Boundaries of Selective MAOI Responders, *American Journal of Psychiatry*, **145**: 306–11.

Quitkin, F. M., Harrison, W., Stewart, J. W. *et al.* 1991 Response to Phenelzine and Imipramine in Placebo Non-responders with Atypical Depression: A New Application of the Crossover Design, *Archives of General Psychiatry*, **48**: 319–23.

Reif, F. and Henry, J. A. 1996 Lofepramine Overdosage, *Pharmacopyschiatry*, **23**(suppl. 1): 23–7.

Rickels, K. *et al.* 1994 Nefazodone and Imipramine in Major Depression: A Placebo Controlled Trial, *British Journal of Psychiatry*, **164**: 802–5.

Royal College of Nursing 1995 *Clinical Guidelines: What You Need to Know*. London: RCN.

Sackett, D. L., Rosenburg, W. and Haynes, R. B. 1997 *Evidence Based Medicine: How to Use Practice and Teach EBP*. London: Churchill Livingstone.

Sackett, D. L., Richardson, W. S., Rosenberg, W. and Haynes, R. B. 1997 *Evidence Based Medicine: How to Use Practice and Teach EBP*. Edinburgh: Churchill Livingstone.

Small, J. G., Kelham, J. J., Milstem, V. *et al.* 1980 Complications with Electroconvulsive Treatment Combined with Lithium, *Biological Psychiatry*, **15**: 103–12.

Swage, T. 1998 Clinical Care Takes Centre Stage, *Nursing Times*, **94**(14): 40–1.

World Health Organisation 1992 Mental and Behavioural Disorders, in *International Classification of Diseases*, 10th edn. Geneva: WHO.

Zigmond, A. S. and Snaith, R. P. 1983 The Hospital Anxiety and Depression Scale, *Acta Psychiatriac Scandinavicaa*, **67**: 361–70.

Classification codes

The following classification codes were used in the guidelines outlined earlier in this chapter:

A = Evidence from well-designed randomised controlled trials, meta-analyses or systematic reviews of randomised controlled trials.

B = Evidence from prospective studies (non-randomised controlled trials or good observation studies).

C = Evidence obtained from retrospective and cross-sectional studies.

D = Evidence obtained from expert committee reports or opinions and/or clinical experience or respected authorities.

UC = Unclassified.

Other references reviewed

Some of the following references were also reviewed in putting together the guidelines outlined in the chapter. Classification codes (see above) are indicated at the end of each reference.

Anderson, I. 1997 Lessons To Be Learnt from Meta-analyses of Newer Versus Older Antidepressants, *Advances in Psychiatric Treatment*, **1**: 94–101.

Beck, A. T., Rush, A. J., Shaw, B. F. and Emery, G. 1979 *Cognitive Therapy of Depression*. New York: Guilford Press (C).

Bethlem and Maudsley NHS Trust 1996 *Prescribing Guidelines*, 3rd edn. London: Bethlem and Maudsley NHS Trust.

Brown, R. A. and Lewinsohn, P. M. 1990 A Psychoeducational Approach to the Treatment of Depression: Comparison of Group, Individual and Minimal Contact Procedures, *Journal of Consultant Clinical Psychology*, **52**: 774–83 (A).

Cluzeau, F., Littlejohns, P., Grimshaw, J. and Hopkins, A. 1995 Appraising Clinical Guidelines and the Development of Criteria – a Pilot Study, *Journal of Interprofessional Care*, **9**(3).

Cowen, P. J. 1997 Pharmacotherapy for Anxiety Disorders: Drugs Available, *Advances in Psychiatric Treatment*, **3**: 66–71.

Dihan, T. G. 1993 Lithium Augmentation in Sertraline-resistant Depression: A Preliminary Dose–Response Study, *Acta Psychiatrica Scandinavica*, **88**: 300–1 (C).

Devereaux, E. and Carlson, M. 1992 The Role of Occupational Therapy in the Management of Depression, *American Journal of Occupational Therapy*, **46**(2).

Dunbar, G. *et al.* 1991 A Comparison of Paroxetine, Imipramine and Placebo in Depressed Outpatients, *British Journal of Psychiatry*, **159**: 394–8.

Edwards, J. G. 1997 Prevention of Relapse and Recurrence of Depression; Newer Versus Older Antidepressants, *Advances in Psychiatric Treatment*, **3**: 52–7.

Elkin, I., Shea, T., Watkins, J. T. *et al.* 1989 National Institute of Mental Health Treatment of Depression Collaborative Research Program: General Effectiveness of Treatments, *Archives of General Psychiatry*, **46**: 971–82.

Frank, E., Kupfer, D. J., Perel, J. M. *et al.* 1992 Five-year Outcome for Maintenance Therapies in Recurrent Depression, *Archives of General Psychiatry*, **46**: 769–73 (A).

Gallagher, D. E. and Thompson, L. W. 1982 Treatment of Major Depressive Disorder in Older Adults Outpatients with Brief Psychotherapies, *Psychotherapy: Theory, Research and Practice*, **19**: 482–90 (A).

Gallagher-Thompson, D., Hanley-Petersen, P. and Thompson, L.W. 1990 Maintenance of Gains Versus Relapse following Brief Psychotherapy for Depression, *Journal of Consultant Clinical Psychology*, **58**: 371–4 (A).

Hotopf, M., Hardy, R. and Lewis, G. 1997 Discontinuation Rates of SSRIs and Tricyclic Antidepressants: A Meta-analysis and Investigation of Heterogeneity, *British Journal of Psychiatry*, **170**: 120–7.

Karasu, T B., Docherty, J. P., Gelenberg, A., Kupfer, D. J., Merrian, A. E. and Shadoan, R. 1993 Practice Guideline for Major Depressive Disorder in Adults: Work Group on Major Depressive Disorder, *American Journal of Psychiatry*, April.

Klerman, G. L., DiMascio, A., Weissman, M. M., Prusoff, B. and Paykel, E. S. 1974 Treatment of Depression by Drugs and Psychotherapy, *American Journal of Psychiatry*, **131**: 186–91 (A).

Kocsis, J. H., Croughan, J. L., Katz, M. M. *et al.* 1990 Response to Treatment with Antidepressants of Patients with Severe or Moderate Non-psychotic Depression and of Patients with Psychotic Depression, *American Journal of Psychiatry*, **147**: 621–4 (A).

McLean, P. D. and Hakstian, A. R. 1979 Clinical Depression: Comparative Efficacy of Outpatient Treatments, *Journal of Consultant Clinical Psychology*, **47**: 818–36 (A).

Nezu, A. M. 1986 Efficacy of a Social Problem-solving Therapy for Unipolar Depression, *Journal of Consultant Clinical Psychology*, **54**: 196–202 (A).

Nezu, A. M. and Perri, M. G. 1989 Social Problem-solving Therapy for Unipolar Depression: An Initial Dismantling Investigation, *Journal of Consultant Clinical Psychology*, **57**: 408–13 (B).

Nutt, D. 1997 Practical Pharmacotherapy for Anxiety Disorders, *Advances in Psychiatric Treatment*, **3**: 66–71.

Nutt, D. and Bell, C. 1997 Practical Pharmacotherapy for Anxiety, *Advances in Psychiatric Treatment*, **3**: 79–85.

Parsons, B., Quitkin, F. M., McGrath, P. J. *et al.* 1989 Phenelzine, Imipramine and Placebo in Borderline Patients Meeting Criteria for Atypical Depression, *Psychopharmacology Bulletin*, **25**: 524–34 (A).

Priebe, S. and Gruyters, T. 1995 The Importance of the First Three Days: Predictors of Treatment Outcome in Depressed Inpatients, *British Journal of Clinical Psychology*, **34**: 229–36.

Prien, R. F., Kupfer, D. J., Mansky, P. A. *et al.* 1984 Drug Therapy in the Prevention of Recurrences in Unipolar and Bipolar Affective Disorders: A Report of the NIMH Collaborative Study Group Comparing Lithium Carbonate, Imipramine and a Lithium Carbonate–Imipramine Combination, *Archives of General Psychiatry*, **41**: 1096–104 (A).

Prusoff, B. A., Weissman, M. M., Klerman, G. L. and Rounsaville, B. J. 1980 Research Diagnostic Criteria Sub-types of Depression: Their Role as Predictors of Differential Response to Psychotherapy and Drug Treatment, *Archives of General Psychiatry*, **37**: 796–801 (A).

Ross, M. and Scott, M. 1985 An Evaluation of the Effectiveness of Individual and Group Cognitive Therapy in the Treatment of Depressed Patients in an Inner City Health Centre, *Journal of the Royal College of General Practitioners*, **35**: 239–42 (A).

Rush, A. J., Beck, A. T., Kovacs, M. and Hollon, S. D. 1977 Comparative Efficacy of Cognitive Therapy and Pharmacotherapy in the Treatments of Depressed Outpatients, *Cognitive Therapy Research*, **1**: 17–37 (A).

School of Public Health University of Leeds, Centre for Health Economics, University of York 1993 *Effective Health Care Bulletin*, No. 5.

Sclar, D. A. *et al.* 1995 Antidepressant Pharmacotherapy: Economic Evaluation of Fluoxetin, Paroxetine and Sertraline in a Health Maintenance Organisation, *Journal of International Medical Research*, **23**: 395–412 (D).

Scott, A. and Freeman, C. 1992 Edinburgh Primary Care Depression Study: Treatment Outcome, Patient Satisfaction and Cost after 16 weeks, *British Medical Journal*, **00**: 883–7.

Scott, J. 1995 Prevention of Depression; Psychological and Social Measures, *Advances in Psychiatric Treatment*, 1: 94–101.

Shea, M. T., Pilkonis, P. A., Beckham, E. *et al.* 1990 Personality Disorders and Treatment Outcome in the NIMH Treatment of Depression Collaborative Research Program, *American Journal of Psychiatry*, 147: 711–18 (A).

Shea, M. T., Elkin, I., Imber, S. D. *et al.* 1992 Course of Depressive Symptoms over Follow-up: Findings from the National Institute of Mental Health Treatment of Depression Collaborative Research Program, *Archives of General Psychiatry*, 49: 782–7 (A).

Sotsky, S. *et al.* 1991 Patient Predictors of Response to Psychotherapy and Pharmacotherapy: Findings in the NIMH Treatment of Depression Collaborative Research Programme, *American Journal of Psychiatry*, 00: 997–1008.

Sturm, R. and Wells, K. 1995 How Can Care for Depression Become More Cost-effective?, *Journal of the American Medical Association*, 00: 51–8.

Tyrer, P. 1997 Pharmacotherapy for Anxiety Disorders Using the Available Drugs, *Advances in Psychiatric Treatment*, 3: 72–8.

University of Leeds School of Public Health 1993 *The Treatment of Depression in Primary Care.* Leeds: Effective Health Care.

Usaf, S. O. and Kavanagh, D. J. 1990 Mechanisms of Improvement in Treatment for Depression: Test of Self-Efficacy and Performance Model, *Journal of Cognitive Psychotherapy*, 4: 51–70 (A).

Watson, L. J. 1986 Psychiatric Consultation – Liaison in the Acute Physical Disabilities Setting, *American Journal of Occupational Therapy*, 40(5).

Wessex Regional Health Authority 1993 *Guidelines on the Rational Treatment of Depression.* Wessex: RHA.

Further reading

Barnes, R. and Hansted, K. 1998 Check-up Time, *Health Service Journal*, 8: 26–7.

Culyer, T. 1994 *Supporting Research and Development in the NHS.* London: HMSO.

Sackett, D. L., Richardson, W. S., Rosenberg, W. and Haune, R. B. 1997 *Evidence Based Medicine: How to Use Practice and Teach EBP.* Edinburgh: Churchill Livingstone.

University of Leeds 1995 Effective Health Care. Implementing Clinical Practice Guidelines: Can Guidelines Be Used To Improve Clinical Practice?, *Effective Health Care Bulletin*, 8: 6.

Walshe, K. and Ham, C. 1997 Who's Acting on the Evidence?, *Health Service Journal*, 7(5547): 22–5.

Walshe, K. and Ham, C. 1997 Acting on the Evidence Progress in the NHS. Research Paper, University of Birmingham Health Services Management Centre.

Useful addresses

Best evidence
http://www.bmjpg.com/data/ebm.htm
Database of summaries of articles from the major medical journals, with expert commentaries. Details on the British Medical Journal site.

Centre for Evidence Based Medicine (CEBM)
University of Oxford, Nuffield Department of Clinical Medicine, Level 5, Oxford Radcliffe NHS Trust, Headley Way, Headington, Oxford, OX3 9DV
Tel: (01865) 221320
Aims to promote the teaching, learning, practice and evaluation of evidence-based practice and to conduct applied, patient-based and methodological research in order to generate new knowledge and to collaborate with other scientists in the creation of a graduate programme to train researchers to perform randomised trials and systematic reviews.

Centre for Evidence Based Nursing
Department of Health Studies, University of York, YO1 5DD
http://www.york.ac.uk/depts/hstd/centres/
evidence/evintro.htm
The centre has the following objectives:

- *to collaborate with nurse clinicians in order to identify research questions and undertake primary research;*
- *to undertake primary research in dissemination and implementation;*
- *to identify those areas in which nurses most urgently require summarised evidence and to carry out systematic reviews;*
- *to support and encourage other nurses to undertake systematic reviews, particularly within the Cochrane Collaboration;*
- *to undertake targeted dissemination activities in areas where good evidence is available;*
- *to design, promote and deliver courses in the area of evidence-based nursing for nurses at pre- and postregistration and undergraduate/postgraduate levels.*

Clinical Effectiveness Network in Dorset (CEND)
http://www.cend.org.uk/index.htm
A collaborative project between the Health Authority, Dorset Research and Development Support Unit, the NHS Trusts and primary care teams in Dorset,

working together to ensure that clinical practice is based on the most up-to-date, well-validated research.

Evidence
http://www.bangor.ac.uk/hs/evidence/
A quarterly newsletter publication funded as a pilot scheme by the Welsh National Board for Nursing, Midwifery and Health Visiting Educationalists.

Evidence Based Nursing (journal)
RCN Publishing Company, Glynteg House, Station Terrace, Cardiff, CF5 4XG
Tel: (01222) 553411

Getting Research into Practice Project (GRIPP)
Project Manager, Anglia and Oxford Regional Office, Old Road, Headington, Oxford, OX3 7LF
Initiated by Oxford RHA in 1993.

Journal of Clinical Effectiveness
Churchill Livingstone, Maple House, 149 Tottenham Court Road, London, W1P 9LL
Bi-monthly journal on training in evidence-based practice

National Guideline Clearinghouse (US)
http://www.guidelines.gov/index.asp
A comprehensive database of evidence-based clinical practice guidelines and related documents produced by the Agency for Health Care Policy and Research in partnership with the American Medical Association and the American Association of Health Plans. It provides information on clinical practice, guidelines to doctors, nurses, other health professionals, health care providers, purchasers and so on.

6

Clinical Governance

This chapter will explore clinical governance, where it came from, what it is all about and its progress to date at the time of writing. At the end of this chapter I have described an instrument called Probe, a system of audit designed to explore the three aspects of governance: corporate, clinical and self. The audit was developed and designed by the current author, and by Gayle Garland from the Centre for Nursing Policy and Practice at Leeds University. At the time of writing this chapter, pilot studies in several Trusts had been successfully completed and the findings were in the process of being published, with the intention of rolling out the programme across the UK.

Over the past ten years a series of major incidents in the NHS have led to a process of review and reform – the Beverly Allitt case, the failure of cervical screening at Kent and Canterbury Hospital and, more recently, the mortality rate of children undergoing heart surgery at Bristol to name but a few. The quality reforms put forward by the government are radical and far reaching but nevertheless vital to improve the quality of care in the NHS today.

The government has introduced a wide range of policies to modernise and improve the National Health Service (NHS), (DoH, 1997); these have been discussed in Chapters 1 and 5. This chapter explains more about the National Institute for Clinical Excellence (NICE), the Commission for Health Improvement (CHI), and the National Service Frameworks. Clinical governance, however, is essentially an operational and local service issue that supports the national policies, and a systematic approach to quality improvement and assurance in the NHS.

In the government's paper *A First Class Service* (DoH, 1998) clinical governance is defined as:

What the quality framework means for patients

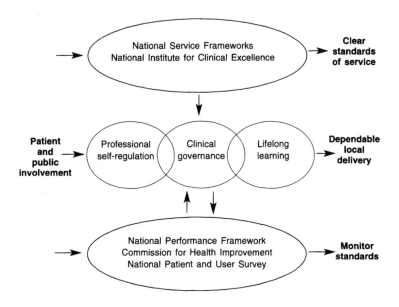

Figure 6.1   The quality framework

a framework through which NHS organisations are accountable for continuously improving the quality of their services and safeguarding high standards of care by creating an environment in which excellence in clinical care will flourish.

The quality framework set out in this document is described in diagrammatic form in Figure 6.1 (DoH, 1999).

Clinical governance requires the development of evidence-based guidelines to set standards of care, and monitoring by health care commissioners to ensure that such guidelines are implemented by clinicians in order to provide clinically effective and economically efficient care (DoH, 1999).

In 1998, the government published a consultation paper outlining their policy for ensuring quality in the NHS. The paper set out the government's plans for standards set by the NICE and the National Service Frameworks, delivered through clinical excellence, lifelong learning and professional self-regulation. These standards would be monitored through the CHI, the National Performance Framework and an annual National Survey of Patient and User Experience of the NHS. The first National Survey of Patient and User Experience was conducted during the winter of 1998, NICE was set up as a Special Health Authority in 1999. CHI was inaugurated as an independent, statutory body, in September 1999. The first clinical governance reports from NHS Trusts are expected to be received in the spring of 2000 (see also Chapter 5).

National Service Frameworks

The Government will work with the professions and representatives of users and carers to establish clearer, evidence-based National Service Frameworks for major care areas and disease groups. That way patients will get greater consistency in the availability and quality of services, right across the NHS. The Government will use them as a way of being clearer with patients about what they can expect from the health service.

The new approach to developing cancer services in the Calman–Hine Report, and recent action to ensure all centres providing children's intensive care meet agreed national standards, point the direction. In each case, the best evidence of clinical cost effectiveness is taken together with the views of users to establish principles for the pattern and level of services required. These then establish a clear set of priorities against which local action can be framed. The NHS Executive, working with the professions and others, will develop a similar approach to other services where national consistency is desirable. There will be an annual programme for the development of such frameworks starting in 1998. (DoH, 1997)

The first National Service Frameworks began with mental health and coronary heart disease, with their priority status being reflected in the guidance given on the development of Health Improvement Programmes. In 1998, the reference groups for the New National Service Frameworks started work, and their findings were due for publication in the spring of 1999. There will then be a roll-out programme of one major new topic every year.

The selection of the future topics will be informal through:

- demonstrative relevance to the Government's agenda for health improvement and tackling health inequalities, set out in *The New NHS, Our Healthier Nation* and wider policies on social exclusion
- an important health issue – in terms of mortality, morbidity, disability or resource use
- an area of public concern
- evidence of a shortfall between actual and accepted practice, with real opportunities for improvement
- an area where care for a patient may be provided in more than one setting (for example, hospital, GP surgery or at home) and by more than one organisation (for example, NHS and/or local authority/voluntary sector)
- an area where local services need to be recognised or restructured to ensure service improvements
- a problem which requires new, innovative approaches.

The programme will also be informed by the Chief Medical Officer's Annual report. (DoH, 1998)

Since 1991 and the birth of the first NHS Trusts there has been a framework of corporate governance. Corporate governance already exists as Trusts are currently required, by law, to break even and to achieve financial objectives set by the Secretary of State. The government plans now to introduce a new statutory duty for Trusts in primary and secondary care, which will make them accountable for the quality of care through their Chief Executives and Boards. The consultation paper states that:

the responsibilities of NHS Trusts and Primary Care Trusts will be reinforced by a new statutory duty in respect of the quality of the services they provide. Quality and financial duties will be given equal weight in statute to reflect their central importance in the new NHS. (DoH, 1998, p. 34)

This new legal duty will provide the control and authority implied by the term 'governance'. Chief Executives will be accountable to Parliament for delivering quality health care provision and implementing guidelines devised by NICE and the National Service Frameworks. The main components of clinical governance are set out in Figure 6.2.

Clear lines of responsibility and accountability for the overall quality of clinical care through:
- the NHS Trust Chief Executive carries ultimate responsibility for assuring the quality of services provided by the Trust;
- a designated senior clinician responsible for ensuring that systems for clinical governance are in place and monitoring their continued effectiveness;
- formal arrangements for NHS Trust Boards to discharge their responsibilities for clinical quality, perhaps through a clinical governance committee;
- regular reports to NHS Trust Boards on the quality of clinical care given the same importance as monthly financial reports;
- an annual report on clinical governance.

A comprehensive programme of quality improvement activities which include:
- full participation by all hospital doctors in audit programmes, including specialty and sub-specialty national external audit programmes endorsed by the Commission for Health Improvement;
- full participation in the current four National Confidential Enquiries;
- evidence-based practice is supported and applied routinely in everyday practice;
- ensuring the clinical standards of National Service Frameworks and NICE recommendations are implemented;
- workforce planning and development (that is, recruitment and retention of appropriately trained workforce) is fully integrated within the NHS Trust's service planning;
- continuing professional development programmes aimed at meeting the development needs of individual health professionals and the service needs of the organisation are in place and supported locally;
- appropriate safeguards to govern access to and storage of confidential patient information as recommended in the Caldicott Report on the Review of Patient-Identifiable Information;
- effective monitoring of clinical care with high quality systems for clinical record keeping and the collection of relevant information;
- processes for assuring the quality of clinical care are in place and integrated with the quality programme for the organisation as a whole.

Clear policies at aiming risks:
- controls assurance which promote self-assessment to identify and manage risks;
- clinical risk systematically assessed with programmes in place to reduce risk.

Procedures for all professional groups to identify and remedy poor performance, for example:
- critical incident reporting ensures that adverse events are identified, openly investigated, lessons are learned and promptly applied;
- complaints procedures, accessible to patients and their families and fair to staff. Lessons are learned and recurrence of similar problems avoided;
- professional performance procedures which take effect at an early stage before patients are harmed and which help the individual to improve their performance whenever possible, are in place and understood by all staff;
- staff supported in their duty to report any concerns about colleagues' professional conduct and performance, with clear statement from the Board on what is expected of all staff. Clear procedures for reporting concerns so that early action can be taken to support the individual to remedy the situation.

NICE = National Institute for Clinical Excellence.

Figure 6.2   Main components of clinical governance – NHS Trusts (DoH, 1998)

As well as the timetable for action at a national level, there was also a schedule for the Trusts at a local level. The key action to improve quality locally was to develop the arrangements for clinical governance. This meant that the Trusts were to have basic arrangements in place by 1999 and to produce their first clinical governance reports in the spring of 2000. The responsibilities of the Trusts included:

- a new statutory duty to ensure that Trusts were accountable for the quality of care provided;
- that Chief Executives would carry ultimate responsibility for assuring the quality of the services provided as well as for the proper use of resources;
- that the Trust Board had to be satisfied that mechanisms were in place to assure responsibilities for the quality of the services provided;
- this mechanism to function through a Board sub-committee, a named person being responsible for ensuring internal clinical governance of the organisation.

The following key elements are essential for clinical governance:

1. Quality improvement processes, such as clinical audit, are in place and integrated with the quality programme for the organisation as a whole.
2. There is good leadership and leadership skills are developed at clinical team level.
3. Evidence-based practice is in day-to-day use, with the infrastructure to support it.
4. Good practice, ideas and innovations, which have been evaluated, are systematically disseminated within and outside the organisation.
5. Clinical risk reduction programmes of a high standard are in place.
6. Adverse events are detected, and openly investigated; lessons learned are promptly applied.
7. Lessons for clinical practice are systematically learned from complaints made by patients.

8. Problems of poor clinical performance are recognised at an early stage and dealt with to prevent harm to patients.
9. All professional development programmes reflect the principles of clinical governance.
10. The quality of data collected to monitor clinical care is itself of a high standard.
11. All clinical staff are to be monitored to ensure that they meet the professional requirements for updating or re-registration, for example Continuing Medical Education and Post Registration Education and Practice.
12. A forum for discussing all clinical practice and for agreeing/reviewing new practices is set up.
13. The culture is open and participative.
14. There is an ethos of teamwork between all staff.
15. The patient is a partner in care.

An example of a Trust's clinical governance framework is shown in Figure 6.3.

Trusts, when preparing for clinical governance will have set up the following:

- An organisational stock-take. The Trusts or Primary Care Group (PCG) would have tested the efficacy of their current systems that contribute to clinical governance, including clinical audit, risk management, audit of consumer feedback, and the development of clinical leadership
- Action plans to implement systems that were lacking and revise those which were not working effectively
- An organisational review to determine whether the current management arrangements supported clinical governance
- A clinical governance committee as a sub committee of the board and educating and training its members
- A campaign to raise awareness throughout the organisation and use it as an opportunity to address staff concerns as well as discuss with them what was to be done
- Discussions between clinical leaders, medical directors, nursing directors, clinical directors in secondary care and GP partners and lead nurses in primary care to discuss in detail how clinical governance would be implemented and achieved throughout the organisation
- A system to ensure that new systems for clinical governance are piloted and evaluated

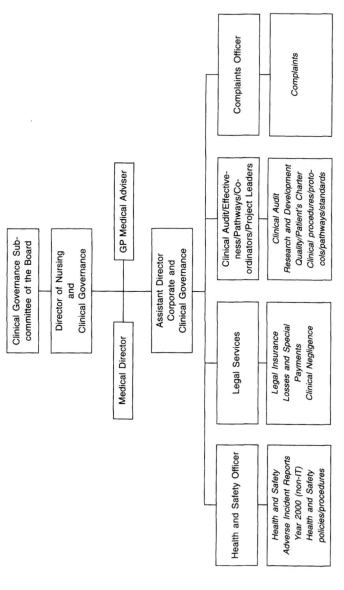

Figure 6.3 An example of a clinical governance framework

- Established constancy of purpose to ensure the programme stays on course and is not deflected from the goals the organisation has set itself
- Systems to support accounting for progress with clinical governance throughout the organisation. (BAMM, 1998)

Monitoring performance

Trusts and PCGs will have reporting mechanisms in place that will produce routine Board reports on progress made in implementing clinical governance. The regional offices of the NHS Executive will have primary responsibility for performance, managing its implementation in NHS Trusts and health authorities, and monitoring improvements year by year. Health authorities will provide the first line of external monitoring for its development in PCGs and primary care Trusts.

The new NHS Performance Assessment Framework will complement the introduction of clinical governance by focusing on the quality and effectiveness of health care, as well as on efficiency.

The CHI will visit each local health system every 3–4 years, subject to legislation expected late in 1999, and self-regulation through the professional bodies will be closely aligned to clinical governance (DoH, 1999).

Also in this publication the government states its 'vision for the next five years'.

For clinical governance to be successful, all health professionals must demonstrate features such as:

- An open and participative culture in which education, research and the sharing of good practice are valued
- A commitment to quality that is shared by staff and managers, and supported by clearly identified local resources, both human and financial
- A tradition of active working with patients, users, carers and the public
- An ethos of multidisciplinary team working at all levels in the organisation
- Regular board level discussion of all major quality issues for the organisation and strong leadership from the top
- Good use of information to plan and assess progress. (DoH, 1999)

This agenda as it stands presents no easy task to the average Trust. As described in Figure 6.3, Trusts have already completed their organisational stock-take, committees and subcommittees are in place, campaigns to raise awareness have been undertaken and reporting mechanisms are in place. Perhaps this development of a formal framework so that professionals can work together is the easiest part of the implementation of clinical governance. The next step is to make it work by creating a culture which values education and research, works as a multidisciplinary team, is open and participative, has good, strong, creative leadership and works in partnership with the patients. Changing the culture to one that is open and participative is perhaps the greatest challenge, although a lot of progress has been made in issues such as dealing with poor performance and the introduction of supervision for nursing and therapy staff and the new performance procedures by the General Medical Council, the changes to the complaints procedure in 1996 reducing the fragmentation and inconsistency of previous arrangements, and introducing more openness and lay participation.

However, there are other issues that concern the Trusts, for example:

- where will the money come from to support the cost of establishing and monitoring clinical governance?
- the lack of information systems capable of delivering good clinical data, particularly in the community Trusts
- problems of reduced staffing levels and lack of resource to bring them up to an acceptable level
- lack of infrastructure in some Trusts to support evidence-based practice and finding time to do the clinical review work as part of the normal clinical work load.

No doubt resources will be required to move the agenda forward, but it is most important to create a culture in which people feel valued, able to question practice and are supported in their efforts for ongoing learning and practising evidence-based care.

For many Trusts and PCGs, the key area has been to carry out an 'organisational stock-take'. The Trust or PCG needed to test the efficacy of its current systems that would contribute to clinical governance, including clinical audit, risk management, audit of consumer feedback, and the development of clinical leadership. Clinical governance is about raising standards and preventing errors and mishaps and it was this concept that led to the development of an audit instrument called Probe.

Probe – an audit of clinical governance

Probe is a system of audit that has been developed in order to enable external auditors to explore the three aspects of governance: corporate, clinical and self. For the purposes of the audit, the three aspects of governance are defined as:

- Corporate governance: the mechanism for decision making and information sharing in the organisation. Through observation of clinical care, review of documents and interviews with staff, probe auditors seek to discover the responsibility and accountability for clinical care in reality.
- Clinical governance: the systematic activities, which support clinical quality. Formal and informal processes of setting standards, measurement and action are reviewed and assessed for their impact on clinical care.
- Self-governance: professional self-management, collaboration, ownership of clinical issues and accountability for clinical outcomes. Through discussion with clinical professionals, a picture is formed of involvement in, and commitment to defining and upholding professional standards of good practice individually and collectively. (Garland, G. and Sale, D. 1998)

The audit process

Probe explores clinical governance within a Trust by examining selected systems of clinical care and the Trust's existing quality systems. Clinical care is evaluated using an in-depth exploration of two clinical processes: medicines and one other clinical process chosen by the Trust. The probe also explores the quality systems that are in place and how they benefit the patient. The auditors look for evidence that clinical care is effective, up to date, evidence based, timely, appropriately resourced, evaluated and consistent (Figure 6.4).

The medicines probe

The reason for choosing medicines as the clinical probe is because almost every member of the Trust is involved in the safe administration of medicines – the Chief Executive, the Director of Finance, the Director of Nursing, the Clinical Governance Committee, the Clinical Audit Committee, the pharmacist, doctors, nurses, therapists and patients.

The outcome standard for this clinical probe is that every patient receives a safe an effective medicine regime. The safe administration of medications is an element of care that has been developed into a probe that can be used to establish good or poor governance throughout the organisation. By following this clinical process with a view to safe and effective patient care, the participation and impact of clinical professionals can be sampled.

At a corporate level, there are issues surrounding policy, procedure, protocols and guidelines, the provision of education and training for staff involved in prescribing and administering medicines, and the provision of an environment and procedures for the safety and security of medications.

The quality probe

The Trust's quality systems are evaluated principally for their impact on clinical care. The auditors look for examples of quality activities that impact positively on the provision of care. Effective systems of quality improvement are characterised as goal/outcome orientated, aligned with the Trust's strategic and business objectives, clinically driven, co-ordinated and evaluated.

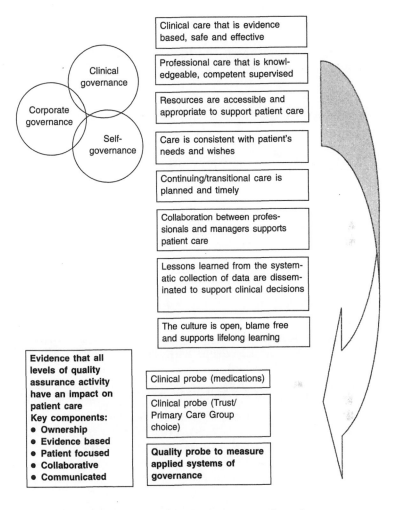

Figure 6.4 Audit of governance – flow chart

Audit planning

The auditors meet with the Trust executive team, including the Board members responsible for clinical governance and other members of staff who will be co-ordinating the audit activities and collecting the documentation for review. The Trust is encouraged to identify its goals for the audit. Goals might include:

- the identification of opportunities for improvement, confirmation of effective clinical governance;
- raising the awareness or understanding of clinical governance among the staff; ʼ
- consultancy on the way forward to implementing clinical governance.

In consultation with the auditors a decision is made about the clinical processes to be included. These decisions are based on the goals for the audit, some examples of which are stated above.

Audit activities

A series of interviews will be undertaken with clinicians and managers at all levels with regard to the clinical processes and the quality activities chosen. Patient care records are reviewed for evidence that standards are being met, and that care is effective and appropriate. Perhaps one of the most useful activities of the audit is the actual observation of care as it is delivered; Trust representatives are welcome to shadow the auditors and usually find the process informative. The auditors are careful to inform staff that the audit is developmental and that the intention is to improve care.

The audit explores the Trust by reviewing the following areas:

- Information required by the auditors includes:
  - medical staffing numbers and costs;
  - nurse staffing numbers and costs;
  - the budget for medicines;
  - policies and procedures concerning the procuring, storing, prescribing and administration of medicines

MENTAL HEALTH TRUST
MEDICINES PROBE

The safe administration of medications is an element of care that has been developed into a probe that can be used to establish good or poor governance throughout an organisation. By following this clinical process with a view to safe and effective patient care, the participation and impact of clinical professionals can be sampled.

Audit Activity Summary:
- Observation of drugs round on ward 1, ward 12 and ward 14.
- Interviews with staff nurses on wards, pharmacist, Director of Nursing, Director of Finance and Consultant Psychiatrists.
- Review of medicines policies, clinical notes and prescriptions.

Outcome Standard: The patient receives a safe and effective medicine regime

Accountability: Function Level of governance	Process Criteria	Findings

**Physician/consultant:
prescribing**
Clinical/self/corporate
	Prescription is evidence based
	Clinical information is up to date
	Laboratory information to support prescribing
	Prescription is – Current
	             – Reviewed
	             – Clearly written
	             – Signed
		Diverse prescribing practices for similar diagnoses
		Consultant participates in clinical trials
		Access to up-to-date professional journals
		Prescriptions are generally current, reviewed and signed –
		handwriting clarity is variable
		Clinical information current

Nurse: Medication administration Clinical/self	Safe administration of medication consistent with professional standards and policy Assessment and alignment of patients' wishes and needs against prescription Demonstration of critical thinking Medication education	Some medication errors undetected by nurses Evidence of patient needs and wishes considered Nurses demonstrate care and attention, knowledgeable of procedures and limits of role Critical thinking surrounding medicines evident Adherence to control procedures
Trust/clinical professionals: Timeliness of treatment and care Corporate/clinical/self	Timely filling of prescriptions and administration of medicines	Stock system avoids delays in filing prescriptions Prompt administration based on patient need
Trust/Clinical professionals: Discharge and transitions to other settings Continuity of care Corporate/clinical/self	Discharge planning that meets the patient's/family's needs and wishes Multidisciplinary planning	Tablets to take out filled on time when ordered in advance Weekend and unplanned discharges problematic Nurses include medication teaching in discharge plan

Figure 6.5 Probe: some examples of the level of governance, process criteria and findings

for the Trust, the wards, departments and the pharmacy;
- incident reports for the previous year, error reports for the previous year, the number of cases and the outcomes;
- information on costs and security;
- the education and training programmes held over the past year and who attended;
- the roles and responsibilities of extended role or specialist nurses;
- the minutes of meetings for the previous year for the clinical governance committee, the pharmacy and therapeutics committees, collaborative meetings and any other relevant meetings.

- Access to the following information:
  - laboratory data used by professionals making prescribing decisions;
  - clinical information on which decisions are based;
  - standards;
  - clinical audit and the results of the implementation of change;
  - integrated care pathways.

- Interviews with nurses, consultants, junior doctors, pharmacists, technicians, porters, laboratory technicians, the Chief Executive, the Director of Finance, the Medical Clinical Director, the Director of Nursing and Quality Assurance, the Chair of Clinical Governance Committee, the lead person for risk management, the lead person/Chair of the Clinical Audit Committee, the Head of Education and Training, patients and their relatives, the person responsible for resuscitation training and the person responsible for the maintenance of the crash trolley.

- Visits to the ward/departments to:
  - review nursing records and case notes to establish whether effectiveness is recorded through evaluation that includes the patient/client's views on the effects of any medication given;

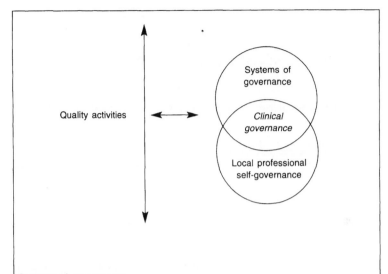

Systems of governance:

● The mechanism for leadership, decision making, information sharing and accountability in the organisation.

Quality activities:

● The shared responsibility of clinical professionals and the organisation. They are formal and informal processes of setting standards, measurement and action to improve care.

Local professional self-governance

● The individual and collective system of professional self-management (standards of professional practice, professional conduct, education and training, professional development and the identification and resolution of poor practice), collaboration, ownership of clinical issues and accountability for clinical outcome.

Clinical governance takes place in the intersection of professional and organisational responsibility, and is delivered through an integrated system of quality activities.

Figure 6.6 A model of clinical governance

- review policy, procedures and guidelines;
- inspect the crash trolley, drug cupboards, controlled drug books and prescriptions;
- observe a selection of drug rounds.

- And to:
  - the operating theatres to review with the anaesthetists the control of medicines;
  - the accident and emergency department;
  - the outpatient department;
  - the pharmacy;
  - the diagnostic imaging areas.

The audit process

Probe was designed to be conducted by experienced auditors with clinical backgrounds. The intention of the audit experience is to be developmental rather than judgemental.

Audit activities are designed to explore the organisation at the clinical level with a view to evolving the systems of clinical governance. Impressions are gathered, examples solicited and information exchanged in such a way as to support staff in their efforts. An example of some of the criteria used is shown in Figure 6.5.

Results

The model of clinical governance (Figure 6.6), which was developed as a starting point for the audit design, forms the basis of the structure of the report that is delivered to the Trust. As patient care processes are investigated, and the quality activities of the Trust reviewed, the auditors gather examples of the three elements of the model. An executive summary gives an overview of the systems of decision making, information sharing and accountability as observed in the clinical settings visited. Professional self-management is also described in terms of how individual clinical professionals interact with their colleagues in order to manage patient care.

Report on the clinical probes

The final report will also contain a description of the patient care processes audited. The following questions inform the findings and recommendations of the report:

- Are professionals who prescribe and deliver care appropriately educated, knowledgeable and up to date with current clinical practice?
- Are the human, financial, material and information resources allocated sufficient for safe and timely care?
- Are standards of care evidence based, communicated and consistently applied?
- Are the outcomes of care measured and used to improve care when necessary?
- Are patients enabled to make informed decisions about their care?

Report on quality

The report on the quality systems within the Trust offers an overview of the quality activities reviewed. Quality activities are evaluated for evidence of the following features:

- There is ownership by clinical professionals involved in patient care.
- Care is evidence based, researched and/or bench marked.
- Quality activity has a defined structure, process and outcome.
- Quality activities are communicated.
- Quality activities are multidisciplinary in design.
- Quality activities are patient focused and impact on patient care.
- Patients are involved in the process of quality, their views being actively sought and acted upon.

Conclusion

The importance of clinical governance is that it brings clinical decision making into the management and organisational arena. In *A First Class Service* (DoH, 1998), it is clear that NHS organisations and individual health professionals are charged with developing 'a framework within which to build a single, coherent, local programme of quality improvement'. It is also clear that patients should ultimately benefit from the implementation of clinical governance, when it is delivered through a service that provides evidence-based care, via guidelines and pathways, to ensure continuity of quality care. Sharing guidelines and pathways with patients will enable more informed patient decisions and choices.

The next chapter looks at the development of integrated care pathways, which are the most effective way of ensuring that patient care is truly evidence based. When every member of the health care teams follows the care pathway, this will ensure continuity of proven, good-quality care.

References

British Association of Medical Managers 1998 *Clinical Governance in the New NHS. London.*: BAMM.

Department of Health 1997 *The New NHS, Modern, Dependable.* London: HMSO.

Department of Health 1998 *A First Class Service – Improving Quality in the New NHS.* London: HMSO.

Department of Health 1999 *Clinical Governance: Quality in the NHS.* London: HMSO.

Garland, G. and Sale, D. 1998 *'Probe', An Audit of Clinical Governance.* Leeds: Centre for the Development of Nursing Policy and Practice, Leeds University.

Useful addresses

NHS Web site:
www.doh.nhsweb.nhs.uk/nhs/clingov.htm

Learning Zone is part of the NHS Web. It has a database called the Database of Service, Delivery and Practice (SDP). NHS staff can enter details of activities designed to improve services for patients, for example implementing clinical governance, managing emergency pressures, or managing waiting lists. Staff can also search the database for relevant examples of good practice across the UK. The site will also contain an NHS Trust Benchmarking Database, which will allow comparisons of cost and outcomes by NHS Trust. High-level indicators of performance by NHS Trusts will be put on to this database at a later date.

From April 1999, NHS Beacon Services will be chosen in six areas of service: waiting lists and times, primary care, mental health, cancer services, health improvement and staff development. A beacon is a service within the NHS that has been selected as a particularly good example of what it does. Beacons will be given financial support to enable them to disseminate learning about their good practices to other NHS organisations.

See also Chapter 5.

7

Integrated Care Pathways

Integrated care pathways (ICPs) are the essential vehicles in turning the concept of clinical governance into reality. A care pathway is the route to delivering evidence-based practice as part of everyday patient care. Care pathways are not packages of care that are taken 'off the shelf' but are developed by a multidisciplinary team of professionals. This process of development means involvement in the process and ownership of the pathway.

This chapter includes three examples of ICPs, all of which are slightly different. The first is a breast-care pathway developed by Nick Carty, a surgeon specialising in breast cancer care, and his team at the Salisbury NHS Trust. The other two pathways originate from the Dorset Community Trust. One is a pathway for the care of people with schizophrenia, which has been developed by the project co-ordinator, Kate Sneidor, and her team from the inpatient and community mental health services. The second was prepared by Carole Annetts, who co-ordinated the development of a day surgery pathway for some of the community hospitals in Dorset. The pathways themselves are excellent, but even more important is the process of developing the pathways and the changes that were made to enable them to be implemented and to improve patient care.

ICPs – where did they originate?

In 1989, Berwick wrote about an approach to quality improvement that is concerned not only with dealing with the problems and deficiencies in health care, but also with finding systems that work better and allow readjustments and continuous improvement to take place (Berwick, 1989). ICPs have been in use in the USA since the late 1980s; there they were also known as anticipated recovery paths and critical pathways.

What is an ICP?

Essentially, a pathway is intended as collaborative guidelines that time and sequence the major interventions, of doctors, nurses and other key professionals and services, in a particular case type or condition. An ICP represents specific practice patterns, patient populations and limits on length of stay. Included in a co-ordinated sequence of events, in the form of guidelines, are the assessments, investigations and interventions that should occur to achieve the desired outcome.

The National Pathways Association defines an ICP thus:

> an integrated care pathway determines locally agreed multidisciplinary practice, based on guidelines and evidence where available, for a specific patient/client group. It forms all or part of the clinical record, documents the care given and facilitates the evaluation of outcomes for continuous quality improvement.

A care pathway sets out the care that should be given to the patient by all the professionals and services involved in his or her episode of care (Zander and McGill, 1994). The care is described, tracked and monitored to ensure that outcomes set along the pathway, as well as the final outcomes, are achieved. Tracking the care follows the patient care journey from wherever it may start, for example home, the GP, the acute hospital or the community hospital, to the patient's return home. If the pathway is at any point not followed, the person delivering that particular aspect of care records the reason for the deviation from the pathway as a variance. Analysis of the variance provides a system for the ongoing monitoring of the quality of care and the pathway. Part of the ongoing review of the pathway is this analysis of the variance, which may lead to changes being made in the pathway.

Care pathways are developed from evidence-based guidelines and are therefore vehicles for implementing evidence-based practice in everyday patient care. The pathway is developed into a multidisciplinary record of care, which is used by each professional to record and evaluate the care given. Pathways are not only multidisciplinary but may also include multi-agency collaboration.

In summary, an ICP:

- is a daily plan of care;
- identifies anticipated progress based on guidelines, protocols and evidence;
- incorporates risk management;
- facilitates the evaluation of goals and outcomes by the professionals who deliver the care;
- requires deviations from the pathway to be recorded as variations, the analysis of the variations resulting in an ongoing monitoring of the quality of care;
- is a multidisciplinary plan of care;
- is a legal record;
- presents a format that helps patients to have a better understanding of their care and encourages greater patient involvement and informed decision making;
- reduces paperwork and improves the accuracy of record keeping by all the multidisciplinary team.

An ICP cycle

In Figure 7.1 the cycle depicts an approach to implementing a care pathway.

Five steps to implementing a care pathway

Step 1: Select an area in which to develop a care pathway

The first step is to assemble the multidisciplinary team, review current practice and decide on a suitable area for a pathway. The following may contribute to the selection process:

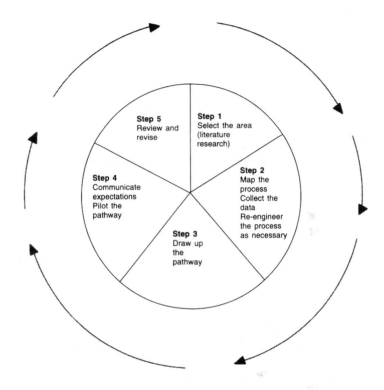

Figure 7.1   Implementing a care pathway

- a high-volume area, for example if the area of specialty is orthopaedics, a high-volume area might be that of first-time hip replacements;
- a high-risk area such as the urgent referral of a patient with a breast lump and the need for early referral, diagnosis and treatment;
- areas of high cost as a result of an extended length of stay;
- choosing an area of care in which there is an enthusiastic leader, which will help to advance the process of developing care pathways;
- an enthusiastic consultant or opinion leader;

- a problem identified through a complaint or an area on which professionals believe that a pathway would improve the quality of care by reducing the duplication of care by different professionals;
- some health authorities working with Trusts to develop care pathways, which may mean that the choice of pathway will be purchaser led.

Step 2: Map the process of care

- Agree the area to be mapped, and set the boundaries around the episode of care.
- Gain the support of directors and senior clinicians for the process.
- Collect the scientific literature through the clinical journals, the Internet, the National Pathway Association, the regional care pathway groups and so on. Gather together any pathways that have already been developed for your chosen topic, and review the evidence.
- Meet with a selection of representative staff to talk through the process and define and agree objectives and goals. Trust staff with a quality assurance background or staff from the education or training department often help by facilitating these meetings.
- Choose the team to drive the process, remembering to include all disciplines.
- Decide who in the team will see the process through, drive the process, agree and meet deadlines and so on.
- Identify and map current practice either by talking through the process using group discussion or brainstorming, or by direct observation and mapping of the process.
- Process mapping is about following the patient's care journey from its start to its end. This can be achieved either by group discussion or by direct observation; in both cases, every aspect of the care journey must be mapped a bit like a road map, noting names, places and road numbers on the way to the final destination. Probably the simplest way to do this is to observe the process of the care journey and note each step of the way on a separate 'post-it' note. These 'post-its' are then

stuck on a wall or a board in the order in which the care actually happened. The observers note only what they see rather than making decisions about what should or should not have happened. Figure 7.2 gives an example of a mapping pathway.

Once the process of the patient's care journey has been mapped, it should be compared with what it should be, based on sound, proven evidence (see Figure 7.2). The processes can then be discussed and changes made to improve the patient's care journey, for example reducing the length of stay, rehabilitating the patient home more quickly and so on.

Process mapping is an effective way of establishing what really happens and not what people think is happening. Experience shows that groups using process mapping were able to:

- improve the patient's care journey;
- reduce length of stay;
- identify activities that did not contribute to care;
- identify those which were repetitious;
- identify activities that were of no real benefit;
- identify those which were duplicated by others, often from different professions.

The role of the team who undertakes the process mapping is to give feedback to the area where mapping has occurred and to challenge practice so that it can be discussed and compared with the evidence reviewed. This will start the process of change management and lead to a consensus on the way forward. Once the process has been mapped, the next stage is to re-engineer the process in the light of the evidence base and the resulting discussions with the group.

Step 3: Draw up the pathway

- Follow the process systematically, ensuring that all the professionals who deliver care are included.

Day of Admission

Process map of current practice	Issues for consideration based on finding and good practice
Patients arrive in the unit – some have the same admission time, some arrivals are staggered	• To have a better control and planning of lists to enable all patients to have a staggered admission time • Health questionnaires to be sent with an admission letter and detailed information regarding sedation or cord spraying *Pre-endoscopy Questionnaire – Form 1, Mobile Gastroscopy Service, Exeter and District Community Health Service NHS Trust (considered good practice)*
Patients are met by the ward clerk or recovery nurse, who arranges a collection time with a relative or friend	• Use of videos to inform patient about the procedure about to be undertaken • To produce a pathway for endoscopy patients to ensure that each patient receives the same standard of care • Consider a named nurse for each patient to build relationships during short stay
Some patients are asked to wait in day room while others are shown to the trolley area[1]	*Panting, A. (1998) Preparing Patients for Endoscopy, Nursing Times, **94**: 27, 60* • Send a consent form with the patient to enable informed consent to be obtained after explanation by a 'knowledgeable practitioner'
Ward clerk checks details for patient administration system (PAS)	*Alexander, J. (1997) Types of consent and the means of obtaining consent. Clinical Risk Management in Day Surgery. IBC UK Conferences Ltd.*
Patient's admission details are taken by nurse	• Obtain consent if not carried out in outpatient department • Ensure that patient is fully informed to reduce stress and that the information given is current, researched and seems acceptable
Procedure is explained to the patient by the theatre nurse Patient is asked to decide whether he or she wishes to have sedation or cord spray Patients for sigmoidoscopy have an enema in the trolley room[1] Patient is informed of approximate time of going into theatre.	*Murphy, D. (1993) Managing Patient Stress in Endoscopy, Society of Gastroenterology Nurse and Associates, **6**: 72–4.* • Consider greater privacy, especially for those having an enema • Surgeon to consent patients in a quiet area • Walk patients to theatre
Patient is prepared for theatre and taken to theatre on a trolley	

1. The trolley room is a small room with eight trolley spaces.

Figure 7.2 Process mapping

- Make sure that the timings of interventions, for example the speed with which the patient moves along the breast-care pathway, are correct.
- Ensure that the interventions are evidence based and that the outcomes are recorded within the pathway.
- Incorporate standards, clinical guidelines and outcome measures.
- Develop the pathway into a single multidisciplinary document to support the recording of interventions completed, one that includes space for recording variances and outcome measurement. Time-based documentation, for example day by day, is easiest to handle.

Step 4: Communicate expectations

- Decide on a minimum period over which to pilot the pathway for example, 3 months or 'x' number of patients.
- Decide where the pathway document will be located, offering easy access for all the team. Include this in your written guidelines for staff.

The project group should take responsibility for:

- developing and circulating guidelines on using the pathway to all staff involved in it;
- discussing the pathway with all the staff in all the departments who will be involved in its use;
- devising ways of ensuring that locum doctors and bank and agency nursing staff are alerted to the pathway's use;
- deciding on ways of providing training for staff to gain their commitment, and ensure that it is used correctly;
- piloting the pathway.

Step 5: Review and revise

- Discuss the pathway with all members of the group and identify any problems.
- Analyse the variances, the completeness of the documentation, alterations that were made, comments from the users and so on.

- Review at least 30 sets of records in order to validate the pathway. To do this, identify 30 patients who have been discharged who used the pathway. Then audit each set of records to establish whether the documentation was completed by all members of the team, and if not, why not. Also to make a note of all the variances and consider the following:
  — If the same variances have occurred in several patient pathways, this may indicate that the pathway needs to be reviewed. For example, if 90 per cent of patients scheduled for discharge on day 6 were actually discharged on day 5, the pathway's length of stay could be reduced.
  — Explore reasons for the variances, which may be patient centred or related to staff not following the pathway because of a lack of understanding of the system.
  — If the variances are patient centred, would a clinical audit or a review of the process resolve the problem?
  — Analyse patients' views on the care received.
- Develop and implement the final pathway.
- Plan the ongoing review of the pathway.

Problems

There are a few problems associated with pathways, one of which is that some staff lack the skills to appraise critically the evidence or research; this aspect may thus need to be supported by additional training.

Another very common problem is that documentation is not completed. The most common reason for this is that, out of habit, some professionals continue to document care within their own system of record keeping. Locum doctors may write in the medical record because they are not involved in the process and may be unaware of the existence of the pathway; the same applies to bank and agency nursing staff.

A further problem may be the location of the pathway. If it does not occur in the right place at the right time, it may not be completed. For example, the patient may receive physiotherapy in the department while the pathway documentation stays on the ward; thus, the physiotherapist will write in the record in the department.

Medico-legal problems may result if the care prescribed in the pathway is out of date or results in poor practice.

Some medical staff have concerns abound individual professional autonomy, describing pathways as 'cookbook medicine'. Nursing staff may also express a concern that the care is not individualised. Such views need to be addressed early in the process.

A lack of time to devote to the development of a pathway can be a problem, but it is time well spent, as can be seen in the benefits listed below.

The project group may resent any criticism of the pathway but need to be open to suggestions and change.

Factors affecting success

- The composition of the team that develops the pathway, for example a group of people who like each other, an opinion leader, a completer and finisher, a good communicator, a scribe, a strong chairperson and a senior clinician.
- The choice of topic area. Choose an area of care that is simple, straightforward and fairly predictable in the first instance. Complex processes and procedures often show most benefit from the development of a pathway. For many patients, such as those admitted for elective surgery, the stages of care are predictable. Medical conditions are less predictable, but often follow a common pattern, as seen in, for example, a patient admitted with a myocardial infarction.
- Care volume. Choose high-volume areas of care because if you want to make changes to the delivery of care, there must be a substantial number of patients using the pathway to make valid changes.

Benefits

A well-planned care pathway will:

- ensure that every patient receives care, from all the health care team, that is planned and evidence based;
- rationalise the process of care;
- promote efficiency, less time being wasted on, for example, unplanned activities and duplication of care;
- prove useful for training and developing staff;
- empower staff;
- encourage critical process analysis;
- reduce the impact of staff rotation;
- through shared structured documentation, reduce paperwork and improve record keeping and communication;
- provide a basis for operational research;
- improve continuity of care, by, for example, the removal of variations in care patterns and outcomes that do not benefit patient care;
- link the process of care to clinical outcome and the monitoring and evaluation of outcome;
- support team building as the various members of the team become aware of each other's role within the care pathway;
- support the analysis of variations from the pathway to facilitate clinical audit, which is more dynamic than previous approaches to implementing changes as a result of a clinical audit;
- improve multidisciplinary teamworking through professionals working to shared goals;
- increase patient understanding: patients can follow the pathway, giving them greater insight into their care and leading to greater co-operation and more informed decision making;
- facilitate the patient's informed participation in the care journey.

The National Pathways Association and National Guidelines Clearing House (USA) support such work; their addresses are provided at the end of this chapter (see also Chapter 5).

Care pathways in practice

To demonstrate how pathways can be used to streamline processes and improve care, three pathways from very different areas have been chosen. The process of developing the pathway will be described, the resulting pathways being included in the format in which they are used on a day-to-day basis. The information is provided with the kind permission of Salisbury Health Care NHS Trust and Dorset Community NHS Trust.

Salisbury Health Care NHS Trust – breast-care pathway

The project (Salisbury Health Care NHS Trust, 1998) started with a memo from the South West Regional Health Authority inviting Trusts to express their interest in being a pilot site for the development of a care pathway and occupational standards, and this Trust was successful in its bid. The team included Mr Carty (consultant surgeon) and his multidisciplinary team, as well as Dr Graham Jagger (GP) and his team.

The process was supported by the ICP co-ordinator and the management consultants, who acted as facilitators and brought a structure to the process. The process included dividing the work on the pathway into subcommittees, each of which took responsibility for the development of an identified part of the pathway. There were five subcommittees, which represented five distinct parts of the process:

- the GP and the referral process (Figure 7.3)
- the one-stop clinic (Figure 7.4)
- the inpatient stay (Figures 7.5, 7.6 and 7.7b)
- oncology and palliative care (Figures 7.8–7.10 and 7.12)
- the community (Figure 7.11).

A steering committee was set up to oversee the progress of the pathway. The pathway took a year to develop and implement, covering primary and secondary care as it traces the patient's entire journey. The process started with a baseline audit of the service before the development of the pathway. At the time of writing, the group, from the hospital, were in the process of reauditing the service and analysing the variances following the implementation of the pathway in October 1998.

There are six parts that make up the pathway:

- primary care (Figure 7.3)
- one-stop clinic (Figure 7.4)
- inpatient episode – the preadmission clinic, admission to the ward, pre- and postoperative care and discharge (Figures 7.5/7.6); reconstructional surgery (Figures 7.7a/7.7b)
- oncology (Figure 7.8) and radiotherapy (Figures 7.9/7.10)
- community and practice nursing (Figure 7.11)
- palliative care (Figure 7.12).

Three parts make up the pathway document (although there were changes in all parts of the process). The pathway is supported by Occupational Standards which contain performance criteria and reflect principles of good practice grounded on explicit values and commitments concerning equality of opportunity and access, the rights of individuals and responsibilities to others.

Inpatient pathway

The inpatient pathway is supported by a general assessment, which is based on an activities of daily living model of nursing (Figures 7.5 and 7.6).

The inpatient episode is also supported by a separate document that summarises and records the operative procedure, the multiprofessional meetings to discuss ongoing treatment and therapy, and the follow-up outpatient visits. This is a patient-held diary, which leads to a sharing of the responsibility for care.

The first part of the pathway is primary care. The information about each of the following six sections was contributed by Mr Carty, Dr Jagger and the pathway working groups and sets out some of the thinking behind the development of the pathways.

Salisbury Health Care NHS
Trust Breast Clinic Referral

Surname	Forename	Hospital No.

Title	Sex: m/f	DoB	NHS No.

Address

Tel No.　　　Work
　　　　　　Home

Postcode

Referring GP

New referral

Re-referral　　　　Date last referred

Reason for referral	Urgent			Soon
Discrete lump	☐	Intractable pain		☐
Asymmetrical lumpiness	☐	Unilateral pain in post-menopausal patients		☐
Abscess	☐	Nipple discharge:		☐
Other*	☐	All women > 50 years		☐
if 'other' please describe,		Blood stained: all groups		☐
for example 'very anxious patient'		Persistent single duct: all groups		☐
		Nipple retraction		☐

Mammogram result in
last 18 months　　　Y/N
Location　　　Date

Eczema/rash　☐

Changing skin contour (puckering)　☐

Recurrent cyst　☐

Family history　☐

Dates not available for appointment

Date referral received

Appt. Date　　　Appt. Time

Please fax this form to the Breast-care Co-ordinator

Figure 7.3　Referral form from the GP

Salisbury Breast Clinic – One-stop

GP name/no.: *(or patient label)*	Patient name: Address:
Date of visit:	Number:

History of presenting complaint: Age:

Last menstrual period/post-menopausal (if cancer suspected)

Past medical history:	Family history:
Drugs:	Previous mammogram:

Examination:

Clinical score =

| Investigations | Requested | Performed | Result | | |
			Provisional	Report	Report filed
Mammogram					
Sono MG					
Fine needle aspiration					
Trucut biopsy					

Provisional diagnosis: Benign/Unsure/Malignant
Information given to patient: Benign/Unsure/Malignant *Breast-care Nurse seen*
Y/N

Plan:

Is patient eligible for clinical drug trial   Y/N   *If cancer – GP letter faxed*   Y/N
For multidisciplinary meeting   Y/N

Proposed operation: L/R   WE/Mastectomy   Axilliary clearance/sample/none

Signature:

Figure 7.4   One-stop clinic proforma

Salisbury Health Care NHS Trust
Surgical Directorate

Ward:_____

Breast-care Pathway – Kardex Record

This document replaces all other nurse documentation, i.e. kardex, care plan, etc. Medical staff will use the pathway as a checklist and write continuation notes in the medical record.

Patient label/details:

Name_____Patient age:_____years

Address:_____

_____

_____

Hospital number:_____

Religion:_____

Relevant Medical History:

Allergies:

GP name:_____

GP contact number:_____

Date of admission:_____

Expected date of discharge:_____

Actual date of discharge:_____

Next of kin:_____

Contact number(s):_____

Figure 7.5   Breast-care pathway – Kardex record (inpatient)

Primary care

Referral process

The GP practice working group had a joint meeting with the one-stop clinic working group to review the process of referral and also to agree referral criteria.

Referral template

A standard template has been developed to facilitate a more efficient referral process (see Figure 7.3). This template contains all the information required to allow the breast-care co-ordinator to make decisions on the urgency of the appointment required and also the need for pre-clinic mammography appointments. GPs have reviewed the template and have requested that it should be made available on computer disks and be developed for transmission via e-mail. Laminated guidelines should be designed to accompany the template.

Referral process (Figure 7.3)

The revised referral process is outlined below. The aims of this revised process are to improve the quality of response to the patient and to improve the efficiency of the process so that the need for patients to phone the breast-care co-ordinator should be eliminated.

- GPs to fax or e-mail the referral template to the breast-care co-ordinator;
- The breast-care co-ordinator to make the appointment on the basis of the GP's indication of whether it should be 'urgent' or 'soon'.
- The patient is advised to phone the GP if she is still waiting for an appointment 7 days from the GP consultation. The patient should *not* be advised to phone the breast-care co-ordinator.
- The fax machine will be switched on at all times (24 hours a day, 7 days a week).

Referral criteria

Criteria for referral between GP practices and the one-stop clinic were agreed and the distinction drawn between 'urgent' and 'soon' referrals. It was noted that no patient has to wait too long as 'urgent' patients are seen on the next clinic and, usually, patients categorised as 'soon' are seen on the next clinic but one.

Discharge information

GP practices receive discharge information from the inpatient episode but are currently not receiving sufficient information from oncology and radiotherapy. In the future information will be provided on:

- drug and other therapies;
- dosage and details of therapy;
- common side-effects;
- when prescribed;
- duration of treatment.

Information regularly required, such as the common side-effects of drugs and therapies, is to be included in the patient's diary.

Follow-up appointments

The pros and cons of acute unit versus primary care follow-ups were reviewed. It was agreed that follow-ups could be shared, where appropriate, with the agreement of the patient and the GP. It was emphasised that continuity of care would be important so that all efforts should be made to ensure that the same person saw the patient for each acute unit visit.

A key objective should be to ensure that patient care is monitored in the longer term. For example, care should be taken to ensure that tamoxifen is stopped, after 5 years.

Information for patients

The working group agreed that it would be important to ensure that patients received consistent messages from primary care and the acute unit and that they were not over-loaded with information. They agreed to use the material developed for the one-stop clinic.

Summary

Changes to process

- Referral criteria agreed;
- Referral template designed;
- Changes to referral process agreed;
- Follow-up appointments process changed.

Benefits of process changes

- Patients will have improved information on the referral process and on when to expect letters and appointments;
- Patients' phone calls to GPs and the one-stop clinic will be significantly reduced;
- The changed process provides a more efficient system for GPs and will remove the need to phone the one-stop clinic to enquire about appointments;
- GPs will have better information on the care process.

Breast cancer services

Care pathway: primary care (Figure 7.3)

Referrals

- Self-referrals
  - symptom(s)
  - family history
  - concerns from screening programme
- District nurses

Presenting symptoms

- Lump(s)
- Lumpiness
- Discharge
- Shape of breast(s)
- Nipple retraction
- Eczema/rash
- Family history
- Mastitis

History

- Menstrual history
- Is the patient post-menopausal?
- Is the patient breastfeeding?
- History and duration of lumps and/or other symptoms
- Family history

Examination

Breasts and under-arms are examined for:

- Lumps
- Lumpy breasts
- Discharge from the nipple
- Shape of breast(s)

- Old scar(s)
- Mastitis

Diagnosis and referral criteria

Patients are categorised against agreed referral criteria as follows:

- 'urgent' referral required;
- 'soon' referral required;
- not to be referred. Patient to be managed in primary care.

Patient management

- Counselling of patients at all stages, both pre- and post-diagnosis and surgery
- Counselling in the longer term
- Monitoring effects of chemotherapy and radiotherapy
- Monitoring effects of tamoxifen
- Removing sutures (on occasion)
- Changing dressings (on occasion)
- Pain control

One-stop clinic (Figure 7.4)

The care pathway covers the one-stop clinic, the post clinic appointment (a review appointment for a small group of patients) and the preadmission clinic. The working group took the opportunity to improve both the quality of care and the efficiency of the care process. The issues addressed and the action planned refer to:

- the referral process;
- mammography appointments;
- information for patients;
- co-ordination of the service;
- preadmission clinic.

Referral process

Two issues were addressed:

- the need for an agreed set of referral criteria;
- the efficiency of the referral process.

Referral criteria

A set of referral critera were agreed with the primary care working group. These criteria will enable GPs to distinguish between those patients who should be referred for an 'urgent' appointment and those who should be categorised as 'soon'.

Process

The one-stop clinic (Figure 7.4) has an excellent record in responding to GP referrals and most patients are seen within a week of the referral being received. However, the working group were keen to improve the user-friendliness and efficiency of the process still further. They identified two areas for review:

- the need for the consultant surgeon to review all referrals;
- the possibility of speeding up the transmission and receipt of referrals.

The working group agreed that the involvement of the consultant could, potentially, delay the process. It was agreed that the medical secretary should process referrals on the basis of the referral criteria and, to facilitate this, a standard clinic booking form has been developed for use in GP practices. This form is based on the referral criteria and also includes the information required to enable the medical secretary to make decisions on pre-clinic mammography appointments.

A further improvement will be the availability of a fax machine (24 hours a day, 7 days a week) for receipt of referrals. It is envisaged that referrals will be transmitted via e-mail in the future.

Mammography appointments

Two issues were identified in relation to the quality of patient care:

- the number of slots available to the clinic does not always match patient demand, so that a small number of patients have to be recalled;
- the timing of the available slots (commencing in the morning) means that some patients have a long period at the hospital before being given a diagnosis.

The working group reviewed this issue with the consultant radiologist and radiographers. As a result, an additional slot has been made available in the afternoon and the pre-lunch slots will start later.

The efficiency of the process and communications between the clinic and the mammography suite is to be improved in two significant ways:

- the patient information obtained in the clinic will be included on the X-ray request form so as to reduce the need for patients to be asked repetitive questions;
- the mammography suite will issue an additional copy of the X-ray report for inclusion in the GP letter, thus reducing the need for photocopying.

As a further improvement, the working group is investigating the possibility of generating request forms with all relevant patient information from the BASO software when it is installed later this year.

Information for patients

The working group identified the need for patients to have improved access to information on the purpose of the clinic, the techniques used, diagnosis and treatment. They have developed a set of posters for display in the waiting area. The information on these posters will also be reproduced as a booklet/diary for patients so that they can study the information in a less hurried way at home. The diary will be designed so that the patient can keep it updated and add additional information during the care process.

Co-ordination of the service

The breast cancer care process involves a complex set of appointments with a wide range of personnel. The working group identified the need for better co-ordination of this process for the patient and for the staff involved. Another key objective was the need to have a 'help line' available to patients and their relatives.

BREAST CARE **PREADMISSION CLINIC**	**Patient name:** **Address:**
Date of Assessment:	**Number:**

Attended One-Stop Clinic   Yes/No/NA
Planned Operation Date:

OPERATION: *(see patient diary/one stop clinic)*

SIDE: RIGHT ☐   LEFT ☐ | Preoperative questionnaire
completed by patient   Y/N
(If No complete now)

Clinical Presentation:	**Previous Treatment/Operation for same condition**

Past/Present Medical History

Hysterectomy	Y/N
Oopherectomy	Y/N
DVT/PE	Y/N

HRT   **Oral contraception**

Duration ☐ years   Duration ☐ years
1. Current   1. Current
2. Ever   2. Ever
3. Never   3. Never

Allergies:

Relevant Family History *(especially breast, ovarian cancer. Include age at diagnosis)*

Number of relatives with breast cancer
1st degree   ☐
2nd degree   ☐

Physical Examination
Weight: kg   Height: cms   Pulse (reg/irreg):   Blood Pressure:

Urine testing: Normal   Blood   Protein   Glucose

Action:

Figure 7.6   Breast care – integrated care pathway documentation

Investigations (all cards to be labelled with admitting ward)	*also do* If reconstructive surgery
FBC ☐ U & E ☐ Group & Save ☐ LFT ☐ CXR ☐ ECG ☐ *(if clinically indicated)* All investigations filed in notes Y/N	MSU ☐ X Match ☐ Photograph ☐ CT Scan ☐ *(if required)*

Interventions:

Consent form signed   Y/N

Drug chart written   ☐ *(antiemetic, tamoxifen, DVT prophylaxis if >75 years with history of DVT)*

Consent to use patient's own
drugs (POD's)   Y/N/NA

Measure for TED stockings: Size:

Special garment measure: (if reconstructive surgery)

Nurse assessment   ☐ Action:

Assessment for early admission   *(see preop questionnaire re anaesthetic status and travel distance)*:

Tuesday admission required   Y/N/NA

Education/Advice:

Assess knowledge and expectations   Y/N

Review of treatment options with patient   Y/N

Explain postoperative exercises/operation recovery   ☐

Explain complications, e.g. haematoma, swelling   ☐

Additional pages added to patient diary   Y/N

Initial information on care of drain and wound at home   Y/N/NA

Explanation of pain relief postop (PCAS etc.)   Y/N/NA

Discharge Planning:

Give approximate discharge date   ☐ *(may go home with drain in situ)*

Assess home, transport needs   ☐

Patient diary updated and explained to patient   ☐

Referrals:

Preoperative:

Anaesthetist ☐   Palliative care ☐   Oncology ☐   Genetics ☐

       Laverstock Ward Sister ☐   Houseman *(if clerking required)* ☐

Follow up: Outpatient appointment made ☐   Date:

Name: **Signature:**

INDICATIONS FOR: ECG
- Patient is over 65 years
- Patient is grossly short of breath (after one flight of stairs)
- Patient has had previous MI, angina, ankle oedema, hypertension

Figure 7.6 *(continued)*

Breast-care pathway	Patient Name:

DAY OF ADMISSION/PREOPERATION ˙   **DATE:**

Clinical progress notes:

Assessment:

Has patient attended Preadmission Clinic   Yes/No *(if no, complete documentation)*

Does PRHO have to clerk patient *(if need highlighted in preadmission clinic)*   Yes/No

Preoperative check list completed   ☐

Investigation/Results:

Group & Save As MG *(if not already taken)*   ☐

All results filed   Yes/No *(check tests taken from Preadmission Clinic/One-stop clinic)*

Inform medical staff of any abnormal results   Yes/No/NA

Interventions:

Apply ID bracelet (× 2)

Apply TEDs *(measured at Preadmission Clinic)*   ☐

Orientate to ward, explain ward routine and facilities   Yes/No/NA

Medications:

As prescribed

Commence patient own drug regime   Yes/No/NA

If minor surgery check TTOs written   Yes/No/NA

Diet:

NBM 4–6 hours preoperatively from   hrs   date.

Mobility:

Up and about:

Education/Advice:

Instruction on postop exercises, answer any queries.

Ensure patient received information leaflet/patient diary

Admitting Nurse Name:	Nocte: AM:
Signature	Signature:

Variance   Yes/No

Figure 7.6 *(continued)*

Breast-care pathway	
RECOVERY **Date:**	**POSTOPERATION** **Date:**
Assessment *(refer to Admission Policy)* Potency of airway Level of consciousness and return of reflexes Pain assessment score: Action:	**Assessment:** Pain assessment scores on postop observation chart Y/N Action: Pressure sore risk assessment: ☐ Action:

Interventions:
Observations *(every 5–20 minutes)*
TPR/BP
Oxygen saturations
Observe skin colour and temperature
Sedation
Nausea:
 	
Check: IV site   ☐
        wound site   ☐
        drain   ☐
Obtain Anaesthetic/Surgical handover
Orientate to time and place.
	Interventions:
	Observations
	TPR and BP *(hourly for 4 hours until stable)*
	PCAS observations
	(15 mins for 1 hour, 30 mins for 2nd hour)
	Check: IV site ☐
	        wound site ☐
	        drain ☐
	Personal hygiene and mouthcare
	Pressure area care
	Check urine output

Medications:
As prescribed
IV fluids   ☐
Pain relief – PCAS   ☐
        – other   ☐
	Medications:
	As prescribed
	IV fluids Y/N/NA
	Pain relief – PCAS ☐
	        – other ☐
	Assess for self-administration Y/N/NA
	Arrange for TTOs *(if day surgery)* Y/N/NA

Diet: Nil by mouth Fluid balance chart	**Diet:** Diet and fluids as tolerated Fluid balance chart
Mobility: Position for comfort	**Mobility:** As tolerated Arm exercises
Education/Advice Refer to discharge procedure Return to ward	**Referrals:** *(day surgery only)* Inform GP Inform community nurse
Named Nurse: **Signature:**	**AM** **PM** **Nights**
Variance Yes/No	

Figure 7.6 *(continued)*

Breast-care pathway	Patient Name:
POST-OP DAY 1	**DATE:**

Clinical progress notes:

Medications:
As prescribed ☐ tamoxifen 20 mgm OD
PCAS ☐ Check TTOs available *(if minor)* ☐ Order TTOs *(if major)* ☐

Investigations:
FBC ☐

Assessment:
Pain assessment score [ ][ ][ ] Action required:.

Pressure sore risk assessment: ☐
Action:

Interventions:
Pressure area care as per policy *(remove TEDs to check heels/toes)*
Personal hygiene and mouthcare.
Remove IV *(if not contraindicated)*   Y/N/NA
Observations (6 hourly) TPR/BP/wound site/drain site
Monitor wound drainage:
Remove pressure dressing   Y/N/NA

Diet:
Full diet and fluids
Monitor input/output
Accurate fluid balance chart

Mobility:
As tolerated
Arm exercises

Education and advice:
Self-care of wound
Self-care of drain

Discharge:
Minor surgery – discharge today.
Check patient has TTOs, follow up appointment.
Fax discharge letter to GP   Y/N
Assessment document to Named Community Nurse   Y/N

Signatures:
AM: **PM:**   **NIGHTS:**

Variance Yes/No

Figure 7.6 *(continued)*

Breast-care pathway		

POST-OP DAY 2   DATE:

Clinical progress notes:

Investigations:

FBC *(if drop is >30 gl of preop value)*   Y/N/NA

Medications:

Self medication   Check TTOs available Y/N/NA

Assessment:

Pain assessment score [| |]   Action required:.

Interventions:
Observations (6 hourly) TPR/BP/wound site/drainage
Remove drain if output <30 ml in 24 hours   Y/N/NA
Apply dry dressing   Y/N/NA
Pressure area care as per policy (including remove TEDs to check heels/toes)
Personal hygiene:

Diet:
Full diet and fluids
Monitor food intake
Accurate fluid balance chart

Mobility:
Independent
Arm exercises

Education and advice:
Explanation re progress and likely discharge date
Explain follow up care
Self-care of drain if not removed   Y/N/NA

Discharge Planning:
Discharge am/pm
Complete HAA form   Y/N
Inform Debbie ext 4989   Y/N
Complete patient diary/explain TTOs/ensure patient competent with drain Y/N/NA
Fax discharge form to GP   Y/N
Fax admission assessment document to Named Community Nurse   Y/N
Extra bags given to patient   Y/N/NA
Drain to be removed when <30 ml/24 hrs or at 9 days post operative

Signatures:
AM: **PM:**   **NIGHTS:**

Variance   Yes/No

Figure 7.6 *(continued)*

Salisbury Health Care NHS Trust

Breast care Discharge summary Admitted on: Discharged on:	Patient name/ label: Address:

Procedure undertaken:
Right/left   Mastectomy/wide resection/lumpectomy/other:

Diagnosis: Benign/malignant/unknown   **Patient informed**:   Y/N

Inpatient stay:
Drain in situ   Y/N/NA
To be removed when drainage <30 ml/24 hrs or on day 7 post operation

---

Medications on discharge: Previous medications unchanged ☐
1. Co-proxamol   ii   *6 hourly*   4.
2. Tamoxifen   20 mgm   *o.d*   5.
3.   6.

Follow-up plan: ,
Home visit   Y/N
Outpatient appointment due at 9 days post-op. Friday ....../....../...... at

Referrals:
Palliative care ☐   Oncology ☐   Radiotherapy ☐

Communications:
If you have any concerns/queries, please do not hesitate to contact a member of the team:

Bishopstone ward

Breast-care co-ordinator

Breast-care nurse

Laverstock ward

Fax copy to GP.   **File copy in medical record.**   **Carbon copy left on ward**

Figure 7.6 *(continued)*

Breast-care pathway   **Patient Name:**

Date	Time	ICP Day	Variance/Reason	Action taken	Sign

SIGNATURE SHEET

Please give your full name, profession, initials and full signature below, if you write in this pathway. This is for legal purposes.

Name	Initials	Signature	Profession	Date

Figure 7.6 *(continued)*

It was decided that the role of the medical secretary should be extended to that of breast-care co-ordinator. The co-ordinator will have responsibility for smoothing the process for the patient and tracking the patient through the system to ensure that all relevant staff are kept informed. It is envisaged that this monitoring of the patient journey will form part of the computer system in the future. The co-ordinator will also be the main point of contact for patients and relatives, referring queries to other personnel as appropriate.

Patient empowerment

A key objective is to empower the patient so that they feel 'in control' of the care process. In this context, the patient information diary (see above) is to be extended to include full details of appointments and follow-up periods. This will enable the patient to track the care process and to ensure that appointments and follow-ups are convenient for her. It will also provide the information required by the staff working with the patient, particularly in the community.

The preadmission clinic (Figure 7.6)

Patients booked for inpatient admission are currently given an appointment with the breast-care nurse prior to admission. It has been decided to extend this appointment to a nurse-led, preadmission clinic to replace the current clinic which is staffed by junior doctors. The nurse-led, preadmission clinic will undertake:

- preadmission assessment, including assessment for early admission;
- initial assessment for anaesthesia;
- diagnostic tests;
- consent to use own drugs;
- psychological and social assessment;

- counselling and review of treatment options;
- patient documentation;
- initial preparation of the patient for the discharge process and drain care at home;
- initial instruction on arm exercises.

Reconstructive surgery

Where a patient has opted for, or is considering, reconstructive surgery, a ward sister will be called to provide additional information and advice.

Appointments

The appointment process has been reviewed to make it more convenient for patients. In future, patients will receive the following dates at the preadmission clinic:

- discharge date;
- postoperative appointment with consultant;
- oncology outpatient appointment.

Benefits of preadmission clinic

The benefits of extending the current breast-care appointment to a nurse-led, preadmission clinic are as follows:

- eliminates the need for a pre-surgery overnight stay for almost all patients;
- reduces the duplication of effort (and poor patient quality) related to patient information being collected by a number of staff (the patient information from the preadmission clinic will not be collected again on the ward). The group identified that similar types of patient information were being collected at least four times in the early period of admission;
- discharge planning and preparation of the patient starts early.

Summary

Changes to process

- Referral criteria agreed;
- Standard clinic booking form developed for use in GP practices;
- Transmission of referral changed from post to fax (and computer in the future);
- Changes to timing of mammography slots and an additional afternoon slot;
- Inclusion of patient information on X-ray request form to avoid duplication;
- Additional copy of X-ray report form to be provided for GPs;
- Breast-care nurse appointment extended to nurse-led preadmission clinic;
- Preadmission clinic patient information to be used on ward;
- Patient to be given dates for discharge, postoperative appointment and oncology outpatient appointment at preadmission clinic.

Information for patients

- Posters in waiting area;
- Patient booklet and diary of appointments.

Changes to work roles

- Consultant removed from referral and clinic appointment process;
- Medical secretary role enhanced to breast-care co-ordinator;
- Breast-care nursing role extended to preadmission assessment and assessment for early admission.

Key messages

- A process which was already efficient has been made even more efficient;
- Professional workload can be delegated so long as the appropriate systems are in place (for example role of breast-care co-ordinator in referral process).

Inpatient episode

There are separate care pathways for:

- inpatient episode for breast cancer surgery (Figures 7.5 and 7.6)
- outpatient clinic for reconstructive surgery (Figure 7.7a)
- inpatient episode for reconstructive surgery (Figure 7.7b)

The text below refers, in the main, to breast cancer surgery but the variations for reconstructive surgery are shown at the end (Figures 7.7a and 7.7b).

Length of stay

The patient length of stay was reviewed in relation to (a) admission the afternoon prior to surgery and (b) recovery post-surgery.

Admission

The current admission process requires all patients to be admitted the afternoon prior to the day of surgery. The justification for early admission is:

- to ensure that preoperative tests and assessments are completed in good time for the surgery list;
- to ensure that there is time for more detailed assessments for those patients at risk from the anaesthetic;
- to avoid the risk of breast cancer patients' beds being allocated to emergency admissions overnight.

The working group agreed that it would improve both quality and cost-effectiveness if patients could be admitted on the morning of surgery and they reviewed the admission process with this as their objective. The only exceptions would be patients requiring a more detailed preoperative assessment or those who lived too far from the hospital to make morning admission convenient. It was accepted, however, that even for this second group of patients, admission times could be staggered.

The planned changes to the admission process are as follows:

- the completion of preoperative tests and assessments to fit with the surgery schedules will be met through the introduction of the preadmission clinic (see section on one-stop clinic);
- most patients will, in the future, be admitted on the morning of surgery. This raises the possibility of admissions being postponed in the event of a severe bed shortage. The working group agreed that it would be unacceptable for breast cancer patients to have their operations postponed and it was decided that no admissions should be postponed except with the agreement of the breast-care co-ordinator. The Trust gives a high priority to ensuring that beds are available for breast cancer patients so that no problems are envisaged because of the change to morning admissions.
- patient admission times are to be staggered during the morning to improve convenience for patients, to smooth the workload and to reduce the likelihood of bed shortages.
- patients will not be requried to phone the unit on the day of admission in future.

Discharge

There are currently wide variations in lengths of stay. The determining factor in most cases is the attitude of the patient to going home with a drain in situ. The working group agreed that patient education on this issue should start with the one-stop and preadmission clinics and be followed through on the ward. It is envisaged that minor surgery patients will continue to go home within 24 hours and major surgery patients will have an average length of stay of 3 days rather than the current 7 days. The working group developing the pathway for community services confirmed that patients with drains in situ could be cared for in the community (see section on community and practice nursing).

It was decided that copies of the discharge information should be kept to a minimum to reduce workload on the ward. One copy will be sent to the named contact in the GP surgery (see section on community and practice nursing) to be shared with the GP. A second copy will be sent to the breast-care co-ordinator.

The care process

The development of the care pathway stimulated a review of all aspects of the care process.

- **Sutures** The consultant surgeon has decided to move towards the use of disposable sutures for all patients so that there will be no need to remove sutures either in the community or in outpatients.

The working group also identified a number of areas where Trust policy needed to be clarified:

- the frequency of postoperative observations;
- the frequency of changing and laundering TED stockings;
- criteria for assessing patients for patient controlled analgesia system (PCA);
- theatre escort: replacement of professionally qualified nurse with HCA.

Patient documentation

The working group identified major inefficiencies in the number of times that patients are asked for the same information. This is not a good experience for the patient and is wasteful of staff resources. It was decided that all disciplines should use the same documentation and that the information collated at the preadmission clinic would be used for the patient stay.

The group reviewed the role of the junior doctor in clerking the patient prior to surgery and agreed that the information collected at preadmission stage eliminated the need for this. It was agreed, therefore, that the junior doctor would not be routinely required for clerking.

Summary: breast cancer surgery

Changes to process

- Majority of patients to be admitted on morning of surgery;
- Admissions to be staggered to improve convenience for patients and to reduce the likelihood of bed shortages;
- The requirement for patients to phone the ward on the day of admission to be eliminated;
- Standard documentation (based on care pathway) to be used by all disciplines and duplication of information collation and recording to be eliminated;
- Patient education on discharge and drains to commence at preadmission clinic and to be reinforced during inpatient stay;
- Average length of stay to be reduced from 7 days to 3 days for major surgery patients;
- Extension of use of disposable sutures to all patients.

Changes to work roles

- Junior doctor role in patient clerking not routinely required.

Key messages

- Improved discharge planning and reduced length of stay is heavily dependent on education of patients and consistent messages from staff.
- There is significant scope for improving both quality of care and cost-effectiveness through the use of multi-disciplinary documentation.

Reconstructive surgery (Figures 7.7a and 7.7b)

There are a number of significant differences in the care process between breast cancer surgery and reconstructive surgery. These are due not just to the requirements of the procedure but to the wider geographical base from which patients are drawn.

		Patients arrive diagnosed	

Assessment		• Repeat history
		  – date of onset
		  – presenting symptoms (including pain)
		  – previous medical history
		  – family history of breast cancer
		• Physical examination
		  – size and location of lumps
		  – symmetry
		  – glands: subclavian and axillary
		  – nipple and skin appearance
		  – previous abdominal scars
			• Preadmission assessment
			  – past medical history
			  – allergies
			• Assessment for early admission
			  – ECG required
			  – Diabetic
			  – Inability to walk upstairs without stopping
			• Psychological and social assessment

Investigations			FBC Electrolytes LFT Group and save Cross match Photograph MSU Chest X-Ray ECG Measure for TED stockings Special garment measure CT scan if required
Medication		Tamoxifen	
Education Information Counselling		Diagnosis Treatment options Support	Assess knowledge/expectations Counselling and support Review of treatment options Discharge of expectations
Discharge		Inpatient admission date	Time of admission

Figure 7.7a Breast cancer outpatients – variations to the pathway for reconstructive surgery

CATEGORY	DAY OF SURGERY	POSTOP DAY 1	POSTOP DAY2	POSTOP DAY 3 – UNTIL DISCHARGE
Assessment and Interventions	Preop check list Fit anti-embolic stockings Postop observations (TPR and BP hourly for 4 hours until stable) PCAS obs. (15 mins for 1st hour and 30 mins for 2nd hour) Pain assessment Wound assessment Appearance Flap obs. 1 hourly for 12 hours Wound drainage Positioning of patient Fluid balance	Pain assessment Appearance Monitor wound drainage Monitor fluid intake and output Remove IV if not contra-indicated Flap obs. 2–4 hourly Observations: TPR and BP 4 hourly Check pressure areas Treat pressure areas Ensure anti-embolic stockings clean Check heels and feet Check dressings	Pain assessment Appearance Monitor wound drainage Observations: TRP and BP 4 hourly Flap obs. 4 hourly Treat pressure areas Ensure anti-embolic stockings clean Check heels and feet Re-apply dressing	Pain assessment Appearance Monitor wound drainage Observations: TPR 4 hourly Flap obs. 4 hourly Treat pressure areas Ensure anti-embolic stockings clean Check heels and feet Re-apply dressing Removal of drains when <30 mls in 24 hours
Diagnostics		FBC (24 hour postop)	Repeat FBC if drop is > 30 grms of preop value	Repeat FBC
Medication	Check if patient on tamoxifen Tamoxifen 20 mg per day Sub-cutaneous heparin preop IV antibiotics in theatre Pain relief Anti-emetics if indicated Anti-coagulants postop Night sedation if indicated	Tamoxifen 20 mg per day Pain relief if indicated Anti-emetics if indicated Anticoagulants Antibiotics for 5 days Blood transfusion if indicated Apply leeches if required Night sedation if indicated	Tamoxifen 20 mg per day Pain relief if indicated Anti-emetics if indicated Anticoagulants Antibiotics Iron supplements Apply leeches if required Night sedation if indicated	Tamoxifen 20 mg per day Pain relief if indicated Anti-emetics if indicated Anticoagulants Antibiotics for 5 days Iron supplements Apply leeches if required Night sedation if indicated

Figure 7.7b Breast cancer inpatients – variations to the pathway for reconstructive surgery

CATEGORY	DAY OF SURGERY	POSTOP DAY 1	POSTOP DAY2	POSTOP DAY 3 – UNTIL DISCHARGE
Nutrition	Preop nil by mouth Postop food as tolerated Intravenous fluids	Full diet Monitor food intake	Full diet Monitor food intake	Full diet Monitor food intake
Mobility	Instruction on exercises Bed rest Up to commode	Monitor arm exercises Bed rest Mobile to toilet Physio: chest respiration	Monitor arm exercises Bed rest Mobile Physio: chest respiration	Bed rest Fully mobile
Education/ Information Discharge and Planning	Introduction to ward routine and facilities Physiotherapist introduction	Leaflets Postoperative information	Special garments Postoperative information	Special garments Postoperative information Supply/check TTOs Dressing TTOs Inform named contact and co-ordinator Plastic Op appt. (dressing and clinic) Advice leaflets Sick certificate Review social and psychological assessments Special requirements

Notes on Pathway

1. Average length of stay 5–10 days dependent on type of reconstruction.
2. No patient discharged with drain in situ.
3. Minimum of 7 days between outpatient appointment and admission.
4. Physiotherapy: patient and type of reconstruction dependent.
5. All patients have OPD follow-up 1 week after discharge.
6. Some patients have second OPD follow-up 10 days afer discharge.
7. Sutures removed 21 days after operation.

Figure 7.7b   Breast cancer inpatients – variations to the pathway for reconstructive surgery *(continued)*

Oncology and radiotherapy

The working group reviewed areas where the quality of care and the efficiency of the care process could be improved. They also took account of the views raised by the other working groups. The areas identified for review and action were:

- process involved in obtaining chemotherapy drugs
- investigation process
- information for patients
- information for the primary care team.

Process for obtaining chemotherapy drugs

There are long delays in treatment due to the need for investigation results being required prior to the chemotherapy prescription being written. There is then a further delay for the pharmacy to process the prescription and provide the medication. This remains an outstanding issue, although work is continuing to find ways of changing the pharmacy process. One option being considered is that, in the future, the primary care team could undertake the investigations so that the results are available on the morning of the scheduled treatment.

Information for primary care team

Currently, GP practices and community nurses receive insufficient information. They have indicated that they require information as follows:

- dosage of drug and details of therapy
- common side-effects
- when treatment commenced
- duration of treatment.

Both the oncology and radiotherapy teams have agreed that this information will be provided in the future. The additional patient information (see below) will also be helpful to the primary care team.

Investigation process

There have been delays at the first outpatient appointment due to the need for X-rays and blood tests prior to the patient being seen by the consultant. It has been recognised that the investigations could be undertaken earlier in the process and changes have been agreed:

- chest X-ray and liver function test will be undertaken at the preadmission clinic;
- results will be filed prior to the first chemotherapy/radiotherapy appointment.

Information for patients

There is an optimum time for receiving chemotherapy and radiotherapy. Patients need to be aware of this since, otherwise, they will be inclined to assume that treatment is being delayed. To overcome this problem, the information on when treatment will start will be included in the patient's diary (see section on one-stop clinic).

Summary

Changes to process

- Investigation timing changed
- Information requirements for GP and community team agreed
- Information for patients agreed
- Process for obtaining chemotherapy – still ongoing.

Benefits of process changes

- Reduced delay at first outpatient appointment
- Primary care/community team better informed and able to reinforce consistent messages to patients
- Patients will have better information on the care process.

Key messages

- Sharing patient information across sectors is important to maintain a credible image of the service to the patient
- Visiting consultants (oncology/radiotherapy) have limited time and processes need to be efficient.

CATEGORY	FIRST APPOINTMENT (2–3 WEEKS POSTOP)	FIRST TREATMENT (7–10 DAYS AFTER FIRST OPA)	TREATMENT 2–6 (9.00 am–2.00 pm)	FOLLOW UP
Source of referral	Consultant Surgeon Radiotherapist GP			3 months 3/12 for 2 years 6/12 for 3 years Annually thereafter
Assess/ Interview	• History • Examination • Eligible trials	General well being Nurse assessment (include HAD) Wig fitted Scalp cooling 30 mins pre-treatment Site IV cannula Treatment and anti-emetic (nurse stays throughout) Scalp cooling 30 mins post-treatment	Check weight Consultant/nurse assessment	• Examination • Local recurrence • Pleural effusion • Metastasis • Liver enlargement
Investigation	Check LFT/CXR/FBC results Height and weight to calculate skin surface		U&E/FBC (and LFT at week 3)	
Medication	Write up and order chemotherapy/TTOs	Chemotherapy Anti-emetics TTOs	Order chemotherapy after blood results reviewed TTOs	
Evaluation/ Information/ Counselling	• Explanation of treatment – side-effects – durations • Pros/cons of treatment • Alternative options • General/specific information sheets given	Treatment and side-effects explained Relative/friend to drive patient home Reduce anxiety	Treatment and side-effects explained Reduce anxiety	

Figure 7.8 Breast cancer – oncology care pathway

CATEGORY	FIRST APPOINTMENT (2–3 WEEKS POST-OP)	FIRST TREATMENT (7–10 DAYS AFTER FIRST OPA)	TREATMENT 2–6 (9.00 am–2.00 pm)	FOLLOW UP
Evaluation/ Information/ Counselling	• Contact names/nos given for 24 hour service • Talk about scalp cooling and show hats • Introduce to staff and show around DDU • Outline what to expect at subsequent visits (bring relative or friend)			
Referrals	l Orthotics for wig l Palliative care if required	Arrange next appointment Give care for blood tests (morning of next treatment)		
Discharge	Date given for starting treatment given (7–10 days' time) Letter to GP/named contact Barbara Borwell/consultant re proposed treatment/ length, side-effects, and so on	GP sent letter Named community contact	*After treatment 5* Radiotherapy (for 3–4 weeks after chemo) *After treatment 6* Consultant surgeon	

Figure 7.8 Breast cancer – oncology care pathway *(continued)*

'Curative Intent' – aim 4–6 weeks post-surgery

CATEGORY	FIRST APPOINTMENT	PLANNING SECOND APPOINTMENT	TREATMENT (5 WEEKS)	FOLLOW UP
Source of referral	95 per cent fellow consultant 5 per cent GPs			
Information required on referral	Pink referral form/letter by Tuesday 11.00 am will be seen within 7 days • Diagnosis • What treatment to date • Stage of disease • What found • What action is required • What does patient know/expect	• Is surgical wound healed • Able to undertake arm abduction to 90 per cent		
Assessment/ Intervention	• Personal details • History of illness • Physical examination • Stage of healing • Location of lump/size (if preoperative)	Mapping (in Southampton Radiotherapy Department)	• Treatment	
Investigations				
Medications		Anti-emetics		

Figure 7.9   Breast cancer – radiotherapy care pathway

'Curative Intent' – aim 4–6 weeks post-surgery

CATEGORY	FIRST APPOINTMENT	PLANNING SECOND APPOINTMENT	TREATMENT (5 WEEKS)	FOLLOW UP
Education/ Information Counselling	• Treatment options • How radiation works • Relevance • Side-effects (common)			
Discharge	• Letter to GP • Letter to referring consultant		Referring consultant	
Issues	• Poor secretarial support Salisbury District Hospital – letters not actioned. • Could sign at clinic • OPD rooms – non-availability • X-rays and results not available at clinic • ↑ radiotherapy demand • delays from GP to diagnosis			

Figure 7.9 Breast cancer – radiotherapy care pathway *(continued)*

'Palliative'

CATEGORY	FIRST APPOINTMENT	SECOND APPOINTMENT PLANNING	THIRD APPOINTMENT
Source of referral	95 per cent fellow consultant 5 per cent GPs		
Assessment/ Intervention	History – spread beyond regional lymph node and beyond axilla • Palliative care • Symptom control • Surgery • Medication Physical examination Palliative radiotherapy may assist symptom control		
Education/ Information Counselling	• Aim for few side-effects to gain quality of life • Side-effects • Length of treatment • Outcome		

Figure 7.10　　Breast cancer – radiotherapy care pathway (palliative)

Community and practice nursing

The working group reviewed the current referral and care processes and agreed that a number of changes should be implemented to improve the quality of patient care and to meet any expansion in demand which results from changes to the pattern of service delivery, for example, reduced lengths of stay and the increasing need to care for patients with drains.

They also reviewed work roles and concluded that the current demarcations between, for example, district nurses and health visitors sometimes resulted in ineffective use of resources because of two members of staff needing to visit a patient. This fragmentation in roles also has implications for the continuity of care. It was agreed that community and practice nursing roles should be enhanced to improve both quality of care and cost-effectiveness.

Co-ordination of referral process

Community nurses do not currently receive the full range of information required to assess the need for patient services. Referrals from the inpatient episode are usually limited to:

- mastectomy patients;
- patients requiring support in the home environment.

The working group agreed that information on all patients discharged was required in order to enable them to assess the service need and to ensure that support for patients and their families is efficiently organised. To meet this need, the referral process is to be revised as follows:

- each GP practice is to decide on a named contact to co-ordinate community services for breast cancer patients. Selection of named contacts will be made irrespective of discipline and it is anticipated that there will be a mix drawn from district nurses, health visitors and practice nurses.
- discharge information is to be extended and sent to the named contact for every patient discharged (see Figure 7.6). The group emphasised the importance of full information being available to the named contact in GP surgeries and, through her, to community nurses. Comprehensive information is important in ensuring continuity of care and also in presenting a credible image of the service to the patient. Community nurses want to move on from the situation where they have to start from the beginning with each patient. The group recognised that the information they require will already have been collected and that it should be relatively easy to adapt the current process to ensure that it is available to them. Discharge documentation is to be amended to meet this requirement and is to be available to the community service from each stage of care.
- the named contact will assess the need for service on the basis of the discharge information (this can be provided either through home support or visits to the surgery). The named contact will also decide which discipline is most appropriate (HV, DN or practice nurse).

- the working group stressed the importance of good communications being established between the breast-care nurse and the named contact.

Postoperative care process

The working group identified three major issues to be addressed in the future planning of services:

- the importance of ensuring that all patients are aware of the service available and that patients in need of support do not 'slip through the net';
- shorter lengths of stay will undoubtedly lead to some increased activity for the community service so that efficient deployment of staff will be essential;
- the need for work roles to be enhanced so as to improve continuity of care and cost-effectiveness.

It has been agreed that patients' diaries will contain information on the community service, giving telephone numbers for the named contacts.

The working group appreciated that the effective use of scarce staffing resources will be highly dependent on good communications between community and practice nurses and also with the GP. In this context, the group agreed that the occasions when two members of staff are involved with an individual patient should be kept to an absolute minimum to improve cost-effectiveness and also to improve quality through the delivery of a more continuous, personalised service. To avoid duplication of home visits, roles are to be enhanced and appropriate training and assessment programmes established. For example, health visitors will require training in dressings and drain care/removal.

The working group noted that patients with drains regularly require an additional outpatient visit just to have the drain removed. They regarded this outpatient visit as an inconvenience for the patient and an inappropriate use of hospital resources. They confirmed that drains could be removed by community/practice nurses either in the patient's home or in the surgery.

Summary

Changes to process

- GP practices to decide on named contacts for the co-ordination of the service;
- Discharge information is to be extended to avoid duplication and to improve the seamlessness of the service;
- Information on the named contact is to be included in patients' diaries;
- Discharge information is to be sent to the named contact for every patient discharged;
- The removal of drains by community nurses will eliminate the need for a special outpatient appointment.

Information for patients

- Information on community services and named contacts is to be included in patients' diaries.

Changes to work roles

- A named contact is to be selected for each GP practice;
- Community and practice nursing roles are to be enhanced to ensure cost-effective deployment of staffing resources.

Key messages

- Sharing of patient information across sectors is important to reduce duplication and, more importantly, to maintain a credible image of the service with the patient;
- Collaboration between disciplines and flexibility in work roles is a key determinant of the effective use of staffing resources and of the delivery of a more personalised service to the patient.

	CARE PROCESS	INFORMATION REQUIRED
Referrals	Discharge information to named contact for: • postoperative patients • plastic surgery patients • radiotherapy • chemotherapy • oncology	Discharge information Information on therapies • name of drug/details of therapies • dosage • date of commencement • planned duration • common side-effects
Service Decision	Named professional within the practice Based on • mobility • wound care including drain • children/family circumstances • psychological support • any other factors	
Assessments and Interventions	Nursing assessment including: • assessment of wound • dressings • psychological and social assessment • symptoms Drain care Remove drain (7 days postop. or when <30 ml in 24 hours) Symptom control Apply dressings	
Education/ Counselling	Self-care of drains Counselling and support Diagnosis, symptoms and treatment plan	
Referrals	If appropriate • Social services for social support and personal care • GP for symptom control • GP, palliative care or breast-care nurse for additional psychological support and symptom control • Voluntary agencies	

Figure 7.11   Breast cancer: community and practice nursing

Palliative care

The working group reviewed the palliative care service in relation to breast cancer patients but recommended no change to the current arrangements. The notes below emphasise some key points in relation to the service.

Role of palliative care service

The palliative care service is mainly enabling, advisory and educational. Educational programmes for patients, family/carers and/or professionals are provided in:

- symptom control
- practical advice/support
- support groups
- disease and treatment options
- other staff groups.

Referrals to the palliative care service

The working group reviewed the current referral process and decided to leave it unchanged. The current process accepts referrals from all professionals working with the patient. However, medical consent is required, either from the GP or the hospital consultant, depending on the stage of the care process.

However, it was noted that the medical consent does not have to be in writing. Referrals can be made by phone, fax or letter but phone and fax are preferred to ensure a speedy response.

The working group emphasised the importance of referrals to the service not being left too late to enable the team to develop a relationship with the patient and make an effective contribution.

Communication of bad news to patients and/or relatives

There have been occasions when palliative care personnel have been asked to break bad news to a patient. They do not regard this as good practice and the working group emphasised that this is the role of the doctor caring for the patient. However, the palliative care team are often involved in follow-up sessions after the bad news has been given and regard this as a good use of their time. They are also available to advise staff on the breaking of bad news.

Information required by community and practice nursing

Patient information

- Age
- Social history and situation
- Children (numbers and ages)
- Mobility
- Drain in situ
- Psychological state/emotional attitude
- Understanding/insight of diagnosis
- Referral to palliative care
- Any other factors deemed relevant

Information on therapies

- Name of drug and/or details of therapy
- Dosage
- Date of commencement
- Planned duration
- Common side-effects

	ACUTE INPATIENT AND COMMUNITY	HOSPICE AND DAY CARE
Referrals	Any professional with consent from GP/consultant At diagnosis, relapse/difficult symptoms or psychosocial issues	Any professional with consent from GP/consultant At diagnosis, relapse/difficult symptoms or psychosocial issues
Service Decision	Based on needs of: ● Patient ● Family/carer ● Professional	Based on needs of: ● Patient ● Family/carer ● Professional
Assessments	Personal details History of illness Symptom control Psychosocial issues ● body image ● expectations/goals ● insight Social ● support/housing ● finances: prescription DLA AA ● Family dynamics/experience/ illness	Personal details History of illness Symptom control Psychosocial issues ● body image ● expectations/goals ● insight Social ● support/housing ● finances: prescription DLA AA ● Family dynamics/experience/ illness
Interventions	Medication Treatments: surgery, RT, CT, nerve blocks Counselling Symptom control Breast-care lymphoedema service	Medication Treatments: surgery, RT, CT, nerve blocks Counselling Symptom control Help with personal hygiene Leisure pursuits
Information and Education *(For patient, family/carer and/or professional)*	Palliative care service Symptom control Practical advice/support Support groups Disease and treatment options	Palliative care service Symptom control Practical advice/support Support groups Disease and treatment options
Referrals	To any appropriate professional/volunteer for example RT, chemo, pain clinic, dentist, clinical psychologist, aromatherapist, volunteer driver/befriender	To any appropriate professional/volunteer for example RT, chemo, pain clinic, dentist, clinical psychologist, aromatherapist, volunteer driver/befriender

Figure 7.12 Breast cancer: palliative care

Summary

This pathway is an example of how the team caring for patients with breast cancer work together in acute and community settings to develop a cohesive approach to managing the patients' care. The process of developing the pathway has enabled the team to address problems, solve problems and streamline the process of care for the patient. Patients are seen and treated more promptly than before and the care they receive is evidence based and of an agreed standard of care.

The pathway has helped both the clinical and non-clinical members of the team to have a better under-standing of everyone's roles and responsibilities in assuring that the process of care meets preset outcomes. As a result of the pathway, the multidisciplinary team now work on the wards and departments on a rotational basis, to ensure that they maintain their skills in all areas of breast care.

The pathway generates a large number of data suitable for audit, thus ensuring that clinical audit is instrumental in effecting changes to improve patient care. As a result of making the processes more efficient, the number of patients being treated has increased and waiting times have decreased, which has been matched by an increase in the number of medical staff. The inpatient length of stay has been reduced, which pleases the patients.

The pathway is supported by an operational policy setting out the occupational standards on which the department is based. These standards ensure that patients are well informed in their decision making and are treated promptly and in a dignified manner.

The information generated through the pathway has been used to write a patient booklet entitled *The Treatment Plan for a Patient with Breast Cancer*. This informative booklet explains all the treatment options and includes a section in which the patient's individual discharge plan details can be entered. The most important aspect of the pathway is that everyone is working to the same evidence base, and there is ongoing monitoring of outcome, which results in good-quality patient care.

Dorset Community NHS Trust – personalised care management project

The pathway for the care and treatment of people with schizophrenia was developed as part of a personalised care management project (Dorset Community NHS Trust, 1998a).

Personalised care management is about:

- integrating the delivery of health services across organisational boundaries to achieve consistent, optimum care for service users, thus developing an integrated care pathway;
- involving service users as much as possible in:
  - maintaining their health;
  - the self-management of their condition;
  - discussing the treatment options available to them;
  - evaluating the care they receive;
- providing treatment and care that are based on clinically effective and best practice;
- measuring outcomes and the appropriateness of care.

Early in 1997, Dorset Health Authority launched several personalised care management projects covering asthma, diabetes, renal disease, heart disease and cancer. Dorset Community Trust was selected to develop a personalised care management for people with serious mental illness. The aim, in the long run, is to disseminate the resulting care pathways across Dorset. Dr Juergen Guenther was seconded from Eli Lilly & Co to work with the Trust and local primary health care teams to develop an integrated care pathway for people with schizophrenia.

A project group was formed that included Dr Graham Gallimore, Consultant Psychiatrist; Roger Wainwright, Nurse Team Leader; Mark Humphries, Team Leader,

Minterne Ward; Peter Daw, Manager Psychology Service; and Kate Sneider, Care Planning Approach (CPA) Co-ordinator. This group reports to a Project Group that includes local GPs and social services representatives.

The project group reviewed the current treatment and care of people with schizophrenia and compared this with gathered evidence and best practice guidelines. Compliance with local protocols, polices and standards was analysed. This resulted in the group agreeing on what constituted best practice in the treatment and care of people with schizophrenia, specific to local need and resources, the areas for improvement and agreed outcome measures to demonstrate change and improvement. The pathway set out in Figure 7.14 is part of an integrated patient file that includes guidelines for practitioners and documentation such as the assessment, contacts, risk assessment, medication, care notes and interventions, CPA care plans, reports, investigations, measures and correspondence.

From this, the group developed the following documentation:

- the standards to support the pathway (Figure 7.13).
- an integrated care pathway, illustrated in Figures 7.14–7.17.
- the pathway documentation (Figure 7.18).

STANDARDS

STANDARD	INPATIENT	COMMUNITY

1. Assessment
• Full clinical assessment undertaken
• Health of the Nation Outcome Scores
    (HoNOS) score taken
• Brief Psychiatric Rating Scale
    (BPRS) measure taken
	Within 7 days
	of admission
		Within 14 days
		of assessment

2. Management • Named nurse (key worker) allocated • CPA registration (new service users) • Care plan • Risk management plan • Telephone or face-to-face contact with carers • Carers' needs assessed • Contact with key worker[1] • Care plan drafted and agreed[2]	Within 7 days of admission	Within 14 days of assessment
3. Review • CPA review/discharge • GP updated • General health check: primary care	Before discharge Before discharge –	Every 6 months maximum

4. Treatment and care
• Education offered to:
   – service user[1]
   – carers[2]
	Within 7 days
	Ongoing
		Within 14 days
		Ongoing

1. inpatient setting.
2. within 1 week of key worker allocation: community.
CPA = care planning approach.

Figure 7.13   Dorset Community NHS Trust: integrated
care pathway for schizophrenia – standards

ACUTE PHASE – FIRST EPISODE

Positive symptoms most prominent Atypical antipsychotic or high-potency conventional antipsychotic	**Negative symptoms most prominent** Atypical antipsychotic

- **ACUTE EXACERBATION DUE TO NON-COMPLIANCE**
  - reintroduce antipsychotic;
  - consider atypical or depot medication;
  - review compliance;
  - monitor for response or relapse.

- **TREATMENT RESISTANT**
  - **partial response: weeks 5–12**
    another atypical or high-potency conventional antipsychotic.
  - **no response: weeks 3–6**
    another atypical or high-potency conventional antipsychotic.
  - **continued non-response**
    clozapine: aim for 360 mg daily;
    consider use of ECT;
    complete review of drug history;
  - withdraw 'ineffective medication';
  - give most effective past drug or alternative untried antipsychotic;
  - lowest effective dose;
  - continuous dosing approach.

- **ADJUNCTIVE MEDICATION**
- **persisting excitement/insomnia**
  - add benzodiazapine;
  - consider more sedative antipsychotic (atypical or conventional);
  - consider lithium carbonate, especially for schizomanic disorder;
  - valproate/carbamazepine – especially if persisting aggression or for mood stabilisation;
  - assess over 4 weeks;
  - consider exceeding benzodiazepine British National Formulary limits for 4 weeks to 3 months
  - unresponsive: consider ECT.
- **persisting anxiety**
  - consider more sedative antipsychotic (atypical or conventional);
  - consider antidepressant (SSRI or tricyclic);
  - consider Buspirone.
- **persisting depression**
  - antidepressant SSRI or tricyclic;
  - consider lithium carbonate;
  - consider ECT.

- **SIDE-EFFECTS OF ANTIPSYCHOTIC MEDICATION**
  - consider reduction of dose;
  - if unsuccessful, switch to another antipsychotic, especially an atypical one;
  - bradykinesia/tremor: add antiparkinsonian drug;
  - akathisia (restlessness): add propanolol;

Figure 7.14   Integrated care pathway for schizophrenia

- sexual dysfunction/troublesome gynaecomastia or galactorrhoea: switch to low prolactin-provoking atypical drug;
- consider amantadine;
- consider clozapine.

Neuroleptic malignant syndrome:
- stop all antipsychotic medication;
- consider involving physicians for support treatment;
- consider use of benzodiazepines after recovery;
- consider slow reintroduction of antipsychotic from another class/group;
- consider clozapine.

STABILISATION PHASE

ANTIPSYCHOTIC MEDICATION UPON DISCHARGE
- provide enough medication to last until first GP contact;
- provide repeat prescriptions for specialist-only prescribing:
  - certain atypical antipsychotics;
  - clozapine (monitor haematology);
- continue same medication dose for 6 months:
  - if originally effective and no emergent side-effects, review compliance and monitor for relapse;
- continue drug treatment education for service user and carers.

ADJUNCTIVE MEDICATION
- review need for continuation of adjunctive medication, especially:
  - benzodiazepines: maximum length of use 4 weeks to avoid potential addiction and need for gradual withdrawal;
  - trial of antiparkinsonian agent: drug's gradual withdrawal;
  - continue antidepressant for at least 6 months.

STABLE PHASE

ANTIPSYCHOTIC MEDICATION
- choice of maintenance antipsychotic:
  - select medication, dose and route of administration most likely to enhance compliance and reduce side-effects;
- duration of maintenance antipsychotic therapy:
  - 12–24 months for *first episode* service users who have gone into remission;
  - longer term (up to lifetime) when diagnosis of schizophrenia is clearly established by multiple episodes and/or persistent symptoms;
- dosing of antipsychotics:
  - continuous dosing: drug holidays and/or intermittent approaches generally not recommended unless the service user refuses continuous maintenance treatment;
- elective dose reductions:
  - taper gradually at 2–4 week intervals over a period of several months, rather than abruptly switching to the targeted lower dose;
- substance abuse complications:
  - maintain continuous dosing at therapeutic dose level even when service user is actively abusing drugs or alcohol.

TREATMENT OF SIDE-EFFECTS OF HIGH-POTENCY CONVENTIONAL ANTIPSYCHOTICS
- refractory EPS:
  - bradykinesia and muscle rigidity: consider atypical agents or switch to low-potency conventional antipsychotic.

ECT = electroconvulsive therapy; SSRI = selective serotonin reuptake inhibitor.

Figure 7.14 *(continued)*

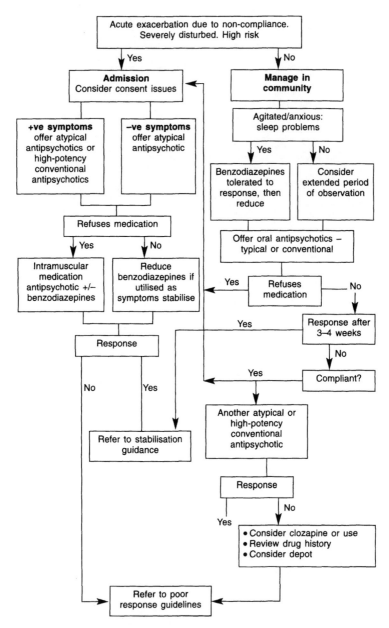

Figure 7.15   Prescribing algorithm for
schizophrenia: acute phase, first episode

- Prior to discharge following an acute episode, patients should be given a programme of self-medication.

- Patients entering maintenance therapy should have their medication titrated to the minimum effective dose.

- Ideally, patients should not be receiving more than one antipsychotic during maintenance therapy.

- Maintenance therapy should include a regular assessment of the patient and the active management of medication side-effects.

- Medication should only be switched to a depot preparation if compliance is a problem in the outpatient setting, or if the patient requests this type of prescription.

- Assertive outreach programmes may be necessary in the first few months of maintenance therapy to promote compliance.

- Ideally, anticholinergic medication should not normally be necessary in maintenance therapy.

- Causes of relapse should be assessed and adjunctive medication prescribed where appropriate.

- If the dose of antipsychotic has to be increased during a crisis, this should be reassessed once the symptoms improve.

- Patients should ideally be assessed every 6 months for cognitive function, behavioural problems and general health.

- The family should be appropriately involved in the care and management of the patient.

- Medication counselling has an important role in maintenance therapy.

Figure 7.16   Points of special note in treatment of schizophrenia

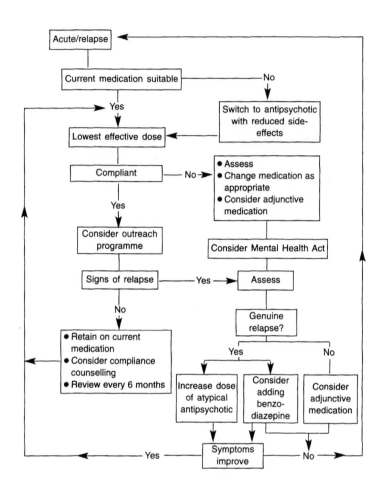

Figure 7.17   Prescribing algorithm for schizophrenia:
stabilisation phase, stable phase

DATE (DAY 1) / /	1	2	3	4	5	6	7	8	9	10	11	12	13	14	3/52	4/52	5/52	3/12	6/12
Assessment																			
• general medical history																			
• general physical/health assessment																			
• psychiatric history																			
• mental state examination																			
• social support																			
• substance misuse																			
• risk (re)assessment																			
• risk management plan																			
• measures: HoNOS																			
BPRS																			
other																			
• neurological evaluation																			
• medical investigations: full blood count																			
liver function tests																			
thyroid function test																			
drug screen																			
other																			
Medication																			
• compliance																			
• review																			
• dosage +/–																			
• adjunctive medication																			
Side effects (rate 1–3) 1 = valid; 2 = moderate; 3 = severe																			
• akathisia (restlessness)																			
• dystonia (abnormal face and body movements)																			
• tardive dyskinesia (grimacing, tongue rolling, bizarre facial and body movements)																			
• parkinsonism (mask-like expression, tremor of limbs, pill-rolling movement of fingers)																			
• other (refer to notes)																			
• LUNSERS																			
Symptoms (rate 1–3) 1 = solid; 2 = moderate; 3 = severe																			
+ve: delusions, hallucinations, thought disorder, inappropriate affect																			
–ve: lack of motivation, social withdrawal, poverty of speech, blunt or flat affect																			
• BPRS																			

continued overleaf

Figure 7.18 Schizophrenia – community care pathway documentation

	DAYS 1–14														WEEKS			MONTHS		VARIANCE
DATE (DAY 1) / /	1	2	3	4	5	6	7	8	9	10	11	12	13	14	3/52	4/52	5/52	3/12	6/12	
Management																				
● key worker allocated																				
● CPA registration (if new service user)																				
● risk management plan																				
● telephone contact with carers																				
● face-to-face contact with carers																				
● carer(s) assessment																				
● CPA care plan																				
● letter/info to referring agent/GP																				
Information given to service user																				
● confidentiality																				
● CPA																				
● advocacy																				
MHA (where applicable)																				
● Supervision Register considered?																				
● S.25A considered?																				
Education (c = carers; s = service user)																				
● evaluate understanding of illness																				
● symptom management																				
● early warning signs/management plan																				
● stress management																				
● problem solving																				
● conflict resolution																				
● social skills																				
Continuing assessment and review																				
● CPA care plan: monitoring																				
● ongoing education/information																				
● compliance																				
● co-morbid conditions																				
● stressors																				
● financial, housing, social care needs																				
● carer's needs																				

Figure 7.18 Schizophrenia – community care pathway documentation (*continued*)

	WEEKS (stabilisation phase)														VARIANCE
	3	4	5	6	7	8	9	10	11	12	13	14	15	16	
DATE (WEEK) / /															
Continuing assessment															
● general physical/health assessment															
● mental state examination															
● social support															
● substance misuse															
● risk (re)assessment: harm to self															
harm to others															
vulnerability															
● medical investigations: drug screen															
other															
Medication															
● compliance															
● review															
● dosage +/−															
● adjunctive medication															
Side effects (rate 1–3) 1 = valid; 2 = moderate; 3 = severe															
● akathisia (restlessness)															
● dystonia (abnormal face and body movements)															
● tardive dyskinesia (grimacing, tongue rolling, bizarre facial and body movements)															
● parkinsonism (mask-like expression, tremor of limbs, pill-rolling movement of fingers)															
● other															
● LUNSERS															
Symptoms (rate 1–3) 1 = solid; 2 = moderate; 3 = severe															
+ve: delusions, hallucinations, thought disorder, inappropriate affect															
−ve: lack of motivation, social withdrawal, poverty of speech, blunt or flat affect															
● BPRS															

Figure 7.18 Schizophrenia – community care pathway documentation *(continued)*

							(stabilisation phase)								VARIANCE

WEEKS (stabilisation phase)														VARIANCE
DATE (WEEK 3) / /	3	4	5	6	7	8	9	10	11	12	13	14	15	16	
Management															
• GP review															
• comprehensive health assessment															
primary health care team/key worker															
• CPA review (discharge plan, inpatient)															
• outpatient review															
• telephone contact with carers															
• face-to-face contact with carers															
• information for GP															
Education interventions (c = carers; su = service users)															
• evaluate understanding of illness															
• symptom management															
• early warning signs/management plan															
• stress management															
• problem solving															
• conflict resolution															
• social skills															
Continuing review															
• CPA care plan: monitoring															
• ongoing educative/information															
• compliance															
• co-morbid conditions															
• stressors															
• financial, housing, social care needs															
• carer's needs/assessment															
• discharge from service															

BPRS = Brief Psychiatric Rating Scale   HoNOs = Health of the Nation Outcome Scores   LUNSERS = Liverpool University Neuroleptic Side Effect Rating Scale

Figure 7.18   Schizophrenia – community care pathway documentation *(continued)*

Dorset Community NHS Trust: community hospitals and district nursing integrated care pathways project

The third care pathway also hails from Dorset Community NHS Trust (1998b), but the staff involved are from the community hospitals. The process for the development of care pathways took a slightly different approach from that for the pathway developed for mental health. The areas chosen for pathways were allocated to individual community hospitals. The decisions for the allocation of the pathways were taken because these were areas of high volume or a perceived problem area that could be improved by the development of a pathway. The areas were as follows:

- Portland Hospital – early transfer from the District General Hospitals to GP beds;
- Blandford Hospital – minor injuries;
- Blandford Hospital – day surgery;
- Yeatman Hospital (Sherborne) – endoscopy;
- Weymouth Hospital – stroke rehabilitation;
- Several hospitals and district nursing – leg ulcers.

The aim was to develop the care pathway in one hospital and disseminate the pathway across all the community hospitals to provide continuity of care that was evidence based and of proven good quality.

The project started with the appointment of Carole Annetts as the project manager, and the setting up of a steering group including the Director of Nursing, the Director of Finance and senior managers from the Trust.

The approach to developing the pathway was as follows:

- Confirm the area for the development of the pathway.
- Identify the key people to work on the development of the pathway.
- Set objectives and goals for each area.

DORSET COMMUNITY NHS TRUST

DAY SURGERY ☐ (Tick Box) . . . . Hospital   Date. . . . . . .

SHORT STAY ☐

Consultant: . . . .

Operation: . . . .

ADDRESSOGRAPH LABEL

Your Named Nurse is:. . . . .   Contact Number:. . . . .

Age: Religion:	Next of Kin: Relationship:
If any of the details on the label above are incorrect please amend below:	Address: Home Telephone No.:
Home Telephone No.: Daytime No.:	Contact/Daytime No.:

HEALTH STATUS QUESTIONNAIRE

Please complete and sign questionnaire. If you require any further information please use contact number or raise any queries at your preopeative assessment. Please bring this form with you to the preoperative assessment.

PLEASE TICK CORRECT BOX ON QUESTIONS 1–20	NO	YES	DETAILS
1. Have you had any operations before?			If Yes, please discuss on admission
2. Do you wear contact lenses, hearing aid or have a pacemaker?			
3. Have you ever had any problems with anaesthetics?			
4. Has any of your family had problems with anaesthetics?			
5. Do you have asthma, bronchitis or other chest disease?			
6. Have you had a serious illness in the past such as heart disease, rheumatic fever, high blood pressure or diabetes?			
7. Do you get breathless or chest pain on exercise or at night?			
8. Do you get swollen ankles?			
9. Have you ever had liver disease or jaundice?			
10. Do you suffer from anaemia?			
11. Do you suffer from blood disorders such as clotting problems?			
12. Do you bruise easily?			
13. Have you ever had a convulsion or fit?			

Figure 7.19   Dorset Community NHS Trust:
health status questionnaire

14. Do you have problems with your hips or back?			
15. Are you currently taking drugs or other medications?			If Yes, please bring with you
16. Do you smoke? (how many per day)			
17. Do you drink alcohol? (how many units per day)			

18. If female – a) could you be pregnant?
       b) are you taking the contraceptive pill?
       c) are you taking HRT?			

19. Do you have any allergies?			
20. Do you understand the information given to you on the advice sheet?			
21. How tall are you?			
22. How much do you weigh?			
23. How will you get home?			
24. Who will take you home?			
25. Who will look after you in the first 24 hours?			
26. Do you have access to a telephone?			
27. Do you anticipate any difficulties in coping at home after your operation, that is dependent relatives, young children?			
28. Do you anticipate any problems with access to your home, toilet facilities, and so on?			
29. Do you have any concerns, which we should know about?			
30. Do you live more than 20 miles from the hospital?			If Yes, which is your nearest hospital?
31. Do you understand what operation you are having?			

I am aware that I am having a general anaesthetic/sedation. I know that I must not drive, make any important decisions or operate a cooker or other machinery for at least **24 hours.**

I am aware that I must have a responsible adult with me overnight.
My operation has been explained to me.

Signature: . . . .

Date: . . . .

Figure 7.19 *(continued)*

- Conduct a literature search, gathering any existing and relevant guidelines and pathways. Review and critically appraise the gathered evidence, guidelines and pathways.
- Map the process by direction observation.
- Re-engineer the process against the gathered evidence.
- Develop the pathway.
- Implement the pilot pathway.
- Review and revise the pathway as necessary.
- Implement the final pathway.
- Plan the ongoing review and revision.

The resulting care pathway for day surgery is illustrated in Figure 7.20. Every patient receives a copy of the health status questionnaire (Figure 7.19) where they are asked to complete, sign and bring their preoperative assessment. When the patient is admitted for surgery the pathway in Figure 7.20 is followed. When the patient attends for their outpatient follow-up appointment the remaining part of the pathway is completed (Figure 7.21).

Carole Annetts and Heather Purse, the Orthopaedic Nurse Practitioner, led this development. The final pathway is well referenced from a strong evidence base. The Trust have sought advice from other Trusts and in particular Chelsea and Westminster Healthcare NHS Trust.

Summary

Process mapping, as a baseline for all the Dorset Community NHS Trust pathways, proved to be a very valuable exercise as it identified variances in practice. The group working on the leg ulcer pathway, which included Erika Delgallo, Lyn Hayward and Carole Annetts, undertook the mammoth task of process mapping the care of leg ulcers in the community hospitals' outpatient clinics and the patients cared for in the community by the district nurses. The results demonstrated a very wide variation in treatments, many of which were neither evidence based nor good practice. Some of the issues that this pathway will have to address concern resources, access to the correct dressings, and training in current, evidence-based practice. The benefit to the patients will be the optimum treatment for their leg ulcer that is proven best practice.

The day surgery pathway is in the pilot stage and will undoubtedly be revised before the final version is reached. Once the pathway has been implemented following the revisions as a result of the pilot, it will be validated. This will be via a structured audit involving the review of at least 30 sets of patient records for each pathway, as described earlier in this chapter.

(Affix patient label)

Patient's Name.	Hospital. . . . .
Medical Record No.	Ward. . . . .
Sex. . . . . . D.O.B. . . . . Age	Consultant . . . .
Named Nurse	Pre-admission Assessment Date. . . . . .
Physiotherapist.	Admission Date. . . . .
Occupational Therapist	Discharge Date. . . . .

1. ABBREVIATIONS USED ON PATHWAY

ASA	American Society of Anaesthesiologists	MG	Myasthenia gravis
B/P	Blood pressure	MI	Myocardial infarction
CXR	Chest X-ray	MND	Motorneurone disease
CVA	Cerebral vascular accident	MS	Multiple sclerosis
DVT	Deep vein thrombosis	N/A	Not applicable
ECG	Electrocardiogram	N/S	Not suitable
FBC	Full blood count	PR	Per rectum
GA	General anaesthetic	PV	Per vagina
ICP	Integrated care pathway	U&E	Urea and electrolytes
IDD	Insulin-dependent diabetic	TED	Thromboembolic device
IV	Intravenous	TTO	Tablets to take out
LFT	Liver function test	V	Variation
LMP	Last menstrual period		

Guidelines for completing the ICP

ICPs are multidisciplinary plans for a given diagnosis or procedure, which identifies best practice to achieve high-quality care and patient-focused outcomes (goals).

This is a record for care for patients attending for day/short-stay surgery. This document is a medico-legal record, which will be kept with the patient during his or her stay and then filed with the case notes. It is meant to replace other existing forms of documentation. There is no need to duplicate the information recorded here elsewhere. It is not intended to replace individual clinical judgement or to be used as a standard for care.

When initiating or using the ICP

- Ensure you have completed the signature page (see over). This page serves as a medico-legal record of your signature as you are only required to initial the ICP.
- Initials. You will need to initial or sign to confirm that an intervention has been carried out and an outcome/goal achieved. Once you have initialled, you do not need to record what you have done anywhere else. If you do not carry out an intervention or meet an outcome/goal, you do not initial but record that a variation has occurred.
- Document variances in care.
- Variation/comments sheet – for indicating where an intervention has not been performed, for example, ECG *not* performed, or outcome/goal is *not* met, for example, not being fit for discharge. If a variation in care occurs, include reasons for the variation as well as any action taken.

Variance takes into account patient individuality. The ICP is a guideline and does not replace professional judgement

Figure 7.20   Dorset Community NHS Trust integrated care pathway (ICP) for day/short-stay surgery

DORSET COMMUNITY NHS TRUST

SIGNATURE PAGE

You must sign and complete this section *once* if you initial the ICP. Since you are only required to initial the ICP, rather than place your full signature, this page serves as a medical-legal record of your signature.

Signature	Printed name	Title	Initials

VARIANCE TRACKING SHEET

Date/Time	Reason for variation	Action taken	Initials

Figure 7.20 *(continued)*

DORSET COMMUNITY NHS TRUST

Age		Next of Kin:		GP:	
Religion		Address:		Address:	
Patient's Home Telephone No.:					
Patient's Daytime No.:		Contact No.:			
		Person collecting:		Tel. No.:	
		Telephone No.			

OUTPATIENT APPOINTMENTS:					
Date	Appointment		Time		Comments
Date of Surgery	Ward/Hospital		Admission Time		Comments

OUTPATIENT APPOINTMENT					
Discipline	Pathway	Date	Initial/time	Outcome	
Consultant	Consultation Surgery discussed with patient Patient's written consent obtained			Patient accepted onto care pathway	
Clinic nurse	Issues patient with relevant information Advise patient that: • Pre-asssessment appointment and Health Questionnaire will be sent to them one month prior to operation date. • To bring completed questionnaire to the pre-assessment appointment			Patient has written information about pending surgery	
Secretary/ admission officer	Puts patient name on waiting list Issues the pre-assessment appointment and date of operation Patients confirms pre-assessment appointment within five working days If no reply within five working days contact patient			Pre-assessment appointment 2–3 weeks prior to surgery Patient is admitted for surgery within 12 weeks	

PRE-ADMISSION ASSESSMENT	
Discipline	
Nurse	**Pre-assessment clinic:** Discuss preoperative questionnaire – date information obtained: / / *Initials* .... Day Surgery Pathway explained to patient. *Initials* .... Check that patient knows what surgery they will be admitted for. *Initials* .... Date information expires (12 weeks from the above date): / / Contact patient if surgery delayed (>12 weeks) to check update information date: / / *Initials* .... Additional information gained:

Figure 7.20 *(continued)*

DORSET COMMUNITY NHS TRUST

HEALTH ASSESSMENT			DATE / /	TIME	
Discipline	Condition	No problems Initial each box	Problems identified Initial each box used		Results
Nurse	Previous problems with anaesthetic. List:				
	Family problems with anaesthetics. List:				
			Refer to anaesthetist Initials:	Yes/No	
	Patient aged >80 years		Check: ECG U&E FBC Results to anaesthetist Initials:	Yes/No Yes/No Yes/No Yes/No	
	Asthma/Bronchitis/ Chest disease		Normal activity limited If well controlled: CXR Spirometry Results to anaesthetist Initials:	N/S Yes/No Yes/No Yes/No	
	Heart disease/ Rheumatic fever/M.I.		Chest pain at rest or walking on the flat If well controlled or only occurs under exceptional conditions request: ECG CXR Pacemaker in situ Refer results to anaesthetist Initials:	N/S Yes/No Yes/No Yes/No Yes/No	
	Hypertension/swollen ankles		Record B/P If >160/100 or >180/100 for Patients over 60 Refer to anaesthetist Initials:	Yes/No	
	Diabetes		If poorly controlled or I.D.D. Initials:	N/S	
	Muscle disease/ Progressive weakness		MS M.N.D. M.G Polio (history of assisted ventilation/ swallowing difficulties Initials:	N/S N/S N/S N/S	
	Breathlessness		Walking on flat or on greater exertion – Refer to: CXR Spirometry Results to anaesthetist Initials:	Yes/No Yes/No Yes/No	
	Liver disease/Jaundice		If jaundice due to gallstones Check – LFT Results to anaesthetist If Hepatitis B and C positive Initials:	Yes/No Yes/No N/S	
	Convulsions or fits		Epileptic fit within 1 year or with an anaesthetic If well controlled with medication Initials:	N/S OK	
	Problems with back or hips		Severely disabled Neck involvement inform anaesthetist Initials:	N/S Yes/No	

Figure 7.20 *(continued)*

DORSET COMMUNITY NHS TRUST

	HEALTH ASSESSMENT *continued*			
Discipline	Condition	No problems *Initial each box*	Problems identified *Initial each box used*	Results
Nurse	Fainting fits Record cause of fainting:		If on exercise or patient >60 years – Refer to anaesthetist Yes/No *Initials:*	
	Kidney/Urinary problems		If the reason for treatment OK If not check: U&E Yes/No Results to anaesthetist Yes/No Problem with micturition Yes/No Refer to anaesthetist Yes/No *Initials:*	
	Indigestion/Heartburn/ Regurgitation		Reliably diagnosed OK ? Prescription of H2 antagonist – discuss with anaesthetist Yes/No *Initials:*	
	C.V.A. Date:		Refer to anaesthetist Yes/No *Initials:*	
	Alcohol Record quantity		Advise patient of the limits. If reason to believe abusing – Check: LFTs Yes/No Results to anaesthetist Yes/No *Initials:*	
	Pregnant		Referring clinician aware Yes/No *Initials:*	
	Smokes How many per day		Advice given re reduction preop Yes/No *Initials:*	
	Concerns/problems with home situation on discharge		Record: Action taken: Problems resolved *Initials:*	
	Patient understands the information leaflet and has signed the Health Questionnaire sent to them. Health Questionnaire attached to ICP Yes/No *Initials:*		Record concerns Action taken *Initials:*	Health Questionnaire is signed
	Anaesthetist's comments:			

Figure 7.20 *(continued)*

DORSET COMMUNITY NHS TRUST

Discipline	PREOPERATIVE ASSESSMENT	DATE / /	TIME:
Nurse	Previous operations – list: Operation: Has patient been in hospital in the last six months Screen for MRSA Yes/No *Initials:. . . . .*	Date Yes/No Results	
	Medical history		
	List medications *including contraceptive pill		
Dr/Nurse Practitioner	Physical Examination: General appearance Circulation Heart Chest		
	Body mass = Body mass index if >34 Refer to anaesthetist – possible N/S Yes/No *Initials:. . . . .*		
Nurse	ASA Grading 1 & 2 – Acceptable Yes/No 3 – Refer to anaesthetist Yes/No 4 – N/S Yes/No *Initials:. . . . .*		
	List Allergies:		

Temperature:	Pulse:	Respiration:	B/P:
LMP:	Weight:	Height:	

Urinalysis results . . . .
Abnormal results identified. . . . .
Refer to anaesthetist   Yes/No
Initials:. . . . .

Patient is suitable for day surgery	**Yes/No**	*Initials:. . . . .*
If Yes continue with ICP		
If No refer back to: GP	Yes/No	*Initials:. . . . .*
Consultant	Yes/No	*Initials:. . . . .*

Figure 7.20 *(continued)*

DORSET COMMUNITY NHS TRUST

	PREOPERATIVE ASSESSMENT DATE / /	TIME:
Nurse	Ask patient:	
	Can he/she have time off work?	Yes/No
	Has patient arranged for someone to collect them?	Yes/No
	(put name and contact number on page 3)	
	Has patient someone who will stay with them for first 24 hours?	Yes/No
	Initials:	
	Patient has visited the unit	Yes/No
	Patient understands the need to fast	Yes/No
	Patient understands the need to bath or shower before admission	Yes/No
	Patient knows where to shave	Yes/No/NA
	Patient understands the need for comfortable clothing	Yes/No
	Patient has been given estimated length of stay	Yes/No
	OUTCOME: Patient can state preparation required for surgery	
	Discuss with patient the events of the day of surgery	Yes/No
	Discuss informed consent	Yes/No
	Discuss postoperative pain control and PR medication	Yes/No
	Discuss what to do in an emergency following discharge	Yes/No
	Discuss follow-up arrangements	Yes/No
	Discuss estimated time for return to normal activity – that is, work/driving/sport/sex	Yes/No
	Information leaflets given	Yes/No
	Inform patient of surgeon carrying out operation. . . . . State who.	
	OUTCOME: Patient can state details of hospital stay **Patient can state details of discharge**	
	Initials:.	
Physio-therapist	Does the patient need referral to other members of the multidisciplinary team?	Yes/No
	If Yes, list those contacted:	
	Initials:. . . . . *date*.	
Occupa-tional Therapist	**MULTIDISCIPLINARY ASSESSMENT** Assessment of patient's postoperative requirements List:	

DAY OF OPERATION	DATE / /	TIME
Nurse	Inform patient of layout of ward	Yes/No
	Check the patient has attended a preoperative assessment clinic	Yes/No
	If NO pre-assess patient as above.	
	Initials:	
	OUTCOME: The patient is pre-assessed before surgery	
	Review vital signs as per anaesthetist's instructions or recent illness Record any changes:	
	Report any changes to anaesthetist	Yes/No
	Initials:	
	Check allergies, if allergies apply red wrist band *Initials:*	
	Confirm discharge arrangements	Yes/No
	Any new problems identified. Action taken:	
	Initials:	

Figure 7.20 *(continued)*

DORSET COMMUNITY NHS TRUST

PREPARE PATIENT FOR THEATRE		TIME:
Nurse	Measure for TED stockings:	
	Right . . . . .cms Left . . . . . .cms	Initals:
	Varicose veins surgery – where required – measure for stockinette	
	Right . . . . . .cms Left . . . . . .cms	
	Apply TED Stockings:	Yes/No/NA
	Initals:	
	PREOPERATIVE CHECK LIST	
	Confirm nil by mouth time	
	Time of last solid food	
	Time of last clear fluids	
	Gown	Yes/No/NA
	Apply identification bracelet	Yes/No/NA
	Remove/cover jewellery	Yes/No/NA
	Remove cosmetics/nail varnish	Yes/No/NA
	Check operation site shaved	Yes/No/NA
	Check contact lenses removed	Yes/No/NA
	Identify any other prosthesis	Yes/No/NA
	Identify whether hearing aid/glasses are remaining until in theatre	Yes/No/NA
	If Yes, state	
	Dentures removed	Yes/No/NA
	Crowns/Caps/Loose teeth identified	
	List:	
	8 7 6 5 4 3 2 1 | 1 2 3 4 5 6 7 8	
	8 7 6 5 4 3 2 1 | 1 2 3 4 5 6 7 8	
	Check allergies	Yes/No
	If Yes, state	
	Apply red wrist band	
	Bladder emptied:	
	Time:	
	Consent form signed	Yes/No
	Notes with patient	Yes/No
	X-rays with patient	Yes/No/NA
	Initals:	
Surgeon	Explain procedure	Yes/No
	Explain use of diathermy/tourniquet if appropriate	Yes/No
	Patient reads, understands and signs consent form, if not already signed at outpatient appointment	Yes/No
	Marks operation site	Yes/No
	Initals:	

Figure 7.20 *(continued)*

DORSET COMMUNITY NHS TRUST

Anaesthetist	Ensures patient is fit for surgery	Yes/No
	Discusses type of anaesthetic	Yes/No
	Discusses postoperative pain relief	Yes/No
	OUTCOME: All preoperative checks were completed	
	Initials: . . . . Date / / Time:	

THEATRE		**TIME**
Anaesthetic Nurse	Checks preoperative list completed	Yes/No
	Checks name band with the patient	Yes/No
	Checks operation details	Yes/No
	Checks operation site marked	Yes/No
	Checks allergies	Yes/No
	Initials:	
Anaesthetist/ Anaesthetic Nurse	Induction time	
	Type of anaesthetic – GA/Caudal/Epidural/Spinal/Local block/Sedation	
	Airway – Endotracheal tube/Laryngeal mask/Oral airway/Mask only	
	IV Access Site – Y Can/Venflon/Other:	
	ECG/Pulse Oxymetry/B/P recording	
	Patient position: Prone/Supine/Lithotomy/Side	
	Diathermy pad – Thigh/Buttock/Abdomen Right/Left	
	Heel pads Yes/No Arm Pads Yes/No Back supports Yes/No	
	Calf stimulators Yes/No	
	Other:	
	Tourniquet TIME ON TIME OFF SITE	
	Right	
	Left	
	Intra-operative analgesia given Drug Time	
	TIME OPERATION COMMENCED	
	TIME OPERATION FINISHED	
	Initials:	

Figure 7.20 *(continued)*

DORSET COMMUNITY NHS TRUST

THEATRE continued	
Surgeon	**OPERATION/PROCEDURE:** Skin closure . . . . Dressings . . . . Drains . . . . Packs . . . . **POSTOPERATIVE INSTRUCTIONS** *Initials:* . . . . Date / / Time:
Scrub Nurse Runner	**Instrument checks:** **Swab, needle and other item checks:** First count Second count First count Second count *Initials:* . . . . *Initials:* . . . . *Initials:* . . . . *Initials:* . . . . *Initials:* . . . . *Initials:* . . . . *Initials:* . . . . *Initials:* . . . . Informs the surgeon all checks correct *Initials:* . . . .
	Attach CSSD Coding stickers

Figure 7.20 *(continued)*

DORSET COMMUNITY NHS TRUST

IMMEDIATE POST OPERATIVE CARE		TIME:
Nurse	Airway – laryngeal mask/Guedel in situ	Yes/No
	Airway rejected at	
	Time patient regained consciousness	
	Cannula in situ	Yes/No
	Time cannula removed	
	Oxygen given	Yes/No
	Oxygen given at . . . .%	
	Vital signs monitored	Yes/No
	Attach print out	Yes/No

Nurse				
	Blood loss: Wound/PR/PV/Packs/Drains – circle			
	Checked	Time		Comment
	1.			
	2.			
	3.			
	4.			
	5.			

PAIN CONTROL
Record observation of patient's pain

KEY
Pain Levels:
1. Pain Free
2. Just noticeable
3. Moderate
4. Severe
5. Excruciating

Time	Level of pain (circle)
1.	1 2 3 4 5
2.	1 2 3 4 5
3.	1 2 3 4 5
4.	1 2 3 4 5
5.	1 2 3 4 5

Postoperative medication given

Drug   Time

Time discharge from Recovery . . . .

Initials: . . . .

Ward Nurse	Time	Wound check/ Action taken	Observations				Pain/action taken	Initials
			T	P	R	B/P		

Figure 7.20 *(continued)*

DORSET COMMUNITY NHS TRUST

Nurse	DISCHARGE ASSESSMENT			DATE / /	TIME:
	Pre-discharge check				
		Time of assessment		Time of re-assessment	
		Yes *Initial*	No *Initial*	Yes *Initial*	No *Initial*
	Patient alert and orientated				
	Observations stable				
	Patient is mobile				
	Patient is pain free				
	Fluids tolerated				
	Patient has passed urine				
	Wound/PV/PR loss				
	Dressings given				
	Cannula removed				
	Escort contacted				
	Time				
	Follow-up appointment arranged				
	Date / / Transfer date to page 3 of ICP				
	Insert date on district spell				
	Practice nurse letter given				
	Discharge summary given				
	Advice leaflets given				
	Patient agrees to 24 hour home check:				
	Contact no.				
	Contact time				
	TTOs given and explained List:				
	Prescription attached to ICP				
	Time of discharge . . . .**Destination** . . . .**Initials**				
	OUTCOME: Patient is fit for discharge **Patient has all the information required to ensure a safe recovery at home**				

Figure 7.20 *(continued)*

DORSET COMMUNITY NHS TRUST

PRESCRIPTION SHEET

Drug – approved name		Dose and frequency		Time ▼							
		Route	Duration								
Pharmacy	Doctor's signature	Date									
Drug – approved name		Dose and frequency		Time ▼							
		Route	Duration								
Pharmacy	Doctor's signature	Date									

ONCE ONLY PRESCRIPTION

Date	Drug – approved name	Dose	Route	Doctor's signature	Time to be given	Time given	Given by	Pharmacy	

AS REQUIRED, FREQUENTLY NEEDED AND VARIABLE DOSE DRUGS

Drug – approved name		Dose and frequency		Date	Time	Date	Time	Date	Time
Pharmacy	Doctor's signature	Route	Duration						

ATTACH TO FORM

Figure 7.20 *(continued)*

DORSET COMMUNITY NHS TRUST

Nursing Notes for overnight stay

HOME CHECK		DATE / /	TIME:
		Advice given/action taken	Initials
Named Nurse	Any post operative problems? List:		
	Any problems related to managing at home? List:		
	Pain controlled	Yes/No	
	Patient requires further information List:		
	Patient requires further follow-up **OUTCOME: Patient is satisfied with pain control Patient is able to manage at home**	Yes/No Person Date Time	

Post discharge wound check (if necessary)		DATE / /	TIME:
Nurse	Reason for check/redressing: Action taken: *Initials:* . . . . **OUTCOME: Wound healing and free from infection**		

Figure 7.20 *(continued)*

DORSET COMMUNITY NHS TRUST

OUTPATIENT POSTOPERATIVE ASSESSMENT FORM

Name . . . .

Hospital . . . .

No. . . . .

	YES	NO	N/A	COMMENT/ACTION
Patient happy with outcome of operation				
Improvement in gait/joint				
Level of activity improved				
Return to work				
Wound healed				
Tenderness – surrounding area				
Swelling – surrounding area				
Calf tenderness				
Pain Constant Intermittent Variable Aggravating activity				
Numbness/paraesthesia Constant Intermittent Specific weakness Sensory nerve loss Reflexes				
MOVEMENT AT SITE OF OPERATION	**Active** Y/N	**Passive** Y/N		
Flexion				
Extension				
Abduction				
Adduction				
Rotation				
FUNCTION BELOW OP. SITE				
Flexion				
Extension				
Abduction				
Adduction				
Rotation				
DISCHARGE				
Advice given re: future care				**Document:**
Patient has no postoperative complications				
Patient happy to be discharged				
Is a further appointment required				**Next appointment:**
Discharge letter to GP completed				
Date sent / /				

Additional Information

FORM COMPLETED BY . . . .   **GRADE** . . . .

DATE . . . .

Figure 7.21   Dorset Community NHS Trust –
outpatient postoperative assessment form

Conclusion

All three examples of pathways demonstrate a structured approach to their development and implementation, as well as to the resulting improvement to treatment and care for the patient. The pathways all look a little different as they have been developed to meet a local need. Some pathways will result in a change to staffing, the environment and the processes of care in order to establish a pathway that is best practice.

Pathways predict the care journey for the patient and their carers. Sharing the pathway with patients and carers will lead to patients receiving better information on which to make informal choices about their care. This will ultimately improve the whole experience for patients and their carers.

ICPs are the vehicles for linking evidence-based clinical guidelines, through multidisciplinary pathways, to achieving ongoing clinical outcome measurement and demonstrating what clinical governance is all about.

References

Berwick, D. M. 1989 Continuous Improvement as an Ideal in Health Care, *New England Journal of Medicine*, **320**: 53–6.

Dorset Community Trust 1998a *Personalised Care Management.* Project Group: Severe Mental Illness. Pilot: Schizophrenia. Working Documents. Dr J. Guenther. Eli Lilly & Co. Bournemouth: Dorset Community Trust.

Dorset Community Trust 1998b *Community Hospitals and District Nursing Integrated Care Pathways Project.* Bournemouth: Dorset Community Trust.

Salisbury Health Care NHS Trust 1998 *Breast Care Pathway.* Salisbury: Salisbury Health Care N HS Trust.

Zander, K. and McGill, R. 1994 Critical and Anticipated Recovery Paths: Only the Beginning, *Nursing Management*, **25**(8): 34–40.

Further reading

Alexander, J. 1997 *Is their Consent Informed? – Techniques and Best Practice*, London: IBC UK Conferences.

Avis, M., Bond, M. and Arthur A. 1997 *Questioning Patient Satisfaction: An Empirical Investigation in Two Outpatients Clinics*, London: Elsevier Science.

Berwick, D. M. 1996 A Primer on Leading the Improvement of Systems, *British Medical Journal*, **12**: 619–22.

Chelsea and Westminser Healthcare Trust 1997 *Integrated Care Pathway: Total Knee Replacement*.

King, M. 1997 *What Advice Should Patient Information Leaflets Include?*, Day Surgery Unit, Royal Devon and Exeter Hospital.

Layton, A. J. and Morgan, G. 1995 The Nuts and Bolts of Patient Focused Care, *Clinical Protocols*, Book 2. Nottingham: Centre for Health Service Management, University of Nottingham.

Penn, S. *et al.* 1966 *Principles of Day Surgery Nursing*, Oxford: Blackwell Science.

Royal College of Surgeons of England 1992 *Guidelines for Day Case Surgery*.

Sutherland, E. 1996 *Day Surgery: A Handbook for Nurses*, Baillière Tindall.

Zander, K. 1992 Critical Pathway, in M. M. Melum and M. K. Sinioris (eds) *Total Quality Management*. New York: The Health Care Pioneer, American Hospital Publishing.

Useful addresses
(See also Chapter 5)

National Guidelines Clearing House (USA)
A comprehensive database of evidence-based clinical practice guidelines and related documents: http://www.guidelines.gov/index.asp

National Pathways Association
Priory Hospitals Group, Broadwater Park,
Denham, Uxbridge. Middx UB9 5HB
Tel: (01895) 836339
Membership secretary: Carole Cairns

8

Accreditation, with a Difference

This chapter explores the developments of accreditation from its origins in the USA to its adaptation for use in the UK and to a system of accreditation with a difference. As discussed in Chapter 5 the need for a multidisciplinary approach to the implementation of evidence-based practice, as well as a fundamental understanding of the process and use of research, is central to the provision of good-quality care. Accreditation is proven as part the process of ensuring good-quality care in large acute hospitals, but this chapter also explores accreditation with a difference, a system that has its roots in the provision of research-based practice delivered by the multidisciplinary team in small, defined clinical areas.

The chapter starts by tracing the history of accreditation on its journey from the USA to the UK and on through the years to the introduction of the principles of accreditation into Practice Development Units (PDUs). However, the adventure does not stop here, instead moving on to the development of a system of accreditation of nursing homes as PDUs. This is still in its pilot stage, but it is nevertheless an exciting development for two nursing homes in Dorset.

Background and history

Accreditation is 'the process by which an Agency or Organisation evaluates and recognises a programme of study or institution as meeting predetermined standards' (WHO, 1986).

Every accreditation system uses a process for measuring an organisation against preselected standards. First, the standards are set by the accrediting organisation, and then the organisation seeking accreditation works towards their achievement. When invited into the organisation, the surveyors will establish whether the standards have been met and award accreditation to the organisation if they comply with the standards.

The first accreditation system started in the USA in 1913, being established to ensure 'that those institutions having the highest ideals may have proper recognition before the profession' (Roberts *et al.*, 1987). The standards that made up the early accreditation systems were focused on creating an acceptable environment in which doctors could practise. This focus on the doctors then moved to the patient and the organisation of the facilities, personnel, procedures and policies that would result in good-quality patient care.

In the 1960s, as a result of changes in the financing of health care through Medicaid and Medicare, the Joint Commission on the Accreditation of Healthcare in the USA changed in order to address the issues of public regulation. There are now a number of health care accreditation organisations:

- in the USA, the Joint Commission on the Accreditation of Healthcare Organizations (JCAHO);
- in Canada, the Canadian Council on Health Facilities Accreditation (CCHFA);
- in Australia, the Australian Council on Healthcare Standards (ACHS);
- in New Zealand, the Joint Commission on Accreditation for Hospitals;
- in the UK, several accreditation systems including:

  - the King's Fund Organisational Audit, London,
  - the Hospital Accreditation Programme, Bristol University.

The JCAHO in the USA was the first system, from which the Australian, Canadian and New Zealand systems were developed. The King's Fund Organisational Audit was developed largely from the Australian model, and the Bristol University system from the Canadian model.

In the USA, accreditation is linked with funding. If standards fall below predetermined levels, the hospital organisation is in jeopardy of losing federal or state funding. These hospital accreditation programmes demand evidence that a hospital has some system of quality assurance. Medical audits have developed into medical record audits, which examine in detail the records post-discharge. Today, these systems are often computerised. Some of these hospitals employ a team of people to examine the records and report their findings to a Quality Assurance Committee

Accreditation is a method that is used to address the issues of evaluating the quality of health services provided. It is the:

> professional and national recognition reserved for facilities that provide high quality health care. This means that the particular health care facility has voluntarily sought to be measured against high professional standards and is in substantial compliance with them. (Limongelli, 1983)

All systems of accreditation are voluntary and are made up of three stages:

- *Stage 1:* the development of organisational standards concerned with the systems and process for the delivery of health care. The standards are developed in consultation with the relevant professional organisations and are revised annually to ensure that they reflect current health care trends.
- *Stage 2:* implementation of the standards. The various accreditation agencies provide support material and guidelines on the interpretation of the standards.
- *Stage 3:* the evaluation of compliance with standards by means of a survey, conducted by a team of trained surveyors chosen for their expertise in a specific health care service.

Accreditation differs from both registration and licensing in that it is not a statutory but a voluntary system. Accreditation was established in the UK in 1995.

King's Fund Organisational Audit

In November 1988, the quality assurance programme at the King's Fund Centre organised a conference to consider the development of national standards for the organisation of health care. Six District Health Authorities – Brighton, East Dorset, North Derbyshire, North West Hertfordshire, Nottingham (Queen's Medical Centre) and West Dorset – were selected to participate in the project. These were joined by two independent hospitals, the Hospital of St John and St Elizabeth and AMI Chiltern.

A project steering group looked critically at existing systems for setting and monitoring national standards, principally those models of accreditation used in the USA, Canada and Australia. The group considered the Australian system to be the most appropriate on which to build its own model, with reference to the Canadian system as appropriate.

The King's Fund Organisational Audit was thus established in 1989, with the development of national standards for acute hospitals. By 1994, approximately 150 hospitals had been surveyed by the King's Fund Organisational Audit, which was extended into health centres and GP practices in 1992 with the Primary Health Care Project, into learning disabilities in 1993, and into community hospitals with a pilot study in 1994.

The King's Fund Organisational Audit system of accreditation is based on:

- standards set for each department, service and group of professionals;
- standards to monitor philosophy and objectives, organisation and administration, polices and procedures, staff, the environment, facilities and equipment, patients' rights and special needs;
- an audit of the structure of the organisation.

Until recently accreditation had concentrated on the environment and organisational structures, and concluded that if these standards were met, it should be possible to ensure good-quality patient care. However, there is an ongoing development and movement towards standards concerning process, outcome and clinical effectiveness. In the Joint Commission's *Comprehensive Accreditation Manual for Hospitals* (1997), an example of this approach is taken from the section on patient care.

The flow chart for the care of a patient (Figure 8.1) illustrates care decision making, the planning of care, the interventions and the decision-making process based on:

- an ongoing assessment and reassessment of the child throughout his or her contact with the organisation;
- ongoing data analysis to determine the patient's needs.

Figure 8.3 illustrates the provision of a variety of hospital care and treatment services that the patient has received.

Preparing for accreditation gives an organisation the opportunity to reflect on what has been achieved, to identify the gaps and to work towards closing them. The most valuable part of this is the process of reflection on care during the preparation phase. There is also the opportunity for the organisation to be reviewed or surveyed by highly skilled people who work within the NHS, have trained as surveyors and offer an independent, objective view of the organisation against preset standards.

Accreditation with a difference

This system of accreditation has been developed by the Centre for Development of Nursing Policy and Practice at the University of Leeds. It was the first system of accreditation for Nursing Development Units (NDUs) and Practice Development Units (PDUs) in the UK.

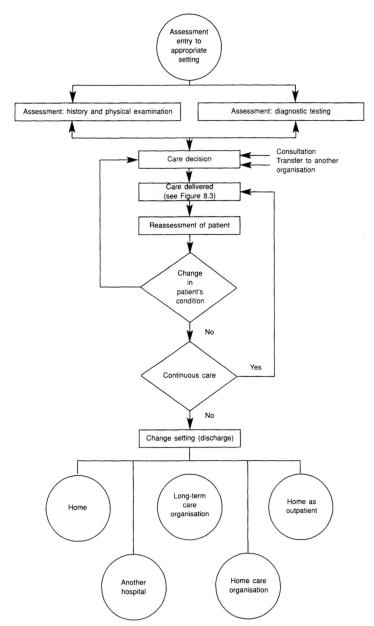

This flowchart and Figure 8.3 represent most of the important processes and activities, particularly the risk points, in the care of patients functions.

Figure 8.1   Care of patients function (Joint Commission, 1997)

Practical application

The flowchart (Figure 8.1) for the care of patients function illustrates care decision making, the primary process in effective, appropriate care. The care planning, orders and interventions shown result from a decision-making process based on:

- ongoing assessment and reassessment of the patient throughout her contact with the organisation; and
- ongoing data analysis to determine the patient's needs.

For the 4 year old girl who was severely injured in an automobile accident, on completion of her assessment in the paediatric intensive care unit (PICU), initial care decisions were made according to PICU protocols. Planning to meet the child's critical care needs began immediately upon her arrival in the PICU and was updated to reflect changes in her condition throughout her stay in the hospital.

The second chart (Figure 8.3) illustrates provision of a variety of hospital care and treatment services. In addition to medical care, the child received:

- emergency trauma services (the full range of services available to any trauma patient);
- operative and other procedures services[1] (thoracic surgery, insertion of central venous lines, insertion of chest tubes, evacuation of cerebral haematoma, insertion of intracerebral pressure monitoring catheters);
- nutrition care (through central line, gastostomy tube, and orally);
- nursing care (trauma team, PICU, paediatric unit);
- intensive care;
- rehabilitation (passive range of motion initially in PICU; full range of physical rehabilitation services including chest physiotherapy later); and
- respiratory care (ranging from full ventilatory support, including arterial blood gases in the emergency room and PICU, to incentive spirometry during her stay on the paediatric unit).

Care planning was updated to reflect the child's progress in key areas.

1. **operative and other procedures** Includes operative and other invasive and non-invasive procedures, such as radiotherapy, hyperbaric treatment, CAT scan, and MRI, that place the patient at risk. The focus here is on procedures and therefore is not meant to include medications that place patients at risk.

Figure 8.2   Practical application (Joint Commission, 1997)

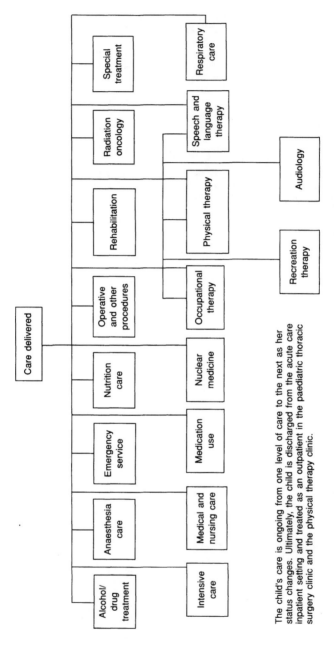

The child's care is ongoing from one level of care to the next as her status changes. Ultimately, the child is discharged from the acute care inpatient setting and treated as an outpatient in the paediatric thoracic surgery clinic and the physical therapy clinic.

Figure 8.3 Types of care delivered in care of patients function (Joint Commission, 1997)

Background information concerning NDUs and PDUs

The first NDU in the UK was established at Burford, Oxford in 1981 (Pearson, 1988) led by Alan Pearson as the Nursing Officer and Dr Sue Pembrey as the Clinical Practice Development Nurse 'at the Oxford Health Authority. Burford is a small community hospital, which at the time was under the threat of closure. The approach used at Burford was influenced by the work of Lydia Hall at the Loeb Centre in New York, and the centres at Rush University and Rochester University in the USA. Other key people in the NDU movement are Stephen Wright and his colleagues at Tameside Hospital. The Tameside team identified some key principles necessary for success, including (Purdy *et al.*, 1988):

- access to opportunities for personal development through a rolling programme organised with the support of continuing education;
- sticking to plans laid;
- funding;
- peer support through groupings of various sorts;
- evaluation to assess progress.

One of the benefits of this approach was demonstrated by the Tameside NDU in 1989. This unit had a waiting list of nurses who wanted to work on the NDU. However, the NDU on Beeson Ward at the Radcliffe Infirmary, Oxford, led by Sue Pembrey, was closed in 1989 as the managers were not convinced that the approach was valuable, even though the research contradicted this view. Coincidentally, the King's Fund Centre was at the same time offering 'pump priming' for 3 years for NDUs, and Brighton, Camberwell, Southport and West Dorset were successful in gaining grants of £90,000 each to support their development over a period of 3 years. By 1992, the Department of Health was also funding 30 NDUs around the country.

NDUs aim to become 'centres of nursing excellence' in their hospital, neighbourhood or health authority. They launch and evaluate experiments in good practice, supported by sound education, management and research. Close relationships with other health staff are also fostered (Salvage, 1989). NDUs are based on the notion that the culture of practice is underpinned by nursing values and beliefs (Allsopp *et al.*, 1998).

Nursing is part of a multidisciplinary, multi-agency system that provides health care, and in this context there are very few issues that can be described as purely nursing. The clinicians from various professional backgrounds need to develop practice together as a team to meet the needs of the patient. This, combined with the health service agenda dominated by the need for patient-centred care, greater user involvement, clinical audit, clinical effectiveness, cost-effectiveness and evidence-based practice, leads logically to the notion of the PDU.

The drivers for a PDU are:

- clinical leadership
- shared multidisciplinary vision and philosophy
- the empowerment of patients
- the empowerment of staff
- the identification of a need to change, with a planned approach to change
- a strong commitment to quality
- the development of research-based practice
- the dissemination of good practice
- the evaluation of practice
- the evaluation of change.

The nursing development accreditation scheme at the University of Leeds

The majority of the King's Fund Centre NDUs were situated within the south of England, with just a few in the north. This prompted the Yorkshire Regional Health

Authority to respond by developing a programme for those units wishing to become NDUs.

The Nursing Directorate at Yorkshire Health created an NDU scheme that had the added benefit of accreditation. Unlike the King's Fund, Yorkshire Health was unable to 'pump prime' organisations financially. Instead, it gave continual support and direction to the developing units.

The accreditation of NDUs was seen as a major step forward for nursing. The 'Yorkshire' scheme was the first of its kind in the UK to offer nurses an objective assessment of their clinical developments. Accreditation was awarded to those units whose innovation and creativity had made inroads into nursing and the delivery of patient care.

The closure of Yorkshire Regional Health Authority saw the Nursing Directorate move from a regional base to an academic setting, in 1993 becoming the Institute of Nursing at the University of Leeds. The creation of the Institute of Nursing meant that, in the future, developments would become national, with a potential to develop internationally.

The spread of NDUs and PDUs has grown dramatically in terms of both specialty and geography. Specialties include:

- drug addiction
- forensic psychiatry
- acute mental health
- elderly mental health
- learning disabilities
- intensive care units
- special care baby units
- surgical wards
- medical units/wards
- elderly wards/units
- paediatrics; rehabilitation and young disabled units
- community mental health teams
- community nursing teams
- housing associations and nursing homes.

The geographical spread of the scheme reaches from Hexham and Newcastle in the north of England to Dorset in the south, Liverpool in the west and Bridlington in the east. More recently, the scheme has spread to Galway in Southern Ireland.

The accreditation scheme is the product of several years of development originating from the work at Yorkshire Health. The process of accreditation is constantly under review and takes place through reflection on visits undertaken, observer feedback, peer review, a formal bi-annual review of criteria, and the Centre's annual review as a department of the University of Leeds. The accreditation criteria are further supported by the findings of *A Delphi Survey of Optimum Practice in Nursing, Midwifery and Health Visiting* (Manchester University, 1994). The accreditation team also publishes an Annual Report for public scrutiny.

Why bother with accreditation?

The Centre's accreditation has a national track record in developing nursing practice and contributing to nursing policy. Clinicians are under no illusions concerning the difficulties of integrating good ideas into the reality of health care delivery. The accreditation process enables the critical independent assessment of a PDU. This assessment goes beyond a process of ticking boxes, which does not reflect the complex nature of practice. Instead, it is a form of peer review against explicit criteria. Accreditation sets a standard. The validity of these criteria rests with the units, which have contributed to their development and to the supporting literature. They are based on a systems approach to organisational development, which reflects the needs of patients, nurses and the other members of the health care team, and on the beliefs established in the principles for achieving best practice, which are set out below.

Principles for achieving best practice

Best practice is the best achievable practice in a given setting. It is influenced by social, economic, political and environmental factors and is dynamic, as the boundary of 'achievable' is constantly redefined as a result of developments in practice. 'Achievable' incorporates the principles of efficiency and effectiveness.

Best practice can only be achieved by empowering the patient. This empowerment is dependent on a strategy that is focused on the patient's participation in individualised plans of care. It incorporates developing staff, facilitating risk taking, encouraging innovation, and evaluation of the impact of new or changed practice on the patient's wellbeing and self-direction.

There are several principles to achieving best practice:

- The process of achieving best practice should be strategically planned.
- The strategy should centre on empowering the patient.
- It requires a multitude of approaches.
- All approaches should incorporate the dissemination of practices that have been tried, tested and evaluated as being successful.
- Developments in practice must be seen to be led and owned by clinical staff.
- All approaches should have links with research and higher education, as well as having organisational support.
- The strategic focus on empowering patients through developing practice enables the development of education, research and management.
- Developments in practice should incorporate interagency and multidisciplinary collaboration.
- Achievement of best practice is not a competitive process but is dependent on networking.
- The strategy should incorporate the process by which best practice influences and is integrated into policy making.

Achieving the criteria ensures that the NDU or PDU is robust enough to ride the waves of change in health care policy in order to reach its expected goals.

The accreditation process

The accreditation process is inextricably linked to a supportive framework for practice development, which includes:

- a practice development network;
- links with those units which have achieved accreditation;
- the team at the Centre.

The accreditation team

Accreditation is led by the accreditation team, but in the longer term functions through self-assessment and peer review. The accreditation team is drawn from the Centre, other academic institutions, the National Health Service and the independent health sector. Its members have expertise in the following areas:

- international health care;
- leadership;
- management – general management, nursing management, commissioning and the Trust Board;
- medicine;
- nursing practice – primary, secondary and tertiary care, adult care, elderly care, mental health, learning disabilities, and children's and women's health;
- nursing theory;
- policy development;
- research and development;
- service and practice evaluation.

There are currently 10 members of the accreditation team, who are responsible for developing and managing the accreditation process and for awarding accreditation. The process is supported by a panel of six assessors.

Achievement of accreditation

The process of accreditation is offered in two stages.

- *Stage 1* – Recognition, for those units which, the accreditation team believes by their submission, are able to achieve accreditation, but on the assessment visit are found to require further time to achieve fully all the criteria. Most units achieve recognition at the first visit, a few receiving full accreditation immediately.
- *Stage 2* is awarded on achievement of all the stated criteria (listed below) for a period of 2 years.

Costs of accreditation

The cost of accreditation is spread over the period of time it takes to become accredited (preferably within 2 years). The first payment occurs when the unit comes forward as a PDU for accreditation, the second when it goes forward for recognition, and the final payment when the unit goes forward for full accreditation.

Criteria for accreditation

The following criteria must be met in order to achieve accreditation:

1. The unit is identified as a defined area or team such as a ward, clinic, community team or GP practice.
2. The team members have chosen the accreditation approach themselves.
3. An NDU or PDU leader is identified who will lead the team in the development, evaluation and dissemination of their work and will have authority for practice within the unit.

4. The team view this concept of change as a positive experience.
5. The accreditation philosophy is used to determine the conceptual framework for organising and developing best practice through decentralised decision making and both staff and patient empowerment.
6. Personal development plans are produced for each member of the team.
7. The business plan includes the process for disseminating evaluated practices both within the organisation and externally.
8. The NDU or PDU operates within baseline resources comparable to those of other clinical care settings within the organisation in order to enable the transferability of developments.
9. The unit's business plan identifies the resource requirements to achieve accreditation, in terms of time, expertise and financial support.
10. Developments within the unit are evaluated and reviewed in terms of their impact on the patient, organisation and staff and the Board or senior management team is informed.
11. The unit should have developed a research-based approach to practice that incorporates a spirit of enquiry and the critiquing and application of research findings leading to a greater participation in individual and collaborative research.
12. There should be a collaboration with higher education to formulate theory and develop staff.
13. The multidisciplinary team should ensure that resources are managed efficiently and effectively, and should facilitate developments.
14. The team needs to act as an agent for change within the organisation, the region and nationally, publicising its success to promote the value of best practice.
15. A steering group is required which must include the NDU/PDU leader, the Chief Executive or Director of Nursing, a senior manager within the organisation and the link member from higher education.

The accreditation journey

The first step is to contact the Centre for the Development of Nursing Policy and Practice, based at the University of Leeds (see Useful address), to express interest. At this stage, there is a need to discuss costs and to decide whether the unit will need consultancy support to prepare the submission. The preparation offered by the Centre is a half-day diagnostic visit resulting in a written report, and then a follow-up visit with workshops if required, and support for the preparation of the submission (Figure 8.4).

The submission must include:

- Evidence of how each criterion is being achieved, including:
  - the NDU leader's job description or role specification;
  - the NDU action or business plan (criterion 7).

- A statement from senior management covering how the organisation's responsibilities as a host organisation are met:
  - incorporating the NDU or PDU into the strategic development of nursing within the organisation;
  - supporting the NDU or PDU in evaluating the impact of its activity on the wider organisation's service delivery;
  - marketing the NDU or PDU's activity and co-ordinating public relations;
  - protecting the NDU or PDU from undue stress related to its profile as a national leader;
  - resourcing specific activity related to agreed development programmes.

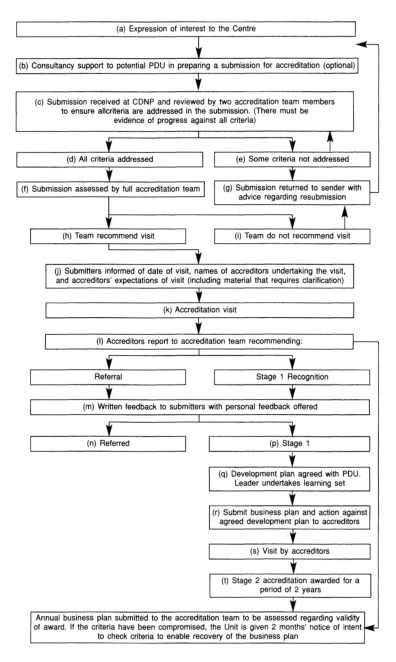

Figure 8.4   The accreditation journey

- A statement from the link education department detailing how the following responsibilities are met:
  - ensuring that the relationship is a reciprocal one;
  - contributing to the advancement of nursing knowledge;
  - disseminating advancements in nursing evaluated by the NDU through its student programmes;
  - ensuring that advancements in the NDU reach a wider audience through publication and educational activities.

The submission is then sent to the accreditation team and reviewed by two members of the team. They look for evidence of progress against all the criteria. If this is the case, the full accreditation team will organise an appropriate time to visit the unit. If some of the criteria are not addressed, the submission is returned to the sender with advice regarding its resubmission.

When the submission has been accepted, the unit goes through to Stage 1 – recognition.

Stage 1 – Recognition

At this stage, the development plan is agreed with the NDU or PDU. The leader is offered a place on the NDU or PDU 'leader learning set' in order to assist in addressing the areas requiring improvement for Stage 2. The learning set centres on a personal leadership development for the leader and preparation of the NDU business plan. This is followed by the submission to the accreditors of the business plan and the results of the action that was agreed concerning the development plan.

Recognition will be awarded if:

- the essential infrastructure is in place (criteria 1–7);
- there is progress on all the other criteria such that the accreditation team expect to be able to award accreditation within a set time frame.

:

The visit by the accreditors is organised and then takes place, resulting in Stage 2.

Stage 2

Accreditation is awarded for a period of 2 years. During those 2 years, an annual business plan is submitted to the accreditation team to be assessed regarding the validity of the award. If the criteria have been compromised, the unit is given 2 months' notice of intent to check the criteria in order to enable recovery of the business plan.

Accreditation of nursing homes – a Dorset project

In December 1997, the Chief Executive of Dorset Health Authority was approached with regard to a suggested pilot project for the accreditation of nursing homes as PDUs. The proposal was put to the Health Authority Board, who were enthusiastic about the idea and agreed to support financially two nursing homes to go through the accreditation process in order to establish whether this approach would improve the standard of care for the residents. One of the non-executive board members was particularly interested in the project and led the selection process.

The reasons for choosing accreditation are:

- To improve patient care.
- To ensure that practice is research-based care.
- To create an environment of intellectual enquiry.
- To raise the profile of nursing homes in the eyes of both the general public and the nursing profession.
- To help with recruitment and retention.

Selecting the two nursing homes

This process took much longer than was initially anticipated. The project commenced with a series of presentations by the accreditation team from Leeds University and
the current author. This travelling road show ensured that
both the east and west of the county had the opportunity
to hear the presentation. We received completed application forms from 14 nursing homes, of which four were
shortlisted. All four nursing homes were visited, the final
two going through to the accreditation process.

The successful nursing homes were Hyde Crook House,
owned by Christopher and Karen Burdon, and Forest Hill
House, owned by the Wilson family. Hyde Crook House is
situated in the west of Dorset Health Authority, in a village
called Frampton, near Dorchester. The home is small,
having just 14 residents. Forest Hill House is in Corfe
Mullen, near Wimborne, and is situated in the east of Dorset
Health Authority; it has 37 residents.

The potential clinical leaders and the proprietors were
all very enthusiastic about their becoming a PDU. Both
the clinical leaders were involved in post-registration studies
at Bournemouth University. The projects started with
meeting the staff at both homes to discuss what being a
PDU meant to them, gathering their ideas about what areas
of care they would like to explore and identifying any
training needs that were required. Representatives from
the accreditation team visited the homes and talked to
staff about their concerns and aspirations. Both homes
completed a needs assessment for all the staff and the clinical leaders.

Unfortunately, the clinical leader at Hyde Crook House
resigned within 6 weeks of the start of this project, which
at first seemed to spell disaster. However, this event helped
to prove the point that skilled and innovative nurses are
attracted to a PDU: it gives them an opportunity to develop
and practice research-based patient care. The response to
the advertisement for a clinical leader for the PDU was
staggering. The number and the quality of the applicants
had never been seen before by the proprietors of the home.

Once in post, the new leader, Piet Bekker, and the clinical leader from Forest Hill, Jules Todd, attended leadership skills workshops in Leeds.

In order to become accredited, one of the key criteria is the setting up of a steering group that meets regularly to oversee and support the PDU in its development. Both nursing homes have steering groups, a key member being a senior lecturer from Bournemouth University. This has proved to be very valuable as he has contributed to the provision of development and training requirements that were identified by the staff as part of their needs assessment. The steering groups also include people from the local community, for example the relative of one of the residents and a retired head teacher.

The topics for the research projects were selected to improve care, including physical, psychological and social care. Both homes felt that the physical care that they delivered was of a good standard but not always researched based. However, they were more concerned about the psychological and social aspects of care, and ideas for the following projects emerged from both the qualified staff and the care assistants.

The skill mix in the nursing homes is about 40 per cent qualified staff and 60 per cent care assistants. This could have presented problems, but it was in fact the care assistants who came up with some of the ideas that eventually led to the development of the projects. The approach to the development of the projects was as follows:

- the identification of the problem;
- an examination and more precise definition of the problem;
- establishing ownership of the problem – who would lead the project, who had the skills the desire, the energy?;
- setting the goals;
- a literature search and review;
- networking with other PDUs;
- an agreement on the approach to gathering and collating the information;
- a comparison of the current situation with agreed goals;

- the selection and planning of agreed change processes;
- the implementation of the findings as a pilot project;
- evaluation;
- dissemination.

The homes have developed several projects, including reflective practice, a gardening scheme with the local garden centre, the creation of a sensory garden with the local agricultural college and the creation of memory boxes. There are plans for other projects, for example, skin care for post-menopausal women, essential oils instead of night sedation, and healthy nutrition. Two examples of these projects and their progress are given below.

The gardening project

The nurses, and in particular one care assistant, felt that the men admitted to the home were not really interested in life in the home as a group and as a result spent a large amount of time doing nothing. The staff decided to establish gardening as an activity to stimulate interaction between the residents. The home is situated in a rural area surrounded by a lovely garden. Most of the residents have lived all their lives in the country and have enjoyed their own gardens and the open countryside.

The first step was to ask the residents what they thought of this idea and to note, in a diary, what they were doing with their time. The project started by linking with a large local garden centre, which involved some of the residents and staff meeting at the centre with a representative of the company.

The staff at the garden centre were very supportive and helped with the provision of plants and plenty of expert advice. The result was that most of the residents have been involved in growing tomatoes and herbs, which they enjoy eating, and there are plants in the pots outside on the patio that have been grown from seed. There is now a garden with raised beds and easy access for people in wheelchairs so everyone can enjoy the garden. Perhaps the most interesting outcome of this study is the effect of the project on one gentleman who previously did not speak to the staff or the other residents and as a result was very isolated. Since the project he has joined in actively and talks about the plants and the residents' plans for the next season, obviously enjoying the activity.

The reminiscence projects

The staff at both the nursing homes developed these projects. Their approaches were different, but the outcomes were the same. The projects were developed from the staff's desire to know more about the residents, their life when they were young, their careers, their family and their experiences.

Before the study started, all the staff wrote down everything that they knew about each resident – which did not amount to much. They then collected information from the staff, family, friends and the resident about the life of each person. The aim was to enable the staff to individualise care to meet the needs of the individual person based on the experiences of a lifetime rather than those of being an elderly person in a nursing home. They hoped to have more meaningful and interesting conversations with the residents and help them to recall the past, all based on the information gathered. In one home, each resident has a memory box full of pictures and details of his or her life. The other home has developed a folder of information. Both homes intend giving the resulting collection of memories to the relatives on the death of the resident. This process now begins before a resident is admitted, and the relatives help to gather the information together.

Once the projects have been completed, the dissemination of the results to other nursing homes in Dorset, to other PDUs and to nursing homes across the UK will be planned. Ideas to date include a newsletter to the nursing homes around Dorset, sharing the findings through the PDU network, the publication of an article on the process of accreditation and the progress of the PDU in a relevant journal, and of course accreditation by University of Leeds.

Difficulties

At Hyde Crook House, there was a definite dip in enthusiasm and focus, and the care assistants encountered problems with their personal development plans. The introduction of reflective practice was proving difficult as people were happy to discuss their problems and achievements but not so enthusiastic about writing them down. To resolve the problem, Mike Harrison, Senior Lecturer at Bournemouth University, led a session on being part of a PDU and what this really means. The result was that the majority of members of staff began to view the concept of change as a positive experience, and several care assistants have now completed their personal development plans.

A further difficulty is that there is a small number of staff in these two nursing homes, which can present a problem in as much as their workload is already high. Despite this, the staff have taken time to attend meetings and become involved in the projects.

Both clinical leaders attended the leadership skills workshops in Leeds at the same time. The two homes were very supportive as their absence left an additional burden on the qualified staff left behind.

Progress for the nursing home PDUs has been slower than for the NDU or PDUs found in the Trusts, but this is probably because they lack the structural and organisational support and multidisciplinary stimulation that might be offered by a Trust.

Positive findings

Several obvious benefits arose:

- when the matron of one of the homes resigned, the home owners advertised for a PDU clinical leader and were amazed at the response. They had never in the history of the home had either the number or the quality of applicants for this post;

- the staff have an opportunity to develop research projects that are supported by Bournemouth University;
- the nursing home PDUs are part of a network of PDUs all over the UK, which leaves them less professionally isolated;
- an opportunity is provided to improve care through evidence-based practice and effective leadership;
- residents and staff are empowered;
- there is the opportunity to raise the profile of nursing homes within the profession of nursing and the eyes of the general public;
- sharing experiences and good practice with other PDUs, both nationally and internationally, is of benefit;
- staff are able to be creative about the provision of long-term care.

When a nursing home becomes a PDU, this not only improves the quality of care, but also raises the profile of this type of nursing care in the profession of nursing as a whole. Nursing homes who become university accredited receive a public acknowledgement of their approach to assuring continuous improvement in the care that they give to their residents. Working in a nursing home is not always seen as a particularly attractive or positive career move, yet the care required for this group of vulnerable people is complex, requiring skills delivered without immediate medical support.

This approach to quality is about continuous quality improvement, having its roots firmly planted in the provision of research-based practice. Staff in nursing homes can be professionally isolated, but being part of the PDU network allows them to share good practice and improve the quality of care for their residents, creating an environment of intellectual enquiry for the staff.

This chapter concludes a book that has covered a wide range of approaches to improving and ensuring the quality of care for patients and their families and carers. Although the quality journey started many years ago, we have arrived at a crucial point in the journey at which the profile of quality assurance has been raised to a national level and is being driven through the service by clinical governance. The focus is on the members of the multidisciplinary team working together to ensure that care is clinically effective and evidence based. Guidelines and care pathways are effective tools that bring together the essential elements of quality assurance, including multidisciplinary teamworking to review current practice, the process of researching and identifying good practice, time spent understanding the roles and responsibilities of the different members of the team, planning and implementing change to improve patient care and ongoing monitoring and review of the care given. The resulting documented guidelines and pathways predict the journey and, when shared with patients and their carers, empower and inform decisions and choices about care. This will ultimately improve the whole experience for the patient and their carers – which is what quality assurance is all about.

References

A Delphi Survey of Optimum Practice in Nursing, Midwifery and Health Visiting 1994. Manchester University.

Allsopp, D., Page, S. and Casley, S. 1998 *The Practice Development Unit: An Experiment in Multidisciplinary Innovation*. London: Whurr.

Centre for the Development of Nursing Policy and Practice 1998 *Criteria for PDU Accreditation,* University of Leeds

Joint Commission on the Accreditation of Hospitals 1997 *Comprehensive Accreditation Manual for Hospitals: The Official Handbook*. Chicago: JCAH.

Limongelli, F. 1983 Accreditation: New Standards Published, *Dimensions in Health Services,* **60**: 18–19.

Pearson, A. 1988 *The Clinical Nursing Unit*. London: Heinemann.

Purdy, E., Wright, S. and Johnson, M. 1988 Change for the Better, *Nursing Times,* **84**(38): 34–5.

Roberts, J., Coale, J. G. and Redman, R. 1987 A History of the Joint Commission on Accreditation of Hospitals, *Journal of the American Medical Association,* **258**(7): 936–40.

Salvage, J. 1989 Nursing Development, *Nursing Standard* **3**(22): 25

World Health Organization 1986 *Glossary of Terms prepared for European Training Course on Quality Assurance*. Geneva: WHO.

Further reading

Christian, S. 1996 Three Years On. How NDUs are Meeting the Challenge, *Nursing Times*, **92**(47): 35–7.

Closs, S. J. and Cheater, F. M. 1994 Utilisation of Nursing Research: Culture, Interest and Support, *Journal of Advanced Nursing*, **19**: 762–73.

Pearson, A. 1997 An Evaluation of the King's Fund Centre Nursing Development Unit Network, 1989–91, *Journal of Clinical Nursing*, **6**: 25–33.

Useful address

Centre for the Development of Nursing Policy and Practice
School of Healthcare Studies, Baines Wing
University of Leeds
Leeds LS2 9JT
Tel/Fax: 0113-233 1378
E-mail: nursm@healthcare.leeds.ac.uk

Glossary of Terms

Accreditation 'the process by which an Agency or Organisation evaluates and recognises a programme of study or institution as meeting predetermined Standards' (World Health Organization, glossary of terms prepared for European Training Course on Quality Assurance, 1986).

Anticipated recovery pathway (ARP) The anticipated pattern of recovery for a patient with a particular case-type or condition. The pathway includes all major interventions and events, in a planned sequence of time delivered by the multidisciplinary team. An ARP is a tool used to review the process of care delivery to patients.

Assessment 'the thorough study of a known or suspected problem in quality of care, designed to refine causes and necessary action to correct the problem' (World Health Organization, glossary of terms prepared for European Training Course on Quality Assurance, 1986).

Care protocol/pathway This is designed to be used as the record of care, which, through charting variance, enables clinical audit to become part of the routine practice of care.

Clinical audit A systematic, critical analysis of the quality of clinical care, which includes the procedures used for diagnosis and treatment, the use of resources and the resulting outcome for the patient.

Clinical care pathways A tool for managing clinical processes and patient outcomes. This includes a multidisciplinary plan of care written by teams caring for particular case types.

Clinical effectiveness The extent to which specific clinical interventions, when deployed in the field for a particular patient or population, do what they are intended to do – that is, maintain and improve health and secure the greatest possible health gain from the available resources.

To be reasonably certain that an intervention has produced health benefits, it needs to be shown to be capable of producing

307

worthwhile benefit (efficacy and cost-effectiveness), and to have produced that benefit in practice.

Clinical guidelines Systematically developed statements that assist the individual clinician and patient in making decisions about appropriate health care for specific conditions.

Clinical governance A mechanism to assure and improve clinical standards at local level throughout the NHS, ensuring that good practice is rapidly disseminated and systems are in place to ensure a continuous improvement in clinical care.

Clinical and health outcomes These refer to the extent to which the expected health benefit (see Clinical effectiveness) is achieved and can be attributed to the relevant clinical and health interventions. The NHS Executive uses the following working definition of health outcome: 'the attributable effect of intervention or its lack on a previous health state'.

Clinical pathway A condensed flowchart (pathway) depicting key sequential events and expected progress through an episode of care. When a patient's progress diverts from the pathway for any reason, this is documented as a variance, along with the reason for the deviance.

Clinical review 'The term "clinical review" is used to describe any evaluation activities that review the care being given to patients and the effectiveness of that care. Included in clinical review may be utilisation review activities.' (Australian Council on Hospital Standards, *Glossary of Terms* (1997).

Clinician All health care professionals (for example medical, nursing, dental and therapy) unless specified.

Commission for Health Improvement A national body to support and oversee the quality of clinical governance and clinical services.

Concurrent audit (open chart audit) An audit or examination of the patient or client's charts and records while the patient or client is still in hospital or being cared for at home, to establish whether outcomes are being achieved for the patient or client.

Concurrent review Methods of assessing the quality of patient care while the patient is still in the hospital or being cared for. Examples include open chart audit or concurrent audit, patient interview or observation, staff interview or observation and group conferences.

Continuous quality improvement 'Consists, at a minimum, of three essential elements:

- efforts to know the customer ever more deeply and to link that knowledge ever more closely to day-to-day activities of the organisation;
- efforts to mould the culture of the organisation, largely through the deeds of leaders, to foster pride, joy, collaboration and scientific thinking;
- efforts to 'continuously increase' knowledge of control over variation in the processes of work through widespread use of the scientific methods of collection, analysis and action upon data.

When all these three efforts are developed in synchrony in an organisation, continuous improvement flourishes.' (Controlling Variation in Healthcare. A consultation from Walter Shewhart and Donald M. Berwick, *Medical Care*, December 1991, **29**(12).

Continuous quality improvement A systematic approach to ensuring that the organisation has a management framework and infrastructure to ensure that there is a continual review and improvement of its processes and systems.

Cost-effectiveness The cost-effectiveness of a particular form of health care depends upon the ratio of the costs of health care to its health outcomes. Cost-effectiveness is central to the meaning of 'clinical effectiveness' in this book, except where a more specific reference is made at appropriate points in the text. Only by choosing more cost-effective services are we able to secure the greatest possible health gain from the resources available.

Criterion

1. 'variable selected as a relevant indicator of the quality of nursing care; a measure by which nursing care is judged as good' (B. W. Gallant and A. M. McLane 1979 Outcome Criteria – a Process for Validation at Unit Level, *Journal of Nursing and Administration*, **9**: 14–20).

2. 'statement which is measurable, reflecting the intent of a standard' (N. Lang 1976 Issues in Quality Assurance in Nursing, *ANA Issues in Evaluative Research*.

Critical path A tool identifying the key elements of patients' care that must occur within planned resources and activities for a specific diagnosis or procedure, and at the same time considers the time frames that must be followed in order to achieve the best possible patient outcome.

Data collection The collection of information concerning the topic to be researched or the patient. For example, data collection concerning a patient would include information about his or her past and present health status and daily living pattern. This would include subjective data as described by the patient or his or her family, objective data gleaned from observation and examination, and documented data from records and reports.

Evaluation The process of determining the extent to which goals or objectives have been achieved.

Evidence-based clinical practice Practice based on recognised research evidence that is proven to be effective.

Indicators Quantitative statements that are used to measure quality of care. Indicators can be used to measure the rate of occurrence of particular cases or events or to identify individual cases or events that are inconsistent with agreed measures of quality.

Integrated care plan Part of a clinical pathway that amalgamates into a written document all the elements of day-to-day care or treatment provided by the multidisciplinary team for each individual patient.

Monitoring 'the ongoing measurement of a variety of indicators of health care quality to identify problems' (World Health Organization, glossary of terms prepared for European Training Course on Quality Assurance, 1986).

National Institute of Clinical Excellence A new national development to promote clinical and cost-effectiveness, as well as the production and dissemination of clinical guidelines.

National Service Frameworks Set national standards, by bringing together the best evidence of clinical and cost-effectiveness with the views of the users to determine the best ways of providing particular services.

Nursing standard 'a valid definition of the quality of nursing care that includes the criteria by which the effectiveness of care can be evaluated'. (K. J. Mason 1984 *How to Write Meaningful Nursing Standards*, 2nd edn. Chichester: John Wiley & Sons).

Outcome criteria Describes the desired effect of care in terms of patient behaviour responses, level of knowledge and health status.

Outcome standards 'define the expected change in the client's health status and environment following nursing care and the extent of the client's satisfaction with nursing care'. (K. J. Mason 1984 *How to Write Meaningful Nursing Standards*, 2nd edn. Chichester: John Wiley & Sons).

Patient choice Information to the patient about the clinical condition, which includes all the available treatment, management options and non-intervention, which is comprehensive and unbiased about outcomes, risks and benefits based on the evidence available and gaps in scientific knowledge and which is expressed in simple and easily understood language.

Patient questionnaire Questionnaires developed to ask patients about care received, either in hospital or at home.

Peer review 'evaluation of the quality of patient care by persons equivalent in status to those providing the care' (Australian Council on Hospital Standards, *Glossary of Terms*).

Philosophy 'a statement of a set of values and benefits which guide thoughts and actions' (Royal Australian Nursing Federation, 1985).

Practice Development Units A multidisciplinary approach to evidence-based clinical care for patients. Units work with a university to seek formal accreditation and must demonstrate enhanced effectiveness of care for patients and their families. Units network nationally and internationally to share good practice.

Process criteria Relate to actions taken by nurses in order to achieve certain results. They include the assessment of techniques and procedures, the method of delivery of nursing care interventions, techniques, how resources are used, and the evaluation of care planned and given.

Protocols A system of tracking either patient care or a service, as well as identifying and documenting the correct processes and activities within set timescales to an agreed outcome.

Quality assurance 'the measurement of the actual level of the services rendered plus the efforts to modify, when necessary, the provision of these services in the light of the results of measurement' (World Health Organization, glossary of terms prepared for European Training Course on Quality Assurance, 1986).

Quality of care Degree of excellence.

Quality control system A system used in industry to check the quality of goods. In nursing, it would refer to the quality of the environment and surroundings in which nurses work and patient care is given.

Quality Improvement Plan/Quality Improvement Programme A specific detailed plan aimed at improving the quality of a specific area or organisation.

Quality improvement team A team of individuals who are directly involved in working with the problem or issue that is to be improved. They meet to agree and complete the Quality Improvement Programme using recognised quality improvement tools and techniques.

Quality planning Involves four components:

- *identifying* the customers of a particular process;
- *measuring* customer needs and expectations of the process and its outputs;
- *designing* a product or service responsive to their needs;
- *developing* the processes capable of producing the desired output.

Quality programme 'a documented set of activities, resources and events serving to implement the quality system of an organisation' (European Organisation for Quality Control 1981 *Glossary of Terms used in the Management of Quality*, 5th edn).

Quality tools Recognised techniques, for example brainstorming, histograms and control charts, to enable practitioners to collect and analyse data.

Research and development (R&D) Research can range from the curiosity-driven end of biomedical research and innovation to the NHS R&D strategy focusing on applied studies designed to improve the quality, effectiveness and cost/benefit ratio of service delivery. The term 'development' covers both the activities intended to produce general models and promote their use within the NHS, as well as the commercial investment in improving and bringing innovations to the market. These terms are used in their widest sense in this book.

Resource management The balance of quality, cost and quantity.

Retrospective audit (chart audit/closed audit) An audit or examination of the patient or client's charts and records after he or she has been discharged in order to determine the quality of nursing care received.

Retrospective review Methods of assessing the quality of patient care after discharge, including retrospective chart audit, post-care interviews, post-care staff conferences, and post-care questionnaires.

Standard

1. 'optimum level of care against which performance is compared' (B. W. Gallant and A. M. McLane 1979 Outcome Criteria – a Process for Validation at Unit Level, *Journal of Nursing and Administration*, **9**: 14–20).

2. 'agreed upon level of excellence' (N. Lang 1976 Issues of Quality Assurance in Nursing, *ANA Issues in Evaluation Research*).

Standard statements Professionally agreed levels of performance appropriate to the population addressed that reflect what is acceptable, achievable, observable and measurable.

Structure criteria Items and services enabling the system to function. These include the organisation of nursing services – recruitment, selection, manpower establishments and skill mix; equipment; ancillary services such as supplies, central sterilising, catering, pharmacy, laboratory services, laundry, paramedical services and the provision of buildings; and agreed rules and regulations, policies and procedures.

Total quality management 'is the system by which quality at each interface is ensured. It is an approach to improving the effectiveness and flexibility of the service as a whole – a way of organising and involving the whole service, every Authority, unit, department, activity, every single person at every level to ensure that organised activities happen the way they are planned, and seeking continuous improvement in performance.' (B. Morris 1989 Total Quality Management, *International Journal of Health Care Quality Assurance*, **2**(3): 4–6).

Valid/validity The extent to which the measures used in an audit give an accurate picture of the care or service being audited. Validity is concerned with the confidence held by an audit group that the group will draw the right conclusions about actual practice and take the right action, based on the measures used in the audit.

Index